# Funding the Ladder

## The Passmore Edwards Legacy

# Funding the Ladder

## The Passmore Edwards Legacy

Dean Evans

Dean Evans
14 May 2011

Frontispiece – Portrait of Passmore Edwards hanging in the Miners' & Mechanics' Institute, St Agnes, Cornwall. Photograph by F Argall, Truro

First published by Francis Boutle Publishers
272 Alexandra Park Road
London N22 7BG
Tel/Fax: 020 8889 7744
Email: info@francisboutle.co.uk
www.francisboutle.co.uk



ISBN 978 1 903427 66 8

Good deeds live on when doers are no more.

( Engraved on trowel used to lay the foundation stone of the Nunhead Free Library.)

# Contents

# List of illustrations

# Acknowledgments

I would like to thank the Arthur Quiller-Couch Memorial Fund for their financial support, which helped with the many journeys to London necessary to compile this record of Passmore Edwards' life and work.

Thanks also need to go to those many librarians and archivists who have responded to my endless requests for information, the countless individuals who have shared information with me and to my daughter, Clare, for proofreading and correcting my drafts.

Dean Evans
March 2011

# Preface

He was called 'Mr Greatheart' by the actor Sir Henry Irving and was often referred to as the 'Cornish Carnegie'; whilst Andrew Carnegie, who said that he was a disciple of Passmore Edwards, dubbed him 'St Passmore' and said that if he had lived but 100 years earlier he would certainly have been canonised.

If you live in Cornwall or London you may know of Passmore Edwards from the name above the door of your local library, but in just fourteen years over seventy public buildings were established as a direct result of his bequests.

There were twenty in Cornwall, but also in Newton Abbot, Bournemouth, the Home Counties, London and the south east.

They include twenty four public libraries; seventeen hospitals and convalescent homes; twelve homes for adults and children with epilepsy and children who were orphaned or disabled; six clubs, settlements and institutes; five schools of art and science, and four art galleries and museums; and many of these continue to serve the community to which they were originally given. There were also many other gifts and donations. He said that if he could fund the ladder, the poor would climb.

In his life he was a journalist and newspaper proprietor, political reformer, Member of Parliament, peace activist and anti-slavery campaigner. He lived at a time of huge political and social reform and was actively involved in many of the major events of the last half of the nineteenth century. As a Radical Liberal he was one of the links between the early radicalism of the 1840s and the later decades of the century,[1] the golden days of the Liberal movement.

But who was Passmore Edwards, what was at the root of his deeply held convictions, and what made him give away such a fortune?

He was not a wealthy landowner with a big country estate. Nor was he a wealthy industrialist like Andrew Carnegie. Whereas Carnegie gave millions, Edwards gave thousands, but more than £250,000 during a relatively short period of his lifetime; and with his giving came a lasting connection with the institutions that he helped.

Not that he died poor; he left a total estate of more than £46,000, all to his family; charity, at least, ended at home.

The British Library copy of Passmore Edwards' autobiography, *A Few Footprints*, has the comment added in pencil 'No biography by author's bequest'.[2] Passmore Edwards wrote in *Footprints*, that he had previously declined requests for a biography because he thought that anything he may have said or done was scarcely entitled to such specific merit. *Footprints* was, he said, written to correct what had been written about him by others. Two years previous E H Burrage published the sycophantic *Life of Passmore Edwards* and, although the *English Mechanic*, owned by Passmore Edwards, carried a review of Burrage's work, reporting that it contained few factual errors, it is clear that it is this biography to which Edwards refers.

According to Edwards, *Footprints* had been originally published only for private circulation but such was demand that a second revised edition was published for sale the following year. Although very few copies of the original autobiography are to be found today, facsimile copies of the second edition are available.

In 1981 Richard Best, former headmaster of the village school at Blackwater, the village of Edwards' birth, wrote an account of Edwards' *Life and Good Works*, based on *Footprints* and including a few local anecdotes and material from J J McDonald's *Passmore Edwards Institutions*, published by Strand Newspapers in 1900. It was this early work which sparked my interest in a man whose name had previously only been known as adorning public buildings across Cornwall.

In 1994 Peter Baynes, privately published a fuller account of Edwards' life with previously unpublished material relating to Edwards's career as a politician and publisher and dealt with his philanthropic work in more depth. I am indebted to Peter for his encouragement in continuing my research into Edwards' life and for sight of his private research notes.

My first thought on reading *Footprints* was that here was an apparently humble man who was extremely good at blowing his own trumpet – and he admits to having played the fife in the Blackwater band at the time of Queen Victoria's coronation, and of being chastised for showing-off, playing too loud and out of tune. In later life, he noted, there were many times when he found himself 'out of tune' and the way to get back in tune was to do the best for the most.[3] But I wanted to know more about the man and to explore those areas of his life, in particular his wife and children, of whom he gives no clues, and to what extent his private life differed from his public life. I also wanted to make the Passmore Edwards legacy available to others who knew nothing or only a little about a man who had done so much for the benefit of others. A hundred years after his death many of the buildings he funded cease to meet today's needs and without the association of the name above the door with the building's use, Edwards' contribution may be forgotten. Peter Baynes quotes from David Owens[4] in saying 'amongst the late Victorian philanthropists, he will survive critical examination better than most. Not only were his motives beyond reproach but his benefactions expressed deeply held and intelligent convictions about conditions of progress in his society'. Many of the issues that concerned Edwards are still of concern today: inequality, education and the need to settle our differences without resorting to armed conflict.

I also wanted to explore the good works that have continued to take place in and around those buildings and institutions that Passmore Edwards readily supported. One can only guess at the countless numbers that have come into contact with, and benefited from, an association with a Passmore Edwards building. Not all went on to find fame, as did Jacob Bronowski (Chapter 15), but the story of Rosa Lewis who found refuge at the Chalfont St Peters Home for Epileptics (Chapter 17) and the many more like her, are just as valid.

It is appropriate, in the year that marks the centenary of his death, to publish this account and to keep alive the memory of one of the great Victorian Cornishmen.

# One
# A Blackwater boy; making of the man

John Passmore Edwards was born 24 March 1823, in Blackwater, a small Cornish village between Redruth and Truro, which had at that time a population of about 200, surprisingly similar to today. The life of Passmore Edwards, as he is most often known, is not strictly one of rags to riches, since his parents were not poor, just a hard-working Cornish family typical of that time, doing whatever was necessary to raise their family.

His father, William Edwards, was a carpenter, and his mother, Susan Passmore, daughter of a saddle maker from Newton Abbot. Susan, baptised as Susannah, had previously married James Craze in Newton Abbot when she was just 20 years old. James was probably from the St Agnes area returning there with his young wife and when he died Susan remained rather than return to Devon. There were no known surviving children from that first marriage and William Edwards and Susan married at St Agnes in 1818.

Passmore Edwards grew up with three brothers: William, the eldest, Richard and James, and he also referred to another brother and a sister, an earlier James and either Susan or Susannah, both having died in infancy. His father had come from a large local family and there were many cousins in and around Blackwater, but Edwards makes no mention of them.

Edwards was born in a small four-roomed cottage but his father borrowed money and built a larger cottage nearby. When the carpentry trade was insufficient to provide for his family he obtained a public house licence, not only serving beer but also brewing and supplying to other beer houses in the district.[1]

Although the brewery and public house featured significantly in family life, as adults both Richard and Passmore Edwards lectured and campaigned on temperance issues and Richard remained teetotal for most of his life, becoming President of the Western Temperance League and serving on the Committee of the National Temperance League. Passmore Edwards was teetotal for a large part of his life and though he drank a little later on, he considered it should be taken for medicinal purposes only.[2]

According to former Blackwater headmaster, Richard Best, in his account of Edwards' life,[3] the cottage is in Impsey Lane, originally a two up and two down building, and a plaque is fixed to this cottage, declaring that Edwards was born there.

The tithe map of 1842, when Edwards was 20 years old, shows William Edwards as occupier of an 'Inn' and land at the corner of Impsey Lane and the road through Blackwater, about 100 yards from the cottage. This property is most likely what was later to be known as the Cornish Miners Arms, possibly built around 1832. The site is now occupied by a private dwelling. Though larger, the property in which Edwards grew up was still clearly lacking as we are told that although there were eight small rooms there were not eight windows. This was the age of the window tax,[4] and this 'tax on air and light' had a significant impact on Passmore Edwards even at an early age. There were no windows in the back bedrooms where the boys slept, the only natural light entering through a tiny window above the stairs. His father discouraged reading during the day when there was work to be done and so it was in the evenings, in the small, candle-lit room in which the family mostly lived, that he read, with fingers in his ears to cut out the family chatter – and he read everything he could get his hands on.

Edwards states that his only schooling was at the local Dame school at 2d a week and that the teacher was James Blackney, an ex-miner. Blackney, though born in Cornwall had been a coal miner in Gloucestershire,[5] returning to Cornwall after being injured in the mine. Blackney's school consisted of only a single room, described at the opening of the Blackwater Institute by Simon Chellow who was at school at the same time as Edwards, as being a place 'where the pupils, of all ages, were packed like herrings in a box' and that the education received was rudimentary.[6] When the Board School opened in 1878, it was recorded that 'most of the children coming from the Dame school are very backward'.[7] Edwards, while acknowledging the limits of his early education, paid tribute to Blackney as being 'a painstaking and conscientious man, who will always have a green spot in my memory'.

THE PENNY MAGAZINE

OF THE

Society for the Diffusion of Useful Knowledge.

423.] PUBLISHED EVERY SATURDAY. [November 3, 1838.

THE AYE-AYE.

Above: *The site of William Edwards' inn was later occupied by the Cornish Miners Arms*

Below: The Penny Magazine

Edwards' father was one of the few people in the village who took a weekly paper, the *Sherborne Mercury*, printed in Dorset but containing a small section of Cornish news. He also took the *Penny Magazine*, and the young lad would read these from cover to cover. One edition of the *Penny Magazine* contained a biographical sketch of John Hunter, the anatomist, and Edwards asked his mother what an anatomist was. She told him to consult a dictionary, which he did. As he read the account, with the continued use of the dictionary, 'he felt for the first time, flutterings of ambition – to become known and useful in some way' – feelings that never left him. It may also have been the *Penny Magazine* that reinforced in him the value of thrift, for on 1 August 1835 there appeared the advice that Lord Burleigh, Lord High Treasurer of England, gave to his son.

> Touching the guiding of they house, let thy hospitality be moderate; and according to the means of thy estate, rather plentiful than sparing, but not costly. For I never knew any man grow poor by keeping an orderly table. But some consume themselves through secret vices, and their hospitality bears the blame. But banish swinish drunkeness out of thine house, which is a vice impairing health, consuming much, and makes no show. I never heard praise ascribed to the drunkard, but for the well-bearing of his drink; which is a better commendation for a brewer's horse, or a dray-man, than either for a gentleman or a serving-man. Beware thou spend not above three of four parts of thy revenues, nor above a third part of that in thy house. For the other two parts will not do more than defray thy extraordinaries, which always surmount the ordinary by much: otherwise thou shalt live, like a rich beggar, in continual want.

Whilst his mother was a Baptist, Edwards described his father as 'though not a Baptist, Calvinist in belief'. On Sundays William would take the boys to the Baptist chapel at nearby Salem in the morning and to the Wesleyan chapel, where William's brother, John, was Sunday-School superintendent, in the afternoon. Passmore Edwards noted that his father would openly criticise the Wesleyan sermons and he had a clear memory of the nightmares that followed the sermons of a Mr Christopher, on the tortures of the damned, though he said that of the hundreds of sermons he heard as a child, he remembered not a word of any.[8] Clearly a god-fearing man, Passmore Edwards did not profess to any single congregation, rather developing his own religious opinions.[9] A family member later referred to him as a Unitarian[10] and there is evidence of this in his work and those he associated with. Unitarians believe that man creates the evils in society, and they can only be remedied by man's efforts, a belief that Edwards' adult life appears to follow.

When Edwards was around ten years old a cholera epidemic spread through the country killing more than 20,000[11] and William senior was one of the inspectors appointed by the Boards of Health, under the Cholera Act, to ensure that nuisances were cleared and additional sanitary requirements complied with. Many years later Passmore Edwards was to take an active interest in housing conditions amongst the working classes and was to fund hospitals and convalescent homes.

A little while later Passmore Edwards left school to help his father, who by now had developed the land and garden around the inn. As well as helping with the brewing, young 'Jack' tended and picked fruit and took it to sell at the markets in St Agnes, Redruth or Truro. Edwards states that the reopening of a local mine drew down the water from their well causing the brewery trade to cease, but the 1841 census still describes William as a brewer rather than a publican or innkeeper. The brewery trade was in existence at least up until the time that Edwards left Blackwater. In a lecture in 1844 he referred to his father being a brewer. The *West Briton* carried an announcement of the sale of an inn in Blackwater in 1847, and this may be the date when the remaining family left Blackwater to live in Phillack, near Hayle.

Edwards would save up the pennies he earned and walk the six miles to Truro to buy a single book at a second hand bookshop, such was his thirst for education. One book he bought was a copy of Newton's *Opticks* but after reading it, he said he was no wiser at the end than at the start. His father attended the Chacewater Scientific Institute, Chacewater being a larger village adjacent to Blackwater, and the boys would accompany him to listen to the lectures. One of the first lectures he heard was a talk on the 'Pleasures and Advantages of Knowledge', by Henry Sewell Stokes, a Truro lawyer and poet, who was later to become his employer.

As a young man Edwards also attended the Carharrack Literary Institute with his uncle John, who by now had moved to St Day to keep a greengrocers shop in Scorrier Street. Carharrack, a mining village near St Day, built an Institute in 1841 though it is not clear whether an association had existed in the village before this date, but it was at Carharrack that Edwards first tried his hand at public speaking. He said that he offered to speak on the subject of 'The Poetry of the Creation' and was surprised when they accepted, as he admitted that he knew little about poetry, and even less about the Creation. However, he wrote out his talk and on the chosen night stood to face an audience most of whom would have been old enough to be his father, and presumably included his uncle if not his own father. He said that he was dismayed that his efforts 'received neither a vote of thanks nor a vote of censure, neither received laughter, nor applause'. Not to be beaten he volunteered to speak at the Young Men's Association, in St Agnes. Although he had attempted to learn his script by heart, after a few minutes he stumbled and had to sit down. Composing himself he stood and carried on, but the words had left him and he sat once more, this time to laughter and ridicule. He said he returned home a sadder but wiser youth. But he was a determined young man and within a few years he was lecturing at institutes in Chasewater and Truro; half a century later, Passmore Edwards was to become a household name. When asked what had been the secret of his success, he answered that he had tried to 'grasp the skirts of happy chance, and breast the blows of circumastance'.

After his disappointing attempts at public speaking, and perhaps inspired by hearing Henry Sewell Stokes at Chacewater, he tried his hand at poetry and sent off verses to the *West Briton*, a Truro weekly newspaper. He said he was again dismayed, the following week, to read that his verse Song of the Rose 'was not worth the space it would occupy, if any space at all'.

When only sixteen he started as a Sunday School teacher in that same Wesleyan chapel he had attended with his father, and, along with a former school friend, John Symons, began a free evening and Sunday morning school to teach the many uneducated men and boys in the area. This was held in a small Bryanite[12] chapel at Wheal Busy, near Blackwater[13] and it was probably their fathers, both carpenters, who fixed tables around the wall of the chapel that could be folded down when the room was used for worship. The school was very successful and continued for many years, long after Edwards had left the area. In later life Passmore Edwards said that he cherished above all others a few letters that he received from men and boys who had learnt to read and write there.

During the nineteenth century the Corn Laws had a great impact on Cornwall with families finding it a struggle to feed themselves. With the founding of the Anti-Corn Law League, heated debate took place across the county over the need for these protectionist measures. Passmore Edwards, then only sixteen,[14] sent for pamphlets about the League's work but was surprised when a parcel of leaflets arrived, with a note asking him to distribute them in the area. This he did, travelling as far west as Penzance, much to the annoyance of Samuel Bedwell, the Mayor of Penzance and a magistrate, whose son brought home one of Edwards' free trade pamphlets. Bedwell threatened that he would have Edwards arrested and put into prison for sedition. This was no idle threat as there was a great deal of unrest throughout the country and the judiciary were ready to give a firm response.

When Robert Lowery and Arbram Duncan were sent to Cornwall that year, to agitate and collect signatures for the Chartist petition, many of the mayors, fearing violence, tried to deter them from speaking in their towns and ordered the town criers not to call the meetings. Lowery said that he found the working population ignorant of politics but when he addressed a meeting in Chacewater the majority of the crowd of 700 were prepared to sign.[15] Whether Edwards, or his father, attended that meeting we do not know but Edwards would have heard the subsequent reports and this might have been the trigger that led him to send for the leaflets.

Although sent away from Penzance with such a threat ringing in his ears Edwards continued to distribute his free trade literature unaware of how this interest in the League was to influence his adult life.

On Monday 13 April 1840 William and James Lightfoot were hung at Bodmin Gaol for the robbery and murder of Neville Norway. The crowds started to arrive in Bodmin on the Saturday and throughout the weekend, with special excursions run to Bodmin Town station. The town took on the appearance of a fair with entertainment in the streets and every public house and beer shop full to overflowing. Passmore Edwards was among the crowd of more than 20,000 that went to see the public hanging.

Afterwards, he walked the 22 miles back to Truro, allowing himself time to ponder on the spectacle he had witnessed. He was against capital punishment from that time on and also campaigned against flogging both in schools and in the military, and later, against the lynching of Negroes in America.

At around the same time his father took him to Truro to see Henry Sewell Stokes who gave him a job as an under-clerk, at £10 a year. He worked there for about 18 months, walking each Monday from Blackwater the six miles to Truro, returning home on Saturday evening. He took with him three of his mother's pasties for his dinner during the first half of the week, and she would dispatch another three by carriers' cart on Thursday, or he would walk home to collect them. He said that dining on cold pasties, often two or three days old, was not very appetising but with the addition of good bread and butter it was sufficient to keep him in good health.

Edwards was one of the first clerks that Stokes employed, recalling that his time there was not very rewarding and that he 'neither received a word of encouragement nor a smile throughout the time he was there'; but it was this period of his life that was to have the greatest influence. As well as being a lawyer and recognised poet, Stokes entered the world of publishing in 1833 by starting the weekly *Cornish Guardian*, which merged with the *West Briton* two years later. A regular visitor to Stoke's office in Quay Street, Truro, was the *West Briton*'s Isaac Latimer, the first verbatim reporter on any Cornish newspaper. Latimer recognised the glint in Edwards' eye and was not surprised when he left Cornwall to follow a journalistic career. Edwards said that he was told that his services were no longer needed but does not clarify whether this was because he was not cut out to be a lawyer's clerk or there was not sufficient work. He first went to see the editor of the *West Briton* seeking freelance work, without success, but there he met a Mr Philip, a representative of a radical London newspaper, the *Sentinel*, who told him that he was looking for a local agent for the paper in Manchester. Hearing of Passmore Edwards' Anti-Corn Law work, he offered him the post at £40 a year.

So, as an inexperienced young man from a small Cornish village he prepared to travel the 300 miles to the industrial town of Manchester. But how to get there? To travel by train was beyond his meagre budget – there were no *super-savers* in 1844 – besides Brunel's bridge across the River Tamar at Plymouth, joining Cornwall to England, was yet to be built.[16]

He reluctantly sold some of his books and with his belongings packed in a small carpet bag made by his mother from a length of stair runner, he first walked to Falmouth and boarded a steamer to Dublin, travelling as a deck passenger for 10 shillings. He described it as 48 hours of misery, huddled under a tarpaulin. From Dublin three shillings bought him passage across the Irish Sea to Liverpool, with a cargo of pigs to keep him company, squealing all the way. Finally, he took a relatively short half-crown rail journey, in what was no more than a cattle truck with seats, to Manchester.

# Two
# The Manchester School

Nothing could have prepared Edwards for his new life in Manchester. He would have been familiar with the smoke and dust of Cornish mines and ore processing works, and poor housing conditions in and around where he had lived, but the scale of the industrialised development as he travelled by rail from Liverpool into Manchester would have proved a stark contrast.

He was fortunate to find lodgings with James Hibbert, a stationer, who, with his sister, kept a small shop in Bridge Street. He tackled his new position as journalist with great enthusiasm, attending meetings and sending accounts back to London for publication. As the *Sentinel* did not identify the author of any of its reports it is not possible to accurately identify all that should be credited to Edwards but much of the editorial content was very much in line with Edwards' thoughts and for the first time the phrase 'from our Own Correspondent' appeared in connection to reports of events in and around Manchester. As well as his journalistic input he called on booksellers and distributors throughout Lancashire and Cheshire promoting the *Sentinel*; but the paper was not a success and over a period of fifteen months he received only £10 for his work.

Edwards said that he managed to supplement his income by giving lectures and talks for a few shillings a time and mostly to Manchester and Lancashire Temperance Societies. Reports of some of these lectures found their way into the *Sentinel* but not always under Edwards' hand, for Society secretaries would often submit their own reports, as club secretaries still do today. One such report was a letter from the secretary of the Chorley Temperance Society. Along with a wordy report on the progress of the Temperance movement in Chorley was an account of Passmore Edwards' visit during the annual fair. Chorley Fair had previously been an opportunity for many of the town folk to engage in drunken high spirits, so the Society decided to become involved, joining in the procession and arranging events during the week. These events included a lecture by Passmore Edwards. Hardly had he arrived he was asked to address an open-air meeting attended by more than 600 people. His address 'completely riveted the attention of a mixed audience. Scarcely a breath stirred or a whisper was heard during its delivery but the soft murmur of applause frequently issued from those that appeared to be deeply interested in what was being advanced'. At the finish, 'although it was a Sunday', there was 'a loud volley of applause'. At 21 years old he was now a skilled and accomplished public speaker. During his time with Henry Sewell Stokes he had honed his skills giving talks at the Truro Institute, founded by Isaac Latimer, and at other village institutes in the area. At Chorley it was announced that he would talk again on Monday evening, this time in the Wesleyan chapel. The crowd began to assemble well before the start time so that the hall was filled to overflowing and many were turned away. At the end of his ninety-minute lecture the applause was 'enthusiastic and deafening', the chairman saying that it was the best speech that he had ever heard. Finally, a third lecture was delivered on Tuesday evening, this time to an audience of over 900 and many still were turned away. Following Sunday's meeting thirty-eight people came forward to sign the pledge, to give up alcohol completely. Another fifty-four signed after Monday's evening lecture and a further twenty-eight on Tuesday. Edwards would have returned to Manchester well-pleased with these results, although little better off. While the people of Chorley may have reimbursed his expenses and provided his board over the long weekend, the chairman thanked him for his 'gratuitous services'.[1] Edwards did not even receive a fee from the *Sentinel* for the report of this meeting but it can only have impressed his employers when the chairman, rounding up the evening, called for a vote of thanks to the *Sentinel* and its editor for their support of the Temperance movement.

At Wigan, towards the end of September 1844 he addressed a very large audience powerfully setting out his beliefs as regards alcohol and his views on the need for abstinence. He said:

> I believe that intelligent Englishmen do not apprehend the value of Teetotalism. Total abstainers were more healthy and cheerful. Perform their labours more regularly and with greater ease and ability. – I have tried the experiment myself and can unhesitatingly assert that the use of intoxicating beverages always disabled me from the performance of my physical or mental employments in proportion to the quantity I took, and though one of the dearest relatives I have on earth is a manufacturer of these drinks and although almost all of his capital is embarked in a concern where such drinks are made, I will assert on this platform, in the presence of this assembly, and in the face of my country and my God, that I positively believe that all the intoxicating drinks, which are so extensively used, are injurious to the physical and mental well being of man when taken as articles of diet or made use of in any way but for medical purposes. I am fully aware of the responsibilities attached to such words as these but a sense of my duty as a member of society and a man, irresistibly impels me to give utterance to my conscientious and decided convictions, convictions founded on the practice of myself and the experiences of others. As a lover of my country and my religion, of my species and my home, I dash pecuniary interests aside and humbly proclaim, as far as my own experience carries me and my own observations instruct me that the use of all drinks that will intoxicate, are pernicious to the healthfulness and happiness of the human race.
>
> I also believe that all who mix with society and investigate the causes of disease and crime so prevalent in or country will gather sufficient reasons provided he investigates with an unbiased and unprejudiced mind to arrive at similar conclusions.
>
> And I am of the opinion that ninety nine out of every hundred who would fairly look into the operations of the teetotal abstinence movement would soon find that

immediate blessings of a high and noble character have almost invariably accompanied its happiness-scattering march. But for want of people giving the principle fair trial and its operations a fair investigation, they are altogether unable to appreciate its value or its utility. Were Teetotalism only instrumental in making the drunkard sober a great good would be affected. But when that soberised man begins to reflect – when he considers that he is a valuable link in the grand chain of humanity and that he may by his own efforts pluck comfort from the scenes of life, and do something so that the means of happiness may be scattered around the path of his brother man – then the instrumentality of Teetotalism is more valuable still.

Teetotallers as reformers not only desire to see the sensualist making a good use of the good things of Heaven, but they tell him that happiness – pure permanent happiness, can never be obtained by gratification of his animal appetites but only by adoring his grand nature with the excellence of a moral and intellectual life. We reformers are not only wishful to snatch the ruined out from shame and guilty woe, but we wish to plant him in the flourishing fields of thought so that he, by culture may arise in the scale of being, and enjoy the smiles of Heaven's gladness, and throw around his perishless existence the embellishments of human greatness. We as reformers are not only wishful to place the rising race of England's future glory on the undeceivable rock of total abstinence, so that they be severed from the invidious encroachments the poisonous wave of intemperance, but we wish to see that race learning from the painful experience of their fathers so that they, by being warned and guided, may shun the dangers and ward off the poverty burdened winds and vice laden gales which too frequently visited those that went and are going before them. We are wishful to see the rising and bursting minds of the youthful portion of society have more advantages for physical and mental improvement placed within their reach. And in order that these things should be more effectually done than they hitherto have been; is it not requisite that the rubbish of ages should be removed? Is it not essential that the vice stained usage and the cruelly destructive conventionalisms of society, should be broken down? And is it not requisite that these infectiously bad examples which now so prevalently disgrace the drinking world should be discountenanced and if possible destroyed, if we really wish that the budding sons and daughters of Britain should expand in the loveliness of virtue and the powerfulness of thought?

Teetotalism goes to the root of two thirds of the pauperism and three quarters of the crime, which disgrace our land. Let them examine parliamentary documents and parliamentary reports as I have done – and they will find that what I say is true. Set them to listen to the surgeons or poor law commissioners, our Magistrates and our Judges and he will find that I have not painted in sufficiently deep colours the woes and the wrongs which flow from the drinking systems of our country. If I had time I would present such fearful amounts of statistical facts as to make every feeling heart shudder and every thinking mind start back aghast.

A week later Edwards addressed a dinner given by Mr Cooke and M Minnie at Warrington for their workers at Hope Mill. Introduced as the 'great gun of the evening' Edwards gave a powerful address of nearly an hour on 'The moral and mental elevation of the people and the tendency of the present age'.[2] During that month he was also to take the chair, and later speak, at a Temperance Festival at Preston, and to give two lectures on the 'Power of Teetotalism as a Reforming Institution' at Clitheroe. In the following month he gave a lecture at Bury, on 'Total Abstinence',[3] and at Padiham,

Lancashire, where after alluding to the 'Peace Principle' in a Temperance lecture, he was asked to give a further lecture three nights later addressing this 'Principle'.

Speaking of the objectives of the Peace Society and the cause and causers of war, he went on to talk about the cure, which was 'love'. 'Love between man and man, nation and nation, continent and continent. A love which knew no bounds and which was a stranger to all limits'. Such a passion or principle was, he optimistically, or perhaps naively, thought, 'growing amongst men, bursting forth between nations and uniting man with his brother man'.[4]

Birkenhead had the honour of receiving his last lecture of that year. One who attended recorded that he had heard different opinions to that of Passmore Edwards but confessed as to having never been better pleased with any advocate he had previously heard. His language 'charmed the soul'.[5]

When writing his slim autobiography in 1904 he noted how, when walking down a street in Liverpool in 1844, he met a 'little blue eyed girl, with hair like woven sunbeam-s' who asked him to buy a brick. This turned out to be small picture of a brick on a card, at a penny, one of the many needed to build a Temperance Hall in Liverpool. He considered his purchase one of the most profitable investments he ever made, and the memory of the incident and the knowledge that he became the joint proprietor with hundreds of others of a Liverpool Temperance Hall, gave him many a pennyworth of satisfaction. Remarking on his good fortune later in life in being able to make larger investments of a similar kind through his public buildings, he hoped that the institutions he had been privileged to build would be so many bricks in the building of British civilisation.

Apart from the Temperance and Peace movements he subsequently became active in a number of other aspects of the *moral reformation* – political and financial reform. In addition to lecturing he also found time to attend classes at the Manchester Mechanics' Institute but it was his work for the *Sentinel*, attending political and social reform group meetings, that was to contribute the most to his education. It was here that he listened to and rubbed shoulders with the likes of John Bright and Richard Cobden, the free traders and founders of what Disraeli was to call the Manchester School, a movement Edwards was to promote and follow for the rest of his life. His involvement in political affairs also included the 'Irish question' a subject that contributed to the end of his political career.

**Father Mathew**

Father Theobald Mathew led a temperance movement in Ireland from 1839 to his death in 1856. Appalled by the widespread drunkenness throughout Ireland he started a Total Abstinence Society, beginning in Cork when, in 1838, he entered his name into a large book. He had signed the pledge. Hundreds and then thousands added their own signatures after hearing Father Mathew speak. By 1843 almost half of the population had signed the pledge. Mathew travelled to Glasgow, and then Liverpool, Manchester and Salford, Yorkshire and finally to London, gathering signatures as he went. Those that signed the pledge were given membership cards and temperance medals, mostly financed by Father Mathew himself and when he got into serious financial difficulties his supporters rallied around to help.

Delivering a lecture to the Clitheroe Temperance Society, Passmore Edwards made his audience aware of Father Matthew's financial plight and said that he had suggested to the Manchester Temperance Society that they organise and coordinate an appeal through the Societies and like-minded organisations. At Warrington, in December 1844, he was one of several speakers to address a public meeting called to raise subscriptions[6] and just a few days later, with John Bright MP in the chair, Edwards, described as a Temperance lecturer from Cornwall, 'spoke at great length' on the work being carried out by Mathew and the debt owed to him by the public.[7] In London a meeting was called at Exeter Hall to discuss the appeal and both Lord John Russell and William Ewart spoke on Mathew's behalf. Edwards' original suggestion had taken on a national scale and his reputation was spreading. Of course there were some factions that considered that Mathew had only himself to blame for poor management of his funds and those that saw it as propping up the Catholic Church but Edwards' view was to be later vindicated when the Government awarded Father Mathew a pension of £300 a year for his work for society.

The potato crop failure of 1844 was widespread in Ireland. Nearly two thirds of the eight million population depended on the potato, which had become their staple food source. In 1845 the potato blight arrived amongst them; a nation began to starve, and the temperance campaign stalled.

Passmore Edwards saw a simple connection between the temperance issue and the famine. In a lecture at Warrington, Cheshire, he said 'Whilst so many men were starving and dying in Ireland and Scotland, and in England, other men were destroying in the process of brewing and distilling the very food which was in such need'. He suggested that there was enough to feed all the starving Irish and Scots. Nearly eight million quarts of corn were used in brewing and distilling trades during the previous year and this was the chief reason why corn prices were then so high. Eight million quarts would be about 10,000 tonnes. Perhaps not enough to feed the millions that were starving but enough to affect grain prices as he indicated.

**Unitarianism**

Hibbert, his landlord in Manchester, who Edwards said spontaneously befriended him, introduced him to the writings and transcendentalism of Dr William Channing, the Bostonian Unitarian theologian. Edwards went on to read and admire the works of Ralph Waldo Emerson. And it was in Manchester that Edwards first heard Dr James Martineau preach. Martineau was a Unitarian Minister and, in 1844, Professor of Mental and Moral Philosophy and Logic at Manchester Col-lege.[8] He was one of the greatest religious thinkers of the time and an advocate of freedom of belief within the Church.

*Bust of Dr James Martineau, presented to the Mary Ward Settlement by Passmore Edwards*

In 1867 Dr Martineau hosted a meeting in

London to launch the Free Christian Union, a society aimed at promoting unity between Christian churches, Dissenters and Anglicans. Edwards, although unable to attend, wrote expressing an interest in becoming a member and paid his first subscription. The Society, however, did not attract a substantial following and was dissolved in 1870.

It was, then, in Manchester that Edwards' political, moral and social ideals developed and matured. But even with the income from his lectures it was only by borrowing small sums from his family in Cornwall, and by the kindness of James Hibbert and his sister, who allowed him several months credit on his rent, that he managed to keep his head above water.

In 1845, after visiting his family and friends in Cornwall, he turned to London, like Dick Whittington with only a few shillings in his pocket, to find work and 'try his fortunes on a wider sea'.

# Three
# Victorian London

The London of 1845, when Passmore Edwards first arrived, was the largest city in the world, the census of 1841 indicating a population of nearly two million people. It was also the city of Oliver Twist with overcrowded housing, poor water supplies, lack of drains and 200,000 overflowing cesspits.[1] Added to this was more than 80,000 tonnes of animal dung deposited in the streets by horses and animals driven to market, the effluent from the treatment of those animals and animal by-products following butchering, and the almost open 'burial' sites scattered about the city. In 1849 cholera was to kill more than 13,000, mainly through water supplies contaminated by nearby cesspits and overcrowded, unkempt housing conditions.

London was expanding at an astonishing rate, drawing people in from across Britain and the world, those escaping from somewhere worse or just looking for a better life, but frequently not finding it.

The contrast between rich and poor went far beyond the West End-East End divide. While the whole of the East End and the area bordering the Thames on the south were given over to the poorer classes there were many areas where the fine houses and rich living of the upper classes – less than four per cent of the population – stood within a mile of where the poor lived in misery.[2] The majority of the working classes, though labouring under difficult circumstances, managed to make some sort of living though the poorest merely existed.

The very poor lived in slums, in rooms, or more likely a whole extended family in a single room, rented for less than two shillings a week, but still a sizeable proportion of their income. There was no provision for cooking so they relied on ready cooked foods from street vendors, hot potatoes, two a penny, or cockles and whelks, which needed no cooking. With little room for furniture, even if it could be afforded, scant ventilation and almost non-existent sanitary arrangements – this was home for thousands. And for as many as lived in these overcrowded conditions, others were sleeping in lodging houses at a nightly rent of a few scarce pence, or homeless, existing the best they could on scraps put out in the street and from what they could beg, earn or steal.

Many men, women and children survived, or existed, through a life of crime; children as young as six begging and stealing. For women it was shoplifting or prostitution; for men, robbery, mugging and burglary. Passmore Edwards came into contact with this side of life one Sunday evening a few weeks after arriving in London, when he stopped to listen to a speaker addressing an open-air meeting. The speaker said that he would prove that eternity had a centre and fixing his eyes on Edwards said that one gentleman present could follow the drift of his argument, the basis of which was that immediately anyone could form a definite idea of time, that moment became the centre of eternity. At that moment a man standing next to Edwards tipped off the hat of the man in front. In the scuffle that followed, in which Edwards was almost knocked off his feet, he was relieved of his watch. The speaker was doubtless in league with those who robbed him while his attention was distracted. Edwards reflected that since then he had had ample time in which to meditate on the centre of eternity, and to take more care of his watch.[3]

Those finding refuge in the workhouse faired little better than those outside. Entering the workhouse meant giving up all self-respect and was to be dreaded. The conditions were harsh, families were separated, the food poor and insufficient, and the work hard, the Poor Law Amendment Act of 1834 ensuring that the poor could not be accused of sponging on their richer neighbours.[4]

The working classes, from the labourers and porters to the skilled artisans and engineers, lived only a little better, perhaps affording to rent two rooms. The Metropolitan Association for Improving the Dwellings of the Industrious Classes was formed in 1841 and started to build tenement blocks where families could be decently housed at a rent of 3 shillings to 3s 6d a week and speculative builders began to expand the residential areas out into the countryside. After becoming the proprietor of *Building News*, Edwards was often invited to attend ceremonies to open these new housing developments and called on the moneyed classes to invest in these schemes, arguing that a fair return on capital could be had by investing in housing for the English working classes, more than could be had by investing abroad. 'Using the capital we have at home in what will pay, and not speculating with it in foreign rubbish, at which game for every stockbroker that achieves a villa and a snug fortune, five hundred people suffer'.

In later life Edwards was criticised for owning houses that were rented out but responded that his ownership always resulted in lower rents, improvements, and better maintenance.

There was nearly always work for women, usually piecework making cheap clothing for the lower classes and fine dresses and hats of the affluent; both areas of labour were poorly paid and equally exploited.

The middle classes, from the lower ranks of clerks upwards, enjoyed a relatively more comfortable life, although for those at the lower end of the class, not much better paid. But whatever their financial standing, they attempted to retain their respectability; for the middle classes a tall hat, no matter how shabby, was preferable to no hat at all, the differential between them and the lower classes. The middle classes also tended to move out from the central slum areas to the suburbs, the more affluent moving to the more distant areas. Thousands of middle class workers walked several miles a day to and from work, whilst still more came into the city by train. Horse-drawn buses ran frequently through the city and out to the suburbs for 6d or less but the road layout had not been significantly improved since the turn of the century and although broad parallel thoroughfares existed, cross routes were often narrow and congested with traffic moving only at the rate of the slowest handcart. For the masses it was shank's pony.

Whilst the majority of the population was crammed together in such unhygienic conditions, Acts of Parliament were passed that allowed the Dukes of Westminster and Bedford to put up gates across the road, at the expense of the ratepayers, so denying access to the general public, and the House of Lords attempted to stop the construction of the Thames Embankment at Charing Cross because the Duke of Buccleuch's garden reached down to the river there.[5] In a similar manner the Chatham & Dover Railway was ordered to part cover the line with glass so as not to offend the residents of Pimlico with billowing smoke from the locomotives, although the railway companies were not obliged to replace the acres of slum housing they cleared to lay their lines into the city. Passmore Edwards was affected in this way when the house in Camberwell Grove where he lived when he first arrived in London was demolished to make way for the railway. The upper classes, though reliant upon the middle and working classes, lived as if in another parallel world.

More than half the children had no education of any value. Children had to earn their keep as soon as they were able, either working long poorly-paid hours or looking after those even younger, allowing the mother to work. If they were lucky they would attend a school organised by the London City Mission, a Sunday School, or one of the Ragged Schools. Teaching methods there were in most instances rudimentary, the 3 Rs, reading, writing and arithmetic, basic social skills and in all cases, religion. In addition the girls might be taught to sew and knit. For older boys there might be an apprenticeship to learn a trade, and for men a few places at classes at the mechanics' institute but nearly forty per cent of the men and women in London at that time remained illiterate.

An inquiry undertaken in London in 1842 showed that the life expectancy of a gentleman was twice that of someone from the working classes, who was unlikely to survive into his thirties. Children under five years of age accounted for more than half of all deaths. The hospitals that existed were run by voluntary contributions and were chronically short of funds. Poor diet and poor living conditions resulted in stunted growth and disease. And though medical progress allowed a more accurate diagnosis there was still no effective cure for the majority of the infectious diseases such as diphtheria, measles, scarlet fever and whooping cough that affected the young; and the widespread epidemics of tuberculosis, typhus, smallpox and venereal disease.

This then was the London to which Passmore Edwards travelled in 1845 and where he spent the rest of his life.

# Four
# In Pursuit of Reform

## Teetotalism

Like the Chartist Robert Lowery, Edwards believed that social reform would be ineffective unless preceded by moral reform. At the root of this was temperance. His speech at Chorley Temperance Society in September 1844 demonstrated the importance Edwards placed on the effects of alcohol on society and the obstacle to human progress that it represented. He openly admitted his family connection with the brewing trade and used that connection to emphasise the strength of his argument. Though he was not to say so in his autobiography, it is likely that he signed the pledge soon after arriving in Manchester. Through publication of the *Temperance Tract Journal* he continued his campaign to promote the Temperance movement and although, in later life, he was to move away from total abstinence, even then he considered alcohol consumption permissible only for medicinal purposes.

## Chartism

It is most improbable that Edwards, as he states in *A Few Footprints*, merely happened to find himself in Nottingham during that Easter weekend in 1848, as England 'edged unsteadily towards revolution'.[1] Protest meetings and demonstrations were taking place in London and across the country with resolutions passed in support of Ireland and the Charter. This was to be the movement's finest hour. Edwards would have not given any other issue a higher priority.

The Chartists were supporters of a mainly working-class movement that existed from the late 1830s through to the end of the 1840s, the Reform Act of 1832 having failed to appease the aspirations of the working classes. The Chartists wanted to bring about sweeping changes to the British Parliamentary system through the adoption of the Charter, which called for every man over the age of 21 to be given the vote and for ballots to be secret; for MPs to be paid a salary and for an end to the property qualification for candidates, to allow for working men to serve in Parliament; and a revision of the constituency boundaries so that each MP represented the same size population. Finally the Charter called for an annual Parliament so that MPs would have to answer to the voters if they did not perform to their liking.

While many of the Chartist leaders believed they could persuade Parliament to accept these reforms through debate and through lobbying and the use of petitions, others within the movement, particularly Feargus O'Connor,[2] proposed the use of less peaceful agitation to force Parliament to listen to their demands. Edwards, introduced to Chartism during his short time in Manchester with the *Sentinel*,[3] remained with the moral force camp, consistently denouncing the use of physical force and coercion.

The Government dismissed earlier petitions drawn up and presented to Paliament in 1839 and 1842, and the leaders, including O'Connor, were arrested and jailed. Violent demonstrations in Birmingham and Newport, Monmouthshire, were dealt with severely by the authorities and Chartist fervour and the threat of revolution diminished. It was not until 1847, when O'Connor was elected to Palrliament as the first Chartist MP, that a revival topok place.

When a new petition was launched thousands flocked to sign it, and with over five million signatures it was to be presented to Parliament in April 1848 after a mass meeting on London's Kennington Common. Similar meetings were planned in Bradford, in the North, and in Nottingham and Loughborough, in the Midlands. It was at these latter meetings that Edwards was to play his public part. Edwards said that he was in Nottingham on business on Saturday 8 April. His business concluded, he made his way to the market square where the Chartist meeting was to be held. Having listened to 'two or three fiery speeches' he pushed through the crowd to the wagon being used as a platform for the speakers, and 'as a stranger from London, asked leave to speak'. Addressing the crowd he sympathised with the Chartist demands but denounced the use of violence as a means to obtain it. The majority of the crowd appeared to agree with his views and the mood of the crowd quietened. Afterwards one of the organisers invited him to attend a meeting in Loughborough the following day and a second rally in Nottingham on the Monday. Edwards told him that he was intending to travel back to London that day, not having the means to stay in Nottingham, and he offered to pay Edwards' hotel expenses if he agreed to stay. On Sunday 9 April Edwards addressed a crowd of over 5,000 at Loughbough, the largest meeting ever seen in the town.

The magistrates met nearby, having sworn in a large number of special constables to support the regular police and a troop of the 4th Royal Irish Dragoons to assist the civil authorities if required. But the meeting concluded without trouble and by five o'clock in the afternoon the town was quiet.[4]

On Monday 10 April Edwards addressed the meeting in Nottingham and condemned the use of violence to gain political aims. As he was speaking, the military marched through the square, causing alarm amongst the crowd, but no trouble ensued.[5] Newspaper reports of the day describe Edwards as a lecturer for the London Peace Society,[6] again casting doubt on the coincidence of his timely presence at these events.

In London the crowds were met by thousands of Special Constables as they descended upon Kennington Common. The military were also waiting to intervene if the Chartists attempted to cross the Thames. The Government's response was sufficient for O'Connor to instruct the crowd to disperse and the petition was delivered to Parliament unaccompanied. By late afternoon the Queen, who had fled from London to stay at Osborne House on the Isle of Wight, was informed that the crisis was over.

The petition was later discredited and rejected after being found to contain a large number of false names and denied the political victory they hoped for, many of the Chartist activists turned their attention to social reform. Two days after the Kennington meeting the Peoples Charter Union was formed at a meeting at Farringdon Hall, with G J Holyoake[7] a founding member. From this Union evolved the Newspaper Stamp Abolition Committee, again involving Holyoake, and finally, in 1851, the Association for the Repeal of the Taxes on Knowledge, with Passmore Edwards as an active committee member.[8]

The six points of the Charter were eventually met over the years, the final parts, the payment of MP's salaries and the fixed term of Parliament being introduced in 1911, the year of Passmore Edwards' death.

**The Taxes on Knowledge**

In Britain newspapers had been subject to taxation since 1712; whereas initially this had been, at a halfpenny, principally as a source of revenue, in 1815 the tax was raised to 4d in an attempt to control the publication of radical propaganda. Average newspaper prices were then 6d or 7d, well out of the reach of the majority of working men earning less than 10 shillings a week. Newspapers were, however, often available to read in beer houses, encouraging drinking.

A rise in civil unrest and violence throughout the country at this time, resulting in the Peterloo Massacre, was met by the introduction of a series of legislative measures including the Newspaper Stamp Duties Act, which further increased control over newspapers and printed pamphlets. The 4d duty was applied to all publications that sold for less than 6d and contained any 'Public News, Intelligence of Occurrences or any Remarks or Observations thereon, or upon any Matter in Church or State', and were published more regularly than monthly. Publishers were also required to deposit a £200 to £300 bond with the Government, as surety against conviction for libel. The fine for possessing or circulating an unstamped newspaper was £20. In addition there was a tax on the paper used, one and a quarter pence per pound, as well as on each advertisement placed in a newspaper. All this increased the cost of newspapers to the extent that only the better off could afford them and the working classes were denied knowledge of the changing world. During the 1830s men such as Richard Carlile and Henry Hetherington refused to pay stamp duties on their papers and pamphlets and were arrested and jailed. In 1836 the campaigners had their first success with the stamp duty being lowered to 1d on newspapers and removed from pamphlets – but the campaign continued.

The stamped newspapers had an advantage over the unstamped publications in that a stamped newspaper could be sent through the postal service free of charge. Often newspapers would be hired out at 1d an hour and at the end of the day put on the train to be sent to country towns along with any other unsold editions that remained, there being no sale or return arrangements. Some papers could be sent six or seven times to different locations at no extra cost.

Following the failure of the Chartists' petition in 1848, the moderates – those abjuring violent agitation – who between them produced a number of radical journals, turned their attention to the tax on knowledge. It was into this arena that Edwards entered in 1850 with the publication of the *Public Good*.

The repeal of the stamp duty and the end to the privilege of free postage did not come until 1870, when it opened the way for cheap newspapers and changing their pattern of distribution.

**The Reform Movement**

The massive growth in the urban areas during the 1800s distorted the image of representation in Parliament. Constituency boundaries had not significantly changed to reflect the new centres of population and the majority of Members of Parliament were country landowners with little interest in parliamentary reform and elected by small numbers of voters. In Manchester, Birmingham and in London huge numbers of people had no means of influencing Parliament. Edwards was an active member of many of the groups associated with the reform movement, including the Ballot Society (1859), the Parliamentary Reform Committee (1860) and the Constitutional Defence Committee. In 1858 Edwards, then a member of the London Political Reform League, argued that there were 72 boroughs in England with a combined population of 459,000 that returned 113 members, while Tower Hamlets, with a population of 539,000 returned only two.[9] There was clearly an urgent need to redistribute the number of seats in Parliament and give the vote to a greater proportion of the population. Speaking at a meeting in Gloucester[10] that year, he said that the people had too long been made the mere playthings of rival statesmen and hoped the time would soon come when principles and not parties would have the most devoted followers. His view was that it was the upper classes that promoted 'the class war' and it was for the middle and working classes to work together to defeat them.

The Reform movement had begun in the late eighteenth century but after the demise of Chartism in 1848 the working classes became more apathetic to the reformers' calls for action.

In 1849 Edwards wrote an essay on what he called the New Movement.[11] He said that the lack of revolution in England was because of the political reform movement and the Anti-Corn Law League, not despite it. The ability to change unjust legislation had strengthened the British political system, not weakened it. But an absence of revolution and civil war was not evidence that there was no unjust legislation needing removal. He emphasised the need for financial reform – the rich were not contributing in relation to their wealth – and for suffrage. The eligibility to vote was a question of great importance and there was a need for greater and more equally distributed political power – all remaining areas of debate today. There was also as great a need for social reform, and Edwards was to devote his life to these aims.

In 1864 both the National Reform Union, which called for the vote to be given to all men, and the National Reform League, allied to the Liberals which did not advocate universal suffrage, were formed. When in June 1866 Gladstone's Reform Bill was defeated by a combination of Tories and the Adullamites (anti-Reform Liberals) the League organised public demonstrations throughout the country. With economic difficulties affecting the whole country the demonstrations were well supported. When a crowd of more than 30,000 turned out for a demonstration in London at the beginning of July, the League's leader, Edmund Beales, called for an even bigger meeting to be held in Hyde Park on Monday 23 July.[12] Passmore Edwards urged them to 'hold meeting after meeting until they surged up to Hyde Park three hundred thousand strong'. The Home Secretary, Spencer Walpole, feared a riot and banned the meeting. The organisers, therefore, amended their plans to march on Hyde Park, planning a retreat to Trafalgar Square for a rally if refused entry. When Beales and his committee arrived at Hyde Park on Monday evening, there were already thousands at Marble Arch. There were also 1,600 police constables surrounding the park and the military were on standby at the barracks. Having been refused entry to the park, Beales, as planned, left for Trafalgar Square leaving League members to divert the crowds in that direction. The crowds, however, were unaware of the new plan and pressed on towards the park. As the railings collapsed under the pressing crowd and supporters spilled into the park, the police charged and the military was summoned. Though it was midnight before the park was cleared the demonstrators were fuelled by excitement rather than malice and there were few injuries. The crowds returned the next day. Although there appeared to be a growing number of troublemakers amongst them they dispersed quietly when met with police resistance.

The Reform League, which prided itself on the peacefulness of its rallies, organised a further rally for Wednesday 25 July and sent a deputation to the Home Office headed by Beales. Beales asked that the rally should be allowed to go ahead without a police presence, leaving the control of the crowds in the hands of the League's stewards. Surprisingly, Walpole agreed and the meeting went ahead, attended without trouble by 40–50,000.

What part Edwards played in this meeting we do not know but when the League organised a further great demonstration in the park for Monday 30 July,[13] Edwards was certainly involved. At the last moment the meeting was transferred to the Agricultural Hall in Islington and more than 25,000 supporters packed the hall, with thousands more filling nearby streets. After several resolutions had been proposed and carried the meeting broke up into a number of smaller groups around the hall, one of which was addressed by Passmore Edwards, no doubt speaking against violence. In spite of such large numbers the meeting passed without any rowdiness and the mounted police standing by at nearby police stations were not needed.

Within months the Second Reform Bill had passed through Parliament and was enacted, the vote extended to hundreds of thousands of additional working men.

Edwards remained a member of the Union and in 1894, when Lord Rosebery became Prime Minister Edwards took his place as President of the London Reform Union. During the run up to the London County Council elections in 1895 he personally funded the printing of three million leaflets to promote the Union's electoral programme, central to which was the extension of direct labour.

## 'The Two Sisters'

Edwards might be thought of as a pioneer of European unity, in so far as he called for greater co-operation with Britain's nearest neighour, France.

During the early 1800s the political unrest in France caused great concern amongst the English ruling classes and any agitation by English radicals received a stern reaction. Edwards saw what he called 'abundant reason and necessity' why England and France should regard each other as natural friends.

In 1848 Edwards wrote an article, 'The Two Sisters', which was first published in the *Peoples Journal*. In it he argued that there was no shadow of reason why the two countries should consider themselves as 'natural enemies', as the military and many of the Press were promoting at that time. 'Why,' he argued, 'should two nations whose geographical positions were so contiguous, whose history moved on somewhat parallel lines, whose institutions were moulded by similar forces, who inherited and enjoyed a common civilisation, and who could, with equal advantage, promote each other's welfare, look upon each other with jealous or angry eyes and make such vast preparations to check, counter or crush each other?' Sections of the article were translated into French and published in France and later Edwards was to become involved in the first exchange trips of working men between Paris and London.

## The London Committee of Working Men

The Working Men's Excursion to Paris was organised in response to a proposed visit to Paris by a group called the Rifle Volunteers.[14] The prospect of such a trip by a military group led the London Committee of Working Men to propose an excursion of working men, who would tour Paris – a pleasure trip with a moral purpose, shaking hands with Parisian *ouvriers* to assure them that they had no desire other than to live at peace with their continental neighbours.

The Committee, presided over by Joseph Paxton, the designer of the Crystal Palace, was, in itself, not a working-class group but the members were men who had risen from humble backgrounds and these included John Passmore Edwards.

The combination of travel with a moral and educational purpose for working-class folk appealed to Thomas Cook, who had been organising excursions and tours for more than a decade, and he wrote to the Committee to offer his services. Visiting Paris he put together a list of reasonably priced hotels and eating houses and was later able to offer vouchers covering a hotel and meals for five to six shillings a day for those that wished to pay in advance, and in sterling.

A party of around 1,700, men and women, made the journey during the summer of 1861, an impressive number, and the visitors received a warm welcome in Paris. It was intended, by the organisers, that the visitors would be able to see and compare living conditions in Paris and London and especially the dwellings built by housing developers for rent. The excursionists might be expected to come to their own conclusions regarding the principles upon which they were erected and whether they were applicable to Britain.[15] They were warned, however, that the visit was in no way connected with politics and if any of them should try to make political advantage of the trip and by so doing find themselves in a French prison, then 'Serve him Right'.

The success of the visit led to a second excursion the following year but the timing clashed with the 1862 London Exhibition and attracted lower numbers. For Thomas Cook the excursions were ones that he later described as 'of love, minus profit' for they were not financially successful.

# Five
# Early Steps in Publishing

On arrival in London Edwards found employment as a clerk in a publishing house, perhaps that of Charles Gilpin, and it is likely that he lived at the home of George Cox, an optician and Chartist, having been given an introduction when he left Manchester. Working days would be long but he still found time to study at the Mechanics' Institute and Birkbeck College and to continue lecturing.

He was lecturing not only in London but also in Cornwall during his annual family visits, and no doubt stopped off on the way to help fund the trip; he also returned to the north of England on several occasions. In February 1847 he was back in Manchester, delivering lectures on Temperance and the Irish Famine;[1] and in March of the following year he was in Chepstow, again to give a lecture on Temperance.

If this was not sufficiently busy, he was sending off articles to newspapers and journals including the *Morning Chronicle*, 'some of which were inserted and others not; and some of those which were inserted were paid for, and others were not'.[2]

### *The Public Good*

As a child Edwards regularly read the *Penny Magazine* published by Charles Knight for the Society for the Diffusion of Useful Knowledge. With illustrated articles on subjects of general interest, short biographies, natural history and descriptions of manufacturing processes, and even some poetry, it was aimed at a working-class readership and was very successful. It is not surprising that Edwards' first steps at publishing should follow this pattern.

By 1850 he had accumulated around fifty pounds capital and began publishing a monthly periodical, which he called the *Public Good*. 'If he could write for others,' he said, 'then he could write for himself.' On the advice of Charles Gilpin, later MP for Northampton (1857–1874), with whom he had worked on several political reform committees, Edwards obtained both paper and printing costs on credit. Initially Gilpin published the journal but to save on publishing costs he took this on as well, first renting a small room in Paternoster Row for four shillings a week where he worked by day, and slept on a cot bed at night. The constant noise, however, in this busy area denied him the sleep he needed and he fairly quickly decamped to lodgings at 16 Hardinge Street, Islington, where at the time of the 1851 census Edwards' brother, Richard, was also living, describing himself as a writer.

Passmore Edwards had been contributing to *Howitt's Journal* for some time, with articles on the 'Mission of Richard Cobden' and reports on the 1848 Peace Conference. The *Public Good* followed the formula originally set by the *Penny Magazine*. 'It (the *Public Good)* was established,' he said, 'to advocate great principles, advance useful institutions, and elevate man.' The preface to the first volume stated that it was 'a book possessing literary charms blended with utility of purpose'. According to Edwards, the mechanics' institutes and literary societies had not prospered as well as they might because they were forbidden from introducing either politics or religion into lectures and debates. As these were two of the 'great realities of life and human society', institutions that excluded them could not expect to win the support of the masses. Many of the cheaper periodicals also excluded the discussion of political subjects whilst Edwards was determined that the *Public Good* was to be conducted on a different principle.

In an early issue of the journal he wrote and published 'The Intellectual Toll Bar', an article published separately as a pamphlet as an open attack on the tax on paper and newspapers. The revenue from the paper tax, he argued, was only around three-quarters of a million pounds in 1848, yet the harm it did in limiting the education of the population was enormous. He later added that the paper tax also increased the price of papier-mâché goods, popular at the time but mostly imported. A removal of the tax would end the import advantage of these articles creating more than 30,000 jobs.

Due to the paper tax the *Public Good* was close printed on pages about seven inches by four inches, not the magazine sizes familiar to us today. Edwards said that the *Public Good* could be made twenty-five per cent larger for the same price, if not for the paper tax. He did not say that the journal might have been profitable if not for the tax. The stamp on newspapers at the same time raised only £360,000, a small amount but again penalising the working classes. Taxes on advertisements, 1s 6d per advertisement since 1833, discriminated against the stable boy who paid the same price when looking for a position as the country gentleman when selling or renting out his estate. Not letting an opportunity slip to promote his pacifist principles he pointed out that the shortfall in revenue could be easily made up by spending less on the armed forces and more economy in the general affairs of state, going on to describe the difficulty of applying the stamp, the need for references from two guarantors, paying the bond, the stamping of each copy of the published journal and payment of duty to the authorities. More than half of the cover price of the *Public Good* was taxation, though it could then be posted free of charge to the purchaser.

Few copies of the *Public Good* exist, the British Library holding only copies from 1850 and 1851. In these, articles are rarely credited with the author's name, although some have the initials 'JPE'. Edwards could not have afforded to commission many articles at this time. One can be fairly sure that the contents do, at least, meet with Edwards firmly held views as they deal with those aspects of society for which he had campaigned and continued to campaign for the whole of his life. An item in the first edition of 1851 considers the role of the mechanics' institutes, the source of much of Edwards' own education, and another on the establishment of 'Two-penny Polytechnics', which bore a greater similarity to community centres than purely centres of education. Pieces on capital punishment, pacifism, financial and political reform, temperance and vegetarianism also appeared, the latter including articles by Edwards' brother, Richard, all in keeping with the issues Edwards considered important

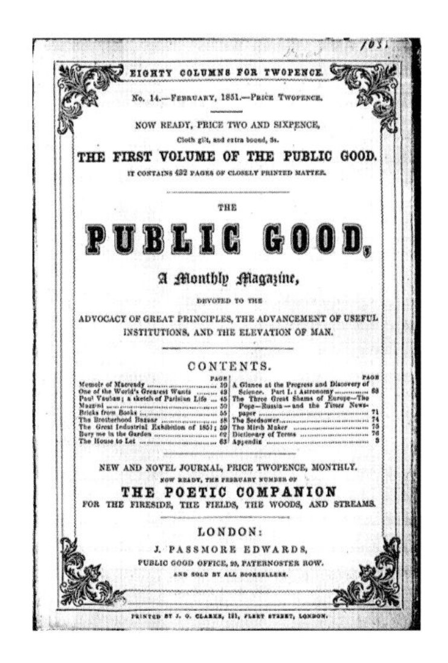
EIGHTY COLUMNS FOR TWOPENCE.

No. 14.—February, 1851.—Price Twopence.

NOW READY, PRICE TWO AND SIXPENCE,
Cloth gilt, and extra bound, 3s.
THE FIRST VOLUME OF THE PUBLIC GOOD.
IT CONTAINS 432 PAGES OF CLOSELY PRINTED MATTER.

THE
PUBLIC GOOD,
A Monthly Magazine,
DEVOTED TO THE
ADVOCACY OF GREAT PRINCIPLES, THE ADVANCEMENT OF USEFUL INSTITUTIONS, AND THE ELEVATION OF MAN.

CONTENTS.

| | PAGE | | PAGE |
|---|---|---|---|
| Memoir of Macready | 39 | A Glance at the Progress and Discovery of Science. Part I.: Astronomy | 68 |
| One of the World's Greatest Wants | 43 | The Three Great Shams of Europe—The Pope—Russia—and the *Times* Newspaper | 71 |
| Paul Vaulan; a sketch of Parisian Life | 45 | The Seedsower | 74 |
| Mazzini | 50 | The Mirth Maker | 75 |
| Bricks from Books | 55 | Dictionary of Terms | 76 |
| The Brotherhood Bazaar | 58 | Appendix | 3 |
| The Great Industrial Exhibition of 1851 | 59 | | |
| Bury me in the Garden | 62 | | |
| The House to Let | 63 | | |

NEW AND NOVEL JOURNAL, PRICE TWOPENCE, MONTHLY.
NOW READY, THE FEBRUARY NUMBER OF
THE POETIC COMPANION
FOR THE FIRESIDE, THE FIELDS, THE WOODS, AND STREAMS.

LONDON:
J. PASSMORE EDWARDS,
PUBLIC GOOD OFFICE, 30, PATERNOSTER ROW.
AND SOLD BY ALL BOOKSELLERS.

PRINTED BY J. O. CLARKE, 121, FLEET STREET, LONDON.

Throughout his adult life Edwards attacked the *Times* newspaper, which he saw as a 'huge intellectual machine without conscience or heart, careless of the blows it gives to liberty or progress so long as it pleases at one time or another a majority of its shareholders'.[3] He believed it held a monopoly position by virtue of the newspaper stamp. The end of the tax on newspapers would 'see this heartless, principle-less paper fall from its lofty heights and eat humble pie while struggling with a host of competitors'. As early as 1844 he had referred to the *Times*' grudging support of the suffrage movement, likening it to its defence of Queen Caroline, which it declared only after it had canvassed public opinion.

The *Public Good* of 1851 contained the first two of a series of articles, written by Edwards under the title 'The three great Shams, The Pope, Russia and the *Times*'. Unfortunately the final part, relating to the *Times* is not at the British Library but it probably concerned the paper's opposition to the Hungarian revolutionary Lajos Kossuth. Edwards delivered a lecture at the Literary Institution, Fitzroy Square, in November 1851, entitled 'The Infamous Policy of the *Times* Newspaper',[4] regarding the *Times*' opposition to the struggle for freedom in Hungary. The reason, argued Edwards, was that the paper was in cahoots with Baron Rothschild, who had financial interests in the area being put at risk by the unrest.

As with many publications of the time there was an annual edition, published at the *Public Good* Office, Lovell's Court, Paternoster Row, containing bound copies of all twelve monthly editions – *neatly stitched in a wrapper, 2s; 2s 6d well bound in cloth; and 3s handsomely bound with gilt edges*. Volume one was advertised as comprising '92 essays and articles; 30 tales and sketches; 30 reviews and notices of books; 20 controversial letters – Edwards would often write letters addressed to 'the Editor' with views that he could then challenge in print – 100 autographs; 75 biographies and biographical notices; 128 poems; 20 anecdotes; five allegories; 43 epitaphs; six suggestions; 46 hints; 12 enigmas, charades etc; 500 paragraphs and extracts from standard books and authors; 47 couplets; 40 student's questions and answers; 230 answers to correspondents, etc, etc'. In case this didn't suit one's needs one could also buy bound collections of eight separate *Public Good Tracts* for 6d, or individual tracts at the rate of four a penny or 1s 8d per hundred. No stone was left unturned in Edwards' attempts at spreading the word, increasing circulation and increasing the viability of the publication.

His declared ambition was to publish 50,000 copies a month, which he is unlikely to have achieved; although he sold several thousands copies monthly, the margins were too small. To increase the price would defeat the primary object of affordability for the working classes, so, in order to help finance the *Public Good* he started a second monthly publication – the *Temperance Tract Journal*.

***Temperance Tract Journal***

The beginning of 1851, the second year of publication of the *Public Good*, was greeted with a prophecy. 'Every January in particular,' he wrote, 'witnesses the birth of a new brood of new aspirants for popular support. It would be unreasonable to suppose that one half of the new candidates will live to see the summer'. No doubt he did not consider that his own publications, in which he had complete confidence of success, would be among the unfortunate half.

The first edition of the *Temperance Tract Journal* appeared on 1 January 1851 and in the opening editorial Edwards wrote that the mission of the Press was to 'mentally and virtually elevate man', and that the penny periodical was 'one of the chief revolutionisers of modern society'. The Temperance movement owed much of its success to the Press and although several Temperance journals were issued monthly there was, he considered, room for one more. What differentiated Edwards' journal from the others was the way in which it was published. Containing essays, Aesop-like tales, reviews, biographical sketches, 'facts and comments', and reports on the Temperance movement throughout the world, the journal was printed so that each copy could be separated into eight distinct and complete tracts. These could then be distributed to others to spread the Temperance message.

> A teetotaller, or any one else, may, for one penny a month, get the journal, read it; and then divide it into eight parts, and distribute them to the best advantage'. 'A Temperance Society, by taking say ten dozen a month, at the rate of nine pence a dozen, may scatter abroad 960 tracts a month for 7s 6d; or 11,520 tracts a year for £4 10s. At this rate, 10,000 teetotallers, for one penny a month, may distribute 960,000 in one year. And one hundred societies, taking ten dozen each a month, would distribute … 2,112,000 temperance tracts in one year. And what tongue can describe, or imagination paint, the possible good such a vast number of useful tracts, judiciously distributed every year, in all likelihood, could do? The great Author of Temperance and Truth, God alone, can tell.

One such tract was 'The Restored Husband' by J Passmore Edwards. Whether fact or fiction, it was the short story of Andrew Jenkin who lived in the village of Jackfield, Shropshire. Andrew was described as being an artist working in the pottery workshops in Coalbrookdale who had taken to drink, abusing his wife and children and falling to a position whereby he could only find irregular labouring work to fund his habit. Andrew junior, his eldest son, left home to work as a stable boy in Wolverhampton, some 15 miles distant but the boy's mother, who was supporting herself and the other four children by whatever work she could find, still walked each week to Wolverhampton to visit her child to keep him from falling into harm. Eventually, after drunkardly walking home one night and falling dead drunk on the edge of an open mine shaft, the father sees the error of his ways, joins the Temperance Society and signs the pledge. Gradually the home and home life is restored and he becomes once again a respected member of the community and is reunited with his son in a tearful reunion. Just a few years later the son meets a young woman at the Wellington Temperance Society summer outing on the top of the Wrekin and they eventually marry. On this happy day, the writer of the article being in the village, is invited to pass the evening with the newly wedded pair and their friends. Of the twenty-five persons present, twenty-two were members of the Temperance Society. Of the eight men, five were reclaimed drunkards. Edwards concludes that the evening passed harmoniously, and the party separated as sober as when it assembled, which is not frequently the case on such occasions as wedding days. While Andrew Jackson does not appear on the census of 1841 or 1851 for Shropshire, Edwards may well have visited the area when he was in Manchester during his days as a Temperance lecturer in the early 1840s and come across such a story.

Edwards also suggested that the public might wish to subscribe to a fund, £50 a year was needed, which would be used to send a copy of the *Journal*, each month, to all of the editors of the estimated 500 daily and weekly newspapers and magazines which were then published in Britain. 'Who can describe the good which this plan, if it were carried out, would do to the world?'

Whether the public were impressed with Edwards' view of the value of such a publication we do not know but *Bibliotheca Cornubiensis*, a catalogue of publications relating to Cornwall, published in 1874, records that only two issues, January and February 1851, were published, and only these two are to be found at the British Library.

### *Biographical Magazine*

As today, the Victorian's were fascinated with the lives of the famous and there was a ready market for their biographies. Edwards had published many accounts of the men that he admired, including the life of Richard Cobden in *Howitt's Journal*, and when the *Temperance Tract Journal* failed to realize the profit levels needed he decided to publish a cheap monthly biographical journal for mass circulation.

In promoting the magazine, he said, 'It will be devoted entirely to the Biography of Great Men, and especially those of the Present Age, and of all Nations'.

The *Biographical Magazine* was first published on 1 January 1852 and included Louis Napoleon, the Bishop of Norwich and Kossuth, the Hungarian democrat. The price was 6d. Generally reviews were supportive, the *Examiner* (London 1852) stating 'we find its papers written with liberality of temper and good sense', and the *Belfast Newsletter* (Belfast 1852), 'Not withstanding its extreme cheapness, 6d each number, it contains forty-eight double columned pages of valuable matter, elegantly printed, and is, on the whole, worthy of extended patronage'.

Again, an annual bound volume was available, entitled *The Lives of the Illustrious*. In the preface to the second volume Edwards expounds on the value of biography, the 'Romance of History'. 'Puppets move and talk upon the stage of life,' he wrote. 'We go behind the scenes and see the wires pulled. The mind of the king is in the hands of a minister. We want to be intimate with the minister rather than the automaton he controls. If a plan of campaign is drawn up by a subaltern, the subaltern is the man for us to know, not the commander who takes all the fame. We yearn to see the secrets of the heart that through other agencies moves the world'. Edwards clearly identified himself with the 'minister' and 'subaltern'.

The *Biographical Magazine* appears to have ceased by the end of 1855 but Edwards was later to find himself a subject of a similar publication, the *Gem Series of Illustrated Biographies*, edited by S G Hobson, and published by P Maurice & Co, New Bridge St, Ludgate Circus in eight parts at 1d each. Part seven contained a single page account of Edwards' *Life*, accompanied by the familiar photo by Elliot & Fry, and was probably published in 1903, before *A Few Footprints*.

### Poetic Companion

Poetry had always played a part in Edwards' life. Although the editor of the *West Briton* had dismissed his earliest attempts,[5] he took the opportunity afforded to him, as his own proprietor and editor, to include his own work, amongst that of others, in his early publications. There were poems included in the *Public Good*, the *Temperance Tract Journal*, and the *Peace Advocate*.

*The Poetic Companion – for The Fireside, the Fields, the Woods and the Streams*, as it was poetically entitled, was first published in January 1851. While the first issue passed into three editions, only two issues are retained at the British Library and it is probable that these were the only issues published. The first issue contained a poem by H J Daniell, a Cornish poet who had occupied on more than one occasion that elusive spot, the poetry corner in the *West Briton*, when Edwards was a youngster.

In 'Lines suggested by witnessing a storm at sea on the North coast of Cornwall', was written

> I stood upon a rock and viewed the sea
> Raging and wild in all its awful might;
> The mighty warrior of infinity,
> Where God is ever present to the sight.

This, no doubt reminded Edwards of his former life in Cornwall and in particular walks along the north Cornwall coastline near Blackwater, a memory he was to refer to in his own autobiography many years later.

The following year a second attempt to publish a periodical dedicated to poetry was made with the *Poetic Review, and Miscellany of Imaginative Literature*, priced 6d. It was to include original poems, whether by Edwards we do not know, biographical sketches of poets, reviews of new poetical works and essays on poets and poems. 'It will show,' said its prospectus, 'the philosophy of poetry and the poetry of philosophy'. This was certainly an ambitious undertaking but the reviewer for the *Examiner* commented 'We doubt whether it will encompass its design'.[6] In later life Edwards is referred to as 'a small poet', in a put-down by a rival journal.[7]

### The Peace Advocate

Charles Gilpin had published the *Peace Advocate*, the monthly journal of the Peace Societies, since 1840. In 1847 the editor announced that he was to resign and the mantle was first taken up by a trio lead by Henry Gardiner Adams. By November 1850, however, Edwards heard that publication of the *Advocate* was to cease and wrote to Adams to say that he would take over total responsibility so that the publication might continue.

The first issue of 1851 carried a message from the new proprietor, pointing out the achievements since the *Advocate* had first been published; the repeal of the Corn Laws in 1846; the defeat of the Government's attempts to establish a militia system in England in 1845; the establishment of the League of Universal Brotherhood in 1847; and the three Peace Conferences, of 1848, 1849 and 1850.[8] All campaigns in which Edwards had played some part.

Circulation was only around 2,500 copies per month, and at 1d Edwards considered that the circulation needed to double for the journal to become viable. *Bibliotheca Cornubiensis* records that Edwards published only the January and February issues for 1851, both retained at the British Library, and these contain several pieces reprinted or rewritten from the *Public Good*.[9]

**Almanacs and Directories**

By the end of 1851 Edwards had dispensed with his single room in Paternoster Row and was at 2, Horse-shoe Court, Ludgate Hill. He published three almanacs during this period. The *Public Good Almanac* for 1852, published on 1 November 1851, price 2d, contained details of all of the charities in London at the time and the work that they carried out. Also included were statistics about public libraries, an unfavourable comparison between Britain and other countries, and statistics revolving around the Great Exhibition that had taken place at Crystal Palace that year. The *Peace Almanac and Moral Reformers' Hand-Book*, published later the same month at 3d, contained a variety of information about the various Peace Societies and Leagues of Brotherhood together with articles on Temperance issues, capital punishment, the Ocean penny post, for which Edwards had campaigned with Elihu Burritt, the ragged schools, and the anti-llavery movement.

Always ready to make use of his skills and experience in support of his many campaigns, Edwards published a set of five 'moral reform' envelopes in aid of the anti-slavery movement, the Ocean penny post, peace, temperance and the Universal Brotherhood. These illustrated envelopes decorated with quotations and tracts were sold for 3d a dozen with the proceeds divided amongst the causes he supported.

The *Literary Almanac and Publishers', Booksellers', Authors', Editors' and General Readers' Directory* for 1852 was published on 1 December 1851, price 6d. It was published, it said, 'to supply a decided want' – but who decided, and whether it satisfied that want, we can only surmise.

Edwards excused any inaccuracies because it was 'got up in a hurry' but promised that there would be no room for a similar excuse next year. However, he said that the best of almanacs had errors because the information they contained was liable to change even during production. Somewhat arrogantly, he said that for some weeks past it had been known that the almanac would be published, plenty of time for publishers, editors, periodical proprietors and secretaries of mechanics' institutions to send in the correct, up-to-date, information for publication. 'Several have availed themselves of the privilege and those who have not should not lay all the blame on the editor's shoulders, if any errors should be found in the work'.

The *Almanac* listed memorable birthdays for each month, a list of books published during 1851; lists of London and provincial newspapers with cost, circulation, date established, political outlook, place, date and time of publication; lists of colleges in London; schools of art; private galleries; mechanics' institutes in England; obituaries of eminent people who had died during the year; literary events that had taken place and statistics for public libraries – again, Britain comparing not very favourably with European towns. There were even hints to advertisers on effective advertising at minimum cost. The advertisements contained in this and other of his publications were mainly of recently published works amongst which were, of course, the *Public Good*, the *Biographical Magazine* and *Familiar Things*.

### *Familiar Things* and *Wonderful Things*

The encyclopaedia that is published in 'inexpensive' weekly parts is well known to us today. Edwards made two early attempts at publishing an encyclopaedia in this way.

A publication called *Familiar Things* was advertised in the *Literary Almanac* – to be published monthly at 2d, four volumes being published in 1851. 'It was,' it said, 'an encyclopaedia of entertaining knowledge; 384 pages, 80 illustrations'. The contents included brief articles on 'a book' – paper making, printing, binding; the needle; 'our cup of tea' – milk, water; the sponge; lamps – street lighting, gas lamps; air; the potter; the piano; and silk production.

Part one of *Wonderful Things* was published in June 1852. To be published 'in 24 weekly parts, again at 2d; each part was to contain 32 pages and several beautiful pictures'.[10] It was 'to give accurate and interesting descriptions accompanied with pictorial illustrations, of the most remarkable wonders of the Ancient and Modern World'. Including such subjects as buildings and ruins, monuments, mountains, caverns, lakes and rivers; earthquakes, volcanoes and tornadoes; and 'the most splendid triumphs of modern times, such as the steam engine, the electric telegraph, the daguerreotype (early photographic process) and the air balloon, 'the work will be, without exception, one of the most interesting and instructive, and at the same time one of the cheapest books of this age of wonderful publications'. The British Library catalogue only refers to parts 1-14 in their archives, through until the end of 1852.

### *The Microscope*

Whereas *Wonderful Things* was written for mass circulation, the *Microscope*, first published in October 1852, set out, not only to 'give a accurate information and beautiful illustrations of the wonders of the unseen world, as revealed by the microscope', but 'will also be found an admirable manual for the use of students in Chemistry, Physiology, Entomology and Botany' a 'Handbook of Scientific Recreation for all Classes of readers'.

Although Edwards intended to publish in twelve monthly parts, at the price of 2d, it is unlikely that the series was completed. The British Library catalogue has no mention of this title by Edwards but issues one and three are to be found in the Wellcome Institute library in London. They give no credit to an author or contributors. In the introduction to the first issue Edwards gives his intentions as publishing 'in simple language and pleasing forms' the principle scientific achievements brought about through use of the microscope by the mid-nineteenth century. Reference is made to the work of several of the leading scientists and microscopists of the time, like the German Christian Ehrenberg, Dr Arthur Hill Hassell, Dr Gideon Mantell and Andrew Pritchard, and it is likely that Edwards simply rewrote, or copied, their work and used their illustrations in his journal. Indeed chapter one of issue one is entitled *Infusorial Animalcules*, the title used by Pritchard for his own book, published a few months earlier in 1852, and illustrations and text are copied from Dr Mantell's *Thoughts on Animalcules*, published in 1846. Edwards even makes use of the same quotation from Dr Thomas Chalmers in the introduction to *Microscope* as used by Dr Mantell in the introduction to his work.

**A Magazine for Children**

Contemporary advertisements also refer to a magazine devoted entirely to children, called the *Children's Favourite*, but alas no copy of this exists at the British Library. However, one can imagine that its flavour resembled his own early reading matter, the *Penny Magazine*, and his encyclopaedias, *Wonderful Things*, and *Favourite Things*, probably including material recycled from earlier publications, rather than the pure entertainment of the twentieth-century *Beano* and *Dandy*.

There was the arrogance of youth in the way Edwards launched these early publications. He expressed a confidence that he was meeting a need and the value that his publications would be to the reader. Apart from the poetry journals, and maybe the *Microscope*, there seems to have been a ready market and good reviews, though he admitted 'The praise I received did not butter parsnips'. He knew that the cover price must be low enough for his target audience to afford, and not above that of similar journals on the market. He clearly could not have reduced his costs further, but in some ways he provided too great a bargain for his readers, enlarging content in order to attract additional sales, rather than reducing it to improve the margins. His objective was, partially, to educate the working classes, and to provide a platform to voice his opinions, rather than to provide him with riches.

To what extent his brother, Richard, contributed we do not know, other than the few articles published under his name. By 1852 Richard had departed London and was living in Bath, leaving his elder brother to carry on alone. The magnitude of the task appears to have overwhelmed him. No matter how hard he worked he sank deeper and deeper into debt, finally owing several thousands pounds.

# Six
# The Darkest of Days

William Barnes Passmore, a cousin of Passmore Edwards, recorded in his memoirs[1] that in 1852 'Passmore Edwards who was proprietor of the *Public Good* and other periodicals appears to have got into difficulties for one morning I received a pressing letter from him to go to see him at Whitecross Street Prison, his stationer having clapped him in prison for debt. This was a very foolish thing to do he being a man of high principle and the difficulty only temporary. I went but could not see my way to help him. I had no position to go bail for him and declined to apply to my employer for assistance, and as he begged of me never to mention the case to my father, I could do nothing. He lost his health which did not surprise me, the place being most vile and stinking, and went to my friends at Kingston to recruit (sic).'

No wonder Edwards described this as the darkest days of his life.

The events of the following two years are unclear. In October 1854 the *London Gazette* recorded that 'Passmore Edwards, late of 15 York Buildings, Adelphi. Middlesex, out of business, in the Debtors Prison for London and Middlesex', had petitioned for bankruptcy and that 'orders had been made Assigning' his 'Estates and effects'.

His early publications appear to have ceased in 1852, apart from the *Biographical Magazine*, which continued under a different publisher until 1855. The British Library holds no copies of later publications and adverts cease to appear in newspapers and journals of the time. There were no reports of Edwards attending political meetings or reform campaigns from the end of 1852 until May 1854. In his autobiography Edwards makes no direct reference to the debtors prison stating that it was his illness, and a subsequent absence from his office 'for a period of ten weeks until he was well enough to resume work', which resulted in his bankruptcy.

In 1854 either the creditors or, as in Edwards' case, the debtor could petition for adjudication in bankruptcy. The official assignee, appointed by the Court, would value and dispose of the assets of the debtor and the money raised would be paid into the Bank of England for distribution to the creditors. After the rate of distribution was agreed with the creditors, but not necessarily before they received all of the money they were due to receive, a request was made for a Certificate of Conformity, a statement that the bankrupt had satisfied all legal requirements. There were three classes of certificate – where the bankrupt was blameless; where some blame could be attributed; and where it was entirely the bankrupt's fault.

Passmore Edwards was summoned to appear before the Court at Portugal Street, Lincoln's Inn, on Saturday 9 December 1854, at 11am. The case files are no longer available, but an account of Edwards' court appearance was widely reported.[2] Edwards, described as the proprietor of the late *Favorite Magazine*, was applying to be discharged from bankruptcy and this was opposed by Messers Magnay, the wholesale stationer. Edwards' losses were attributed to several publications, the sum of £1,500 being the loss from *Uncle Toms' Companions*, *Familiar Things*, *Poetic Companion*, *Wonderful Things*, *Biographical Magazine* and the *Public Good*. Magnay complained that Edwards had entered into contracts for the supply of paper for his publications without a reasonable expectation of being able to pay for it. Referring to the *Favorite Magazine*, Edwards said that the reason why this did not succeed was the high cost of paper. He estimated that the magazine would have made a profit with sales of 10,000 copies and the first number sold upwards of 7,000. He reduced the size of the magazine and this should have been profitable with 5,000 sales, but did not achieve this number. It appeared during the examination that Edwards was also writing articles for the *Empire Newspaper* at one guinea a time. Magnay, most likely William Magnay, who was also declared insolvent a few years later, argued that the publication of the *Favorite Magazine*, with little hope of success, constituted a 'waste of property' and as such Edwards was not justified in entering into the debt. The examining Commissioner, however, sided with Edwards, expressing the view that some latitude should be given to literary publications suggesting that otherwise many popular works would not have been published. Adjudication was made on 18 December 1854 with Edwards being discharged 'forthwith'. Passmore Edwards later stated that his debts totalled several thousand pounds and that sale of his assets brought in sufficient to pay his creditors only five shillings in the pound.

His absence from the public eye due to his financial problems and subsequent illness extended to more than 12 months. This was a long time for someone with such burning passions as Passmore Edwards.

**The Road to Recovery**

Just one of Edwards' earlier publications, the *Biographical Magazine*, remained in publication for a while after his bankruptcy, published by Partridge Oakey & Co, Paternoster Row, with Passmore Edwards as editor.

Although legally clear of his debts he resolved to pay back every penny he owed. There were, he said, one or two things he wanted to do in life and could not do with this moral debt weighing him down. He resolved to redeem his credit and pay everyone in full. He felt that every man should be as good as his word. He had borrowed on a promise to pay back and felt bound to fulfil that promise, 'even if it were at the expense of inconvenience or sacrifice', and maintained that 'no lapse of time, no statute of limitations, no receipts in full, no legal release, not even insolvent debtors' court or Queen's Bench prisons, can pay just debts'. Perhaps he had the words of Dr James Martineau in mind, 'Whoever avails himself of mere legal release as a moral exemption, is a candidate for infamy in the eyes of all uncorrupted men'.[3]

Though struggling to recover his name and his career he did not forget the struggles of others and his work for social and political reform, through the many organisations that fought to bring about change, continued.

By May of 1854, Edwards was back in the newspaper reports, attending a Peace Society meeting at Finsbury Road chapel, Moorfields, and a month later chairing a public meeting in relation to the abolition of capital punishment. Within a few months he had written, *The War; A Blunder and a Crime*, debating and arguing against the British and French campaign against Russia, the Crimean War. Published as a pamphlet with over 50 closely printed pages it was to find its way, in September 1855, into the hands of William Gladstone who, after resigning as Chancellor was at his holiday home in Wales. He noted in his diary 'Read Edwards on the War',[4] referring, of course, to Passmore Edwards' pamphlet, although we are not fortunate in knowing just what Gladstone thought about the merits of this work. To have financed the publication of this pamphlet a few months after being discharged for bankcrutpcy was a measure of his immense selfless principles.

He is known to have written for both the *Eclectic Review*, a London magazine, and *Tait's Edinburgh Magazine*, in the late 1850s,[5] and no doubt there were many other contributions as Edwards struggled to regain his livelihood.

In 1857 Edwards turned his pen to denouncing the opium traffic between India and China and the complicity of the British over this 'odious trade'. The result was a pamphlet entitled *The Triple Curse*, delivered as a lecture at the Guildhall, Bath, on 9 January 1858. The blame was laid squarely on the shoulders of the East India Company, which was growing the opium on its plantations in India and selling it in China. The Chinese Government had attempted to prevent the importation of opium and destroyed all that they could seize. When 20,000 chests of opium were seized and destroyed the East India Company, through the British Representative in Canton, demanded compensation. When this was not paid, Britain went to war. Wooden sailing junks were no match for iron gunboats and a bombardment of Canton killed more than 30,000 Chinese.

In August 1864 Edwards turned up at the Welsh National Eisteddfod in Llandudno. As a Celt he was, no doubt, made welcome and as a writer, biographer, minor poet and publisher, he was either invited to speak, or some how arranged to do so. Whether his controversial speech was welcomed is not recorded; he remarked that a certain English production, likely to be Milton's *Paradise Lost*, should not and could not be translated into Welsh, and as a consequence English should be taught in all Welsh schools so that everyone could appreciate the works of one of the masters of English.

By May 1865 Edwards had paid off his creditors, with interest.[6] Edwards said that he had done what everyone who had it in his power ought to do. He did not recognise the fact that the law exonerates a man from a just debt. As soon as he had sufficient to pay off his creditors he did just that, against the advice of his friends who suggested that he should secure a greater surplus of capital first.

His action so surprised his creditors – all, that is, apart from William Magnay – that they arranged to hold a banquet in his honour and presented him with an inscribed gold watch. When the idea of a testimonial was first put to Edwards he tried to discourage them, saying that three things had motivated him: first a duty to himself, second a duty to his creditors and third a duty to society.

Held at the Albion Tavern, Aldergsate Street, and with John Hodges of Spalding &

Hodge (Stationers) in the chair, the proceeds of the evening were widely reported in the press.[7] During the evening, between the speeches, a soloist gave a rendering of a song entitled 'Let us speak of the man as we find him'.[8]

# Seven
# A Foot Soldier for Peace

In June 1846, Edwards arrived in Truro to speak at the Bible Christian chapel on 'The principles of peace'.[1] It was an address he was to make on many occasions, the first being in Lancashire two years earlier. He continued to express these views for the rest of his long life, often at odds with popular opinion but never retracting from his firmly held convictions. Though perhaps not a major player he was always to remain a loyal foot soldier in the struggle for peace. It was his 'favourite footprint'. He was a 'pacificist', believing that war was only justifiable as the last resort in self-defence,[2] rather than a pacifist, opposed to war under any circumstances. 'Unfortunately,' he said, 'Governments declared that all wars were now fought in the interests of defence.'

After speaking at the Chartist meetings in Loughborough and Nottingham in April 1848 Edwards received a letter from the Secretary of the London Peace Society inviting him to attend the first International Peace Congress in Brussels in September, offering a free delegate ticket and free lodgings for the period of the Conference. On the boat crossing the channel he met the former Mayor of Nottingham who told him that after he had addressed the crowds in Nottingham it had been agreed to thank him for his involvement in the demonstration and they had collected ten pounds, which he had not been able to hand over as they did not know his address. Not only was he to attend what was the most significant event, to date, in the history of the Peace movement, all expenses paid, and in company of Richard Cobden, but he received this unexpected ten pounds as well.

Edwards also attended the following two Peace Congresses: in Paris in 1849 and Frankfurt in 1850, and recounted his experiences and his meetings with people such as Victor Hugo in his journal, the *Public Good*. The anti-war campaign also saw an outlet in the *Public Good*, in a feature headed 'Small Shot from the Peace Arsenal', containing short items of news and anti-war quotations, such as 'War is bankruptcy, and bankruptcy is revolution'.

In 1853 following the collapse of Edwards' early publishing enterprise, Russian troops occupied Turkish outposts, and in March 1854 France and Britain declared war on Russia, in defence of Turkey. One of the first new publications Edwards announced following his own bankruptcy was *Shot & Shell*, to be published in 1855 at 1d a week; this did not materialise, being overtaken by the cessation of the war and a subsequent lessening of anti-war feeling amongst the public.[3] The feature was, however, to reappear many years later in the *Weekly Times & Echo*.

Richard Cobden argued that the alternative to war was arbitration and put a motion before Parliament calling for international arbitration treaties to be drawn up with other governments. The Peace Congress Committee, of which Edwards was a member, organised meetings throughout the country to gain support for the petition. Passmore Edwards, together with the Rev Jerome Clapp, later to become the father of the writer and humorist Jerome K Jerome, toured Cornwall to drum up support. Over two weeks they visited and spoke at the Wesleyan School Rooms in Hayle, where Edwards addressed the audience for more than two hours;[4] at the town hall, Helston; the subscription rooms, Launceston; and the town hall, Bodmin; as well as at Truro, St Ives, Penzance and Falmouth. Each meeting was well attended and the pair were met with a great deal of enthusiasm and support for the petition.

When in 1850 the journal of the Peace Society, the *Peace Advocate*, got into financial difficulties, Edwards had taken over the responsibility for the editing and its finances rather than to see it go under. It is, therefore, significant that the first reappearance of Passmore Edwards in contemporary newspaper reports after his publishing failure was his attendance at the thirty-eighth annual meeting of the Peace Society in London, where he spoke in support of one of the motions condemning the Crimean War. But many saw the war as a crusade, a war of liberation and peace protestors were accused of being unpatriotic. The Peace Society confined itself to general declarations of opposition to war and there was a call for a more vociferous vehicle from the more active anti-war campaigners such as Edwards. The gap was filled by the Stop the War Committee and Passmore Edwards was amongst its members.[5]

His views on the evils of war did not change in later life. He had campaigned as being 'anti-war' at the parliamentary election at Truro in 1868 and was to do so again in his successful election campaign in Salisbury in 1880. During his time in the House he criticised both the Government's military campaign in Egypt, which lead to the death of Gordon at Khartoum, and, as President of the Transvaal Independence Committee, was an advocate of the Transvaal's claim to independence, which was gained in 1881. He was a firm believer in arbitration as the peaceful alternative to warfare, as a means of solving international differences. When the International Arbitration and Peace Association (IAPA) formed in August 1880 he was elected Vice President, alongside John Bright, resigning from the executive of the Peace Society in consequence. Hodgson Pratt, the international agent of the Workingmen's Peace Association, was elected chairman and acknowledged leader. In 1885 Edwards introduced Andrew Carnegie, the Scottish-American steel multi-millionaire to the IAPA, who offered to clear the society's deficit of £574 after attending the annual meeting. The IAPA differed from the Peace Society in that it rejected the abstract doctrine that all war was wrong and recognised the justification of defensive war and even, under certain circumstances crusades against oppression and internal fights for liberation. Both the American War of Independence and Garibaldi's liberation of Italy were seen as justified acts of physical force.

### Garibaldi

When General Giuseppe Garibaldi, a republican who called for the legal and political emancipation of women, racial equality and the abolition of capital punishment – the man who was, seemingly single-handedly, unifying Italy – visited Britain in 1864 it was clear that Passmore Edwards would be involved.

Edwards was elected Treasurer of the Garibaldi Demonstration Committee, which held its first public meeting in September 1862[6] at the Whittington Club, in the Strand, but it was to another eighteen months before the visit came about.

Garibaldi landed at Southampton in April 1864 and after resting on the Isle of Wight, travelled to London, arriving at Nine Elms station. The crowds were immense and it took more than four hours for his carriage to travel the three miles to the Duke of Sutherland's home, where he was to stay, 'the crowds along the route exceeding anything ever witnessed in the metropolis'.[7] The Government took little part in the proceedings leaving the organisation entirely to the Garibaldi Reception and Testimonial Fund Committee – of which Edwards, again, was a member – the Working Men's Committee and the Italian Committee, composed of Garibaldi's compatriots. On Edwards' recommendation the Reception Committee wrote to the Prime Minister, Lord Palmerston, asking for use of the volunteer brigades to line the streets for the procession, but this was turned down as likely to show political support for Garibaldi. Instead thousands of workingmen 'volunteers' lined the route to keep order amongst the onlookers. Although there had been great concern about disturbances during the visit, and even a repeat of the Hyde Park riots, there were no reports of trouble.

Even though the Government distanced themselves from the proceedings, it seemed as though London shut down for three days as Garibaldi met prominent men. The Queen did not meet him but Members of Parliament, noblemen and many of the leading figures of the time sought his acquaintance. Though Edwards' name does not appear in contemporary news reports he was honoured by a private visit from the great man himself.[8]

### Russia and Turkey

In 1878 the situation that had arisen between Russia and Turkey prompted Benjamin Disraeli to call out the Reserves and rumours of impending war spread throughout the country. The Workingmen's Peace Association organised a Workingmen's Anti-War and Arbitration Conference at the Memorial Hall, in Farringdon Street, London, funded by Arthur Albright, the Quaker chemicals manufacturer. A second conference at the Memorial Hall, and similar meetings in Birmingham, Leeds, Liverpool, Glasgow and Edinburgh, were funded by Albright, John Horniman and Passmore Edwards. There was a strong anti-war spirit existing amongst the working classes at that time and these conferences were all very well attended.

### Afghanistan

Just as the British fear of Russian expansion led to the Crimean War, concern over encroachment on the Empire's north-west Indian border resulted in war with Afghanistan. The first Afghan war, from 1839 to 1842, helped to create a buffer between Russia and British India but by the late 1870s British influence in Afghanistan had fallen to a low point, while Russian influence was growing. When in 1878 the envoy Sir Neville Chamberlain was refused entry into the country, Britain invaded.

The first campaign began in November 1878 and ended in May of the following year with the displacement of the Amir and the arrival of the British envoy, Sir Louis Cavagni, in Kabul. In September Cavagnari and his military escort were massacred and the conflict recommenced.

General Roberts was in command at Kabul. He was a close friend of Cavagnari and emerged as the central figure in the Afghan war, declaring that anyone who resisted the British forces would be treated as a rebel. He ordered a systematic search, not only for those involved in the attack on the envoy, but those who had resisted the British invasion by defending their country. Those arrested were then executed, in public, on charges of rebellion. Many others, identified only because their names were on lists of particular regiments, were arrested at their homes and strung up on the spot with no trial or investigation into their links with the attack on the envoy.

When details of the events taking place in Kabul filtered back to London, Passmore Edwards was one of more than sixty prominent men, including Leonard Courtney, William Morris and Joseph Chamberlain, who put their name to a petition addressed to Disraeli denouncing Roberts' revengeful retaliation. Such actions were, they said, contrary to the practices of civilised warfare and certain to be followed by disaster and dishonour. Resistance to invasion could not be converted into mutiny and insurrection by a proclamation of the invading forces, especially when the invaders had destroyed the government that had previously existed. Referring to military sources it was claimed that the public executions of Afghans had no military objective other than political vengeance.

The petition concluded with a call for an independent enquiry into these actions, which they claimed affected the honour of the nation, the army and the sovereign. There is no evidence of an official inquiry taking place. By the time Roberts' report reached London, Parliament was in recess and with the Viceroy supporting Roberts the petitioners could not keep up the momentum of the charges when Parliament reconvened.

In July 1880 Afghan forces defeated British troops at Maiwand and went on to besiege the garrison at Kandahar. Roberts set out from Kabul with an army of 10,000 to relieve Kandahar, more than 300 miles away. After marching for more than three weeks under extreme temperatures, Roberts arrived at Kandahar and the next day engaged and defeated the Afghan army. With the installation of a new Amir more sympathetic to British interests the conflict was over. Roberts was the country's hero.

### The Egyptian War

In 1882 when Arabi Pasha, an Egyptian colonel led a revolt against the dual control of Egypt by the British and French. The two governments, fearing loss of control of the Suez Canal sent a combined fleet to Alexandria to protect the European population there. Calls for non-intervention from the peace associations came to no avail. The arrival of the fleet caused even more unrest and riots broke out. Arabi began to strengthen the fortifications around the city, but was sent an ultimatum by Admiral Sir Beauchamp Seymour. When Arabi failed to dismantle the fortifications as demanded, Seymour ordered a bombardment of the city. Gladstone justified the bombardment not as protecting British interests but as intervention to restore order against military violence. The French ships did not take part.

Edwards had been elected to Parliament in 1880, and although Bright resigned his seat in the Cabinet few of the Radicals, Edwards included, were willing to criticise Gladstone, their leader, and protest against the bombardment. Sir Wilfrid Lawson MP described the bombardment as an atrocity, 'a cowardly, a cruel, a criminal act' and objected to 'the blood of a single English soldier being shed on the behalf of the bondholders' (of the Suez Canal).[9] Edwards' silence in the House was broken only by a question to Gladstone asking him whether he had seen reports in that morning's *Times* which had translated and published stories from two Italian newspapers describing the bombardment of Alexandria and the damage to European property amounting to hundreds of millions of pounds. Was the Government, he asked, prepared to consider compensation claims from foreign citizens and Governments? Gladstone dismissed the question saying that the Government would never think it necessary to take notice of such anonymous stories.[10]

But when the House divided on the issue Edwards abstained and later defended his action in not supporting his government at a meeting of the Workingmen's Peace Association (WPA). The meeting was held at the Westminster Palace Hotel on 14 July 1882, to protest 'against any further slaughter of the Arabs and against a continuance of the interference of the Government in the affairs of the Soudan'. Lawson and Edwards were two of several MPs present. Edwards denounced the action of the Government in bombarding Alexandria. On suggestions that he was injuring the Liberal party by speaking out, he said that he was not injuring the Liberal Party, which was strong when it was consistent, but he would rather injure the Party than injure the nation, and he would rather injure the nation than humanity.[11] As a result of the WPA meeting the Anti-Imperial Egypt Committee was formed at a meeting at Memorial Hall, with Lawson becoming organising chairman and Edwards one of the officers.

By the end of July the Government decided to invade to restore order. When Sir Garnet Wolseley landed a British force and defeated the revolutionaries, the church bells were rung throughout the land. Arabi was arrested, tried and sentenced to death, but reprieved and sent into exile in Ceylon. Wilfred Blunt, the British explorer, helped defend Arabi at his trial, paying the legal fees out of his own pocket. Later Passmore Edwards was one of several, including Randolph Churchill, who wrote to the *Manchester Guardian*, seeking public subscriptions to reimburse Blunt's costs.

### South Africa

In 1877 the British Government had annexed the Transvaal, an area in South Africa predominately populated by Boers, the descendants of Dutch-speaking settlers. When first diamonds and then gold were discovered there was a massive influx of *Uitlanders* from all over the world, but mainly from Britain. In 1880 the Boers struck out over growing British influence in the area and the first Boer War began. Hostilities continued until March 1881 when Gladstone, concerned about the high costs of continuing a distant conflict, ordered a truce. The cause of the conflict, however, was unresolved and in 1899 the tensions erupted again, as the Second Boer War. By now further gold discoveries in the area meant that the Government thought that the costs of war were sustainable – but by the time hostilities ceased in May 1902, the final cost was more than 20,000 British and colonial soldiers killed and over 50,000 Boers and black Africans, the majority civilians; men, women and children, who died in British concentration camps.

A number of groups and committees formed to campaign against the wars in Africa, many of them interconnected. One of these was the Transvaal Committee, an offshoot of the Transvaal Independence Association founded in 1881. With Edwards in the chair, radicals dominated it and its work fed into the South African Coalition Committee of which Passmore Edwards again was chairman.[12]

Edwards was to oppose the South African Wars as strongly as he had opposed the Crimean and the Opium wars half a century earlier. In January 1900 Silas Hocking, the Cornish author and nonconformist preacher, called a meeting at Exeter Hall, in London, to discuss the situation in South Africa and to agree a number of resolutions to be put to the Government. With public feeling as it was the meeting was held in private, 350 attending and more than a 100 being turned away through lack of space. Edwards was one of those present, along with W T Stead, W H Massingham, Lloyd George, Keir Hardie and Dr Derby, then Secretary of the Peace Society. Two resolutions were passed, one to denounce the war as a disgrace to civilisation and to seek an end to hostilities through a negotiated settlement in accordance with the Hague Conference, and the second a declaration that the war had been brought about by the circulation of misinformation and conspiracy within the Government and Colonial Services. A committee, the Stop the War Committee, was formed of around thirty of those present, to which Hocking, Edwards, Lloyd George and Stead were appointed.[13] Given that Hocking was a Cornish Liberal it is surprising that in his autobiography he speaks of Lloyd George, Stead and Leonard Courtney MP, but makes no mention of Edwards. Being written some twelve years after Edwards death, did he consider Edwards a spent force, his name no longer sufficiently well known to be included?

When a young lady wrote to Edwards seeking a subscription to a Redruth bazaar in aid of the soldiers' widows and orphans fund he sent a copy of his response to the *West Briton* for publication.

> I suppose, though you do not say so, it is for widows and orphans of soldiers who are being killed daily in South Africa. Now, as few of our soldiers are married, and will leave no widows and orphans, and as most of the Boers who are fighting and falling for their homes and their independence are married and will leave widows and orphans, would it not be more humane and Christian to hold a bazaar in Redruth for their benefit? I think so; and should such a bazaar be held I would gladly contribute to it. Millions of efforts are being made in this professedly Christian and very rich country at the present time on behalf of our own soldier's widows and orphans, but nothing is being done for the still larger number of widows and orphans that our soldiers are making in South Africa. If

> you and others would hold a bazaar for this benefit you would no doubt be sneered at by many of your neighbours but you would have the blessing of God, who is no respecter of persons and who has made of one blood all the peoples who dwell on the earth.
>
> J Passmore Edwards.[14]

Eleanor, Edwards' wife, who he married in 1870, shared her husbands' views on the war, adding her name to a manifesto addressed to women, published by the Women's Movement for Stopping the War.

As with Hocking, who had to climb over a wall at the back of a church he was preaching in to escape from a rowdy mob, Edwards also came in for public abuse over his opposition to the war and his opposition was to cost him the one honour he would have cherished. After being given the Honorary Freedom of three Cornish boroughs and of the Boroughs of East and West Ham it was suggested that he should be granted the Freedom of the City of London. However, feelings were so high at the time that his nomination was not accepted.

In 1901, following the introduction of the Nobel Peace Prize, Edwards commented that everyone was then working for the Nobel Peace Prize, but few were working for peace.

Within a few years of Passmore Edwards' death, both his son – Harry, and three of his grandsons – Harry's two sons – the twins Ellis and Jack Passmore Edwards, and Robert Ingham Clark, eldest son of Passmore Edwards' daughter, Ada, together with the spouses of his granddaughters, Hesketh Adair Ramsden and William Sommerville, were drawn into the war to end all wars, the First World War. When asked, if he thought any lessons had been learned from that war, Gunner Harry Patch, the last British survivor of the conflict, who died in 2009 aged 111, answered 'No, not a thing'. No doubt Passmore Edwards would have agreed with him.

# Eight
# Crime and Punishment

From the time in 1840, when Edwards witnessed the executions of William and James Lightfoot at Bodmin, he was of the opinion that capital punishment, in any form, was wrong and ineffective. One of his earliest return visits to Cornwall was to give a series of lectures on the subject in Truro and at Hayle. In June 1846, he appeared at Mount Pleasant Chapel in Hayle to lecture on the 'Inefficiencies and ineffectiveness of capital punishment'.

When in November 1849, Frederick Manning and his wife Maria were hanged side by side on the roof of Horsemonger Lane Goal, after being found guilty of the murder of Maria's lover, Patrick O'Connor, Edwards used the first edition of the *Public Good* to attack the system. 'What has the world gained?' he wrote. 'The sightseers' – more than 30,000 had witnessed the public execution – 'pot-houses and inns, the newspapers and the spirit of revenge have had fresh opportunity for growth, but are the crowds in higher morals than before?' He went on to question those who said that the Mannings deserved to die, asking what the reader deserved if justice was to be levied against them and whether they would take the place of the executioner. 'Does Christ tell us to kill our enemies, to throttle those that break the laws of the State? Would they think it proper for Christ to perform the role of hangman? Can a man be made better by killing him?'

### Dr Smethurst and Dr William Palmer

Passmore Edwards' concern over capital punishment resulted in his showing an interest in individual murder trials and guilty verdicts, which were publicly considered unsound. One of these was the case of Dr Smethurst who in 1859 was convicted of poisoning the wealthy Isabella Bankes, whom he had bigamously married some time earlier.

At his trial the medical evidence presented by the prosecution was discredited when it was shown that the arsenic found in tests could actually have come from contamination of the equipment used. Although several other medical men came forward to give possible explanations for Isabella's death, other than poisoning by arsenic, the judge gave a damning summing up and Dr Smethurst was found guilty and sentenced to be hanged. There was a great outcry from the public following the case in the daily papers. Passmore Edwards wrote to several newspapers, and on more than one occasion.

'If Smethurst be executed,' he wrote 'it will materially advance the anti-capital punishment sentiment in the community because the execution will do violence to the feelings and opinions of thousands who are now in favour of punishment by death for murder. Smethurst's gallows, should it ever be built, will do more than any anti-capital punishment platform ever erected'.[1]

The Home Secretary considered the case, overturned the verdict and released Smethurst, only to see him re arrested for bigamy and sentenced to twelve months in prison. On his eventual release, he sued for Isabella's estate, as she had changed her will shortly before her death, and disappeared from public life with the money and, it is said, with the original Mrs Smethurst, who had sent an emotional appeal to the Queen to save her erring husband.[2]

In the case of Dr William Palmer, who was hanged at Stafford gaol in June 1856 before a crowd of 30,000, it was strychnine that was alleged to have killed John Parsons Cook, although, due to a botched post-mortem, no strychnine was found in the body.

Palmer and Cook were friends and horse race followers and Palmer, who was heavily in debt, was alleged to have murdered Cook to steal his winnings. Although only charged with the one murder rumour was that he had killed as many as 15 others, all by poisoning, and he came to be known as the Rugeley Poisoner. Feelings were so high in the Staffordshire town that the trial was moved to London. Although there was only circumstantial evidence against Palmer he was found guilty and sentenced to death.

Passmore Edwards, an active member of the Society for the Abolition of Capital Punishment, took the chair at a public meeting in St Martin's Hall on 10 June 1856.[3] The meeting was to consider what action could be taken to delay the hanging to give time for further medical investigation. Edwards said that he neither knew Palmer, nor had any sympathy for him. He did not know whether he was guilty but there had been doubtful and conflicting testimony. A resolution was passed that the Home Secretary should be petitioned to delay the execution but the Minister refused to meet Edwards and the other organisers of the meeting and no stay of execution was granted. The execution took place just four days later.

In 1866 a Royal Commission came out in favour of 'private' executions and two years later 18-year-old Thomas Wells became the first person to be hanged inside a prison. The abolitionists' argument that execution was a cruel spectacle was severely weakened by the introduction of the more humane form of execution, their support diminished and the Society for the Abolition of Capital Punishment disbanded.[4]

Although the last hanging took place in the Britain in 1964 it was not until January 1999 when the Home Secretary signed the 6th protocol of the European Convention of Human Rights in Strasbourg that the death penalty was formally abolished.

**Flogging**

Although incidents of flogging in the army decreased during the early part of the nineteenth century it was not until 1881 that it ceased altogether in both the Army and the Navy. Passmore Edwards, as a member of the committee for the Abolition of Flogging in the Army and Navy, actively campaigned against this system of punishment. At a meeting in London in 1859, he argued that although there were no fewer than one hundred and twenty three Army officers in Parliament they showed no disposition to put an end to this pernicious system. Stating that the British soldier was treated no better than the felon, he called for a petition to be presented to the Queen and for Prince Albert, who, he pointed out, received £6,000 a year as a Field Marshal, to 'do something to remove the evils of the army system'.[5]

There is no indication in *Footprints* of corporal punishment being applied when Edwards was at school, or at home, despite having a Calvinist father, but he was as opposed to the use of the cane as much as to the whip. In September 1856 Edwards wrote to the *Daily News* on the subject of flogging in schools. He spoke of schools where pupils 'are flogged unmercifully by their teachers' and was sorry to add that 'some of these cruelties were perpetrated by clergymen'. He had, he said, within the last few days written to one of these schools threatening to publicly expose them unless they ceased the practice and was pleased to report that they had done so.[6]

## Penal Reform

The mid-1850s saw a significant increase in violent crime. Transportation of convicted criminals to Australia and Barbados had ceased and a 'ticket of leave' system had been introduced which, similar to the present day parole, released convicted criminals before they had completed their sentence and these 'ticket of leave' men were often held to be the cause of the increase in crime.[7]

Still recovering from his financial setbacks, and no doubt with vivid memories of his enforced stay at Whitecross Street debtors' prison, Edwards actively campaigned for improved penal legislation. In January 1857, he was in Chester to address a public meeting on crime and criminals. He said that the present was a favourable opportunity not only for promoting legislative reform but for attacking the causes of crime; amongst which he enumerated and commented on, popular ignorance, neglect of pauper and vagrant children, the game laws, the gallows, social and political inequality, intemperance, reckless competition in the pursuit of wealth, and the current system of prison discipline. The list is, with few exceptions, as valid today. In particular he attacked the treatment of prisoners, declaring that productive labour should be the basis of all penal education. He also denounced transportation as having singularly failed, tending to increase rather than to diminish crime, and that it had induced the people to neglect their social and moral duties by getting rid of the criminals in that way.[8]

Earlier, in London,[9] he said that considering the difficulties that the 'ticket of leave' men experienced when trying to gain an honest living once released from prison, the system had worked favourably. He hoped that a new system of prison discipline would be established, so that the prisoner should come out of prison a better man, by virtue of the industrial training he was subjected to while undergoing punishment.

When Edwards was a schoolboy in Blackwater, his father had employed a local man identified only as Hales to extend the boundary wall around his property. Hales, who had previously been in trouble with the law, and as a result found it difficult to obtain employment, had offered to do this for a very reasonable price, using stones scavenged from disused mine shafts in the area. Passmore Edwards commented in *Footprints* that acquiring these stones was a dangerous business where one slip could mean a thousand foot fall into the mines below. The legality of ownership of these stones is not mentioned but Hales proved to be a hardworking man on this occasion and having completed his task was duly paid. However, Edwards remarks that not long after Hales again found himself in trouble with the law. Arrested for stealing, he was found guilty and transported to Botany Bay, never to be heard of again. No mention is made of the fate of his wife and children, already living in the poorest conditions in the village. Edwards thought he deserved a better fate, and 'had fortune during his earlier years been more favourable he might, and probably would, have become a law abiding and useful, if not a leading, member of our village society'. 'Poor old Hales!' he concludes.

# Nine
# Newspapers & Publishing

### *Mechanics' Magazine* and *English Mechanic*

It is surprising that Edwards stated that he had been the proprietor of the *Mechanics' Magazine*[1] yet makes no reference to the *English Mechanic*. The *Mechanics Magazine* had first appeared in 1823, published by Knight & Lacey, and was described by Dr George Birkbeck, the President of the Mechanics' Institution, in his inaugural address to the Institution as 'the most valuable gift that the hand of science has yet offered to the artisan'. Such was its standing that a copy of the tenth issue of the *Mechanics' Magazine* was sealed within the foundation stone of the London Mechanics' Institute when it was laid on the 2 December 1824.

The magazine's success continued until about 1850, when it became the property of a firm of patent agents, who could not make it pay. Passmore Edwards was first appointed editor, taking over from Edward Beed on his appointment to the Admiralty in 1860, and then bought a seven year lease of the magazine and under his management once more made it pay. However, the magazine had lost contact with the needs of its readers and changes in its form and policy were essential if it were to continue to be a successful undertaking, and these Passmore Edwards could not get permission to carry out. So in 1867 he gave the paper back to its owners and turned his attention to a similar publication, the *English Mechanic*.

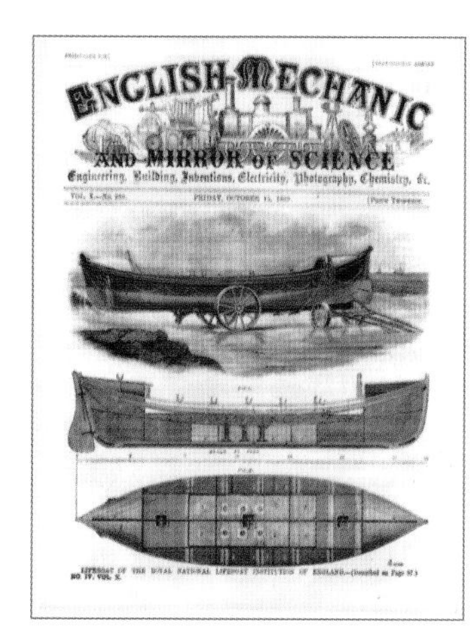


The *Mechanics' Magazine* was later sold to the proprietors of the *Engineer* who in turn sold it to the publishers of a new paper called *Iron*, which after some initial successes finally collapsed.

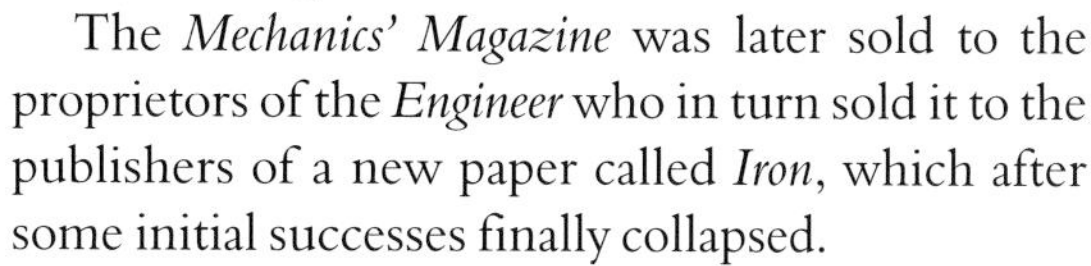

On 26 April 1869 Edwards took over as owner of the *English Mechanic* or, to give it its full title, *The English Mechanic. A Record of Mechanical Inventions, Scientific and Industrial Progress, Building, Engineering, Manufactures, and Arts*, and moved publication to the *Building News* office at 31 Tavistock Street, Covent Garden.

The first edition of the *English Mechanic* under Edwards' ownership was published on 7 May 1869,

The English Mechnic

with E J Kibblewhite as the editor. Although predominantly a science and mechanics journal Edwards often made use of the pages to express his views, whether on the causes of emigration, the loss of agricultural land to game preservation or the promotion of a Bill to introduce tramways to the streets of London.

Key to the success of the *English Mechanic* under Edwards' control was its readership. It was published at a time of great advances in both science and engineering, when the country was rapidly changing from agriculture to industrial pursuits. Contributions from a working man, titled gent, or the greatest living scientist appeared side by side in the same issue, creating a brotherhood of mutual help amongst contributor and reader. In fact everyone could be both a contributor and reader. The feature that most assured the success of 'Ours', as the *English Mechanic* was soon affectionately termed by its readers, was the 'Letters to the Editor'. By issue ten the number of letters, including queries, had grown to such an extent, that it was necessary to increase the size of the paper. The edition appearing on 12 January 1866 was almost doubled in size, but double the price, at 2d. The title was also shortened to the *English Mechanic and Mirror of Science and Art*.

In this issue a new feature was introduced, the 'Subscribers' Exchange Club'. Readers could advertise to exchange equipment free of charge but paid a small fee to advertise items for sale. The 'For Sale' columns were for many the only opportunity of buying items of scientific apparatus or engineering equipment at a reasonable cost.

By 1867, when volume four appeared, much of the content was being supplied by the readers. Much more space was given up to 'Letters to the Editor'; 'Queries' had a separate heading, and was accompanied by 'Replies to Queries'. In 1870 Edwards acquired three more journals to merge with the *English Mechanic*. The *Mechanic*, a 1d publication, absorbed from 25 March 1870, followed by the *Scientific Opinion* and in July, the *British & Foreign Mechanic*. The resulting journal was advertised as having a larger circulation and more correspondents than all similar journals combined. By 1871 more than 27,000 copies of the *English Mechanic* were being sold each week.

For more than 50 years, the *English Mechanic* influenced the engineering and scientific world, being the only journal available to readers wishing to exchange views and get information on a wide range of subjects. In November 1892, when Edwin Holmes discovered a new comet, it was to the *English Mechanic* that he turned to announce his discovery.

> On Sunday night, Nov. 6th at 11:45, I found a new comet in Andromeda. It was bright enough to be visible in an opera glass through the haze prevailing. Nucleus bright, with surrounding nebulosity 5' in diameter. No tail visible. I made the position 0h 46.8m + 38deg 32" exactly 1m 10s preceding Sigma 72. My surroundings prevented me from watching for any motion. I think it must have approached rapidly, for I observed that region on Oct. 25th and observed nothing special.
>
> Edwin Holmes.

Edwards, with Kibblewhite as editor, maintained the quality of the published content making the *English Mechanic* a good standard reference journal. The *English Mechanic* also played a major part in the development of small, and not so small, industries and businesses. Articles describing the construction of the bicycle and, in 1896, the first detailed instructions on how to build an automobile appeared, some months before an Act of Parliament permitted their use on the highway, and led to many entrepreneur engineers entering into production. A design for a 1hp oil engine resulted in the construction and sale of these engines, essential equipment for providing power to small industrial workshops. In Manchester and Edinburgh readers formed *English Mechanic* Scientific Societies where they could meet to air their views and exchange experiences.

The journal also covered the development and use of electricity, the wireless telegraphy and telephony, and it was regarded as the leading journal for both astronomical and microscopical subjects. Since scientific apparatus was difficult, and costly, to purchase, articles on its construction, repair and adjustment were frequently included.

The journal became one of the three titles held by the Strand Newspaper Company Ltd when it formed in 1893 and continued within the company until 1926 when it was sold to Gilbert Wood & Co Ltd, ceasing publication during the Second World War.

### The *English Mechanic* Lifeboat

The 15 October 1869, edition of the *English Mechanic* contained a detailed account of the design and build of an English lifeboat. There had been a number of lifeboats built by subscription through publications of the day[2] and the account was sufficient to arouse an interest amongst a number of *English Mechanic* readers to do likewise.

George Luff, of Ashby de la Zouche, suggested that with a readership of 100,000, a contribution of a 1d, would raise the required £400 to build a fully fitted out boat and that a further ¼d a year would adequately support its operation.

Passmore Edwards was at first apprehensive but agreed to support the appeal and offered 'to head the subscription list with a hundred guineas'.

As contributions arrived at the *English Mechanic*, often in the form of unused postage stamps, they were acknowledged in the following edition, whether a few pence or several pounds. In keeping with the tradition of the magazine many of the contributors used pseudonyms, contributions being credited to *Semper Paratus* (1 shilling), *Two at sixpence each or six at one penny each* and *A little collection amongst the bicyclists and their friends at the Bromsgrove Railway Station* (7 shillings). However, in spite of the contributions from the more enthusiastic contributors such as Mr Luff, who in February 1870 sent in the results of his first collection, amounting to £10 6s 3d, and the proceeds from concerts, such as the £3 6s 0d sent in after a concert at the headquarters of the 1st Essex Engineers, the fund grew very slowly. It was not until October 1870 that the contribution list, inc-

*The* English Mechanic *lifeboat*

luding the results of Mr Luff's third collection, £2 2s 0d, passed £200; sufficiently slow for Passmore Edwards to question the enthusiasm of the readers. Rallying appeals appeared, such as that, in February 1871, signed by 'A Fellow of the Royal Astronomical Society', 'The Harmonious Blacksmith', 'Sigma', and others who, after calculating that a lifeboat would save two to three hundred lives in its career, suggested that 'A hundred wives will have their husbands restored to them' and 'Three to four hundred children will have been saved from orphanhood'.

The list remained open but did not reach the £400 target until August 1875, appropriately with contributions of £2 19s 6d, collected by Mr Luff. This was followed, in January 1876 by the news that the *English Mechanic* lifeboat was to be stationed at Boughty Ferry, near Dundee, as a replacement for the *Mary Hartley*, which had been instrumental in saving upwards of 60 lives.

The launch of the *English Mechanic* took place on Whit Monday, 5 June 1876 and an account of the launch and of an almost immediate call to arms was reported in the *Dundee Advertiser* and repeated in the *English Mechanic* journal on 16 June.

Many thousands assembled to watch the new boat on its cradle – masts rigged and fully manned, process through the town to the King William's Dock where it was met by local dignitaries and a densely packed crowd of onlookers.

Passmore Edwards was not present to hand over the new boat to the Royal National Lifeboat Institution, having sent his apologies that he was unavoidably detained in London. After naming, the lifeboat was plunged into the dock, pulled back to the quay, and after the crew had disembarked, and with the use of ropes attached to a crane, the boat was overturned to demonstrate its self-righting ability. Within 25 seconds the boat had righted, drained of the water she had shipped.

Immediately following the self-righting demonstration the boat set sail down the river to undertake exercises, the dignitaries following in the steamer *Fairweather*. Arriving off Boughty Ferry a telegram was relayed to the *Fairweather* that a schooner had been observed riding close inshore and in danger of being driven ashore by the strong winds. The two boats set off down river to the schooner's position, the lifeboat running with full sails set. The schooner was the *Brothers* of Sunderland. Her sails were split and she was making water, although not yet aground. Five lifeboat crew were put on board and soon had the vessel under way and manned the pumps. Taken in tow by the *Fairweather* and escorted by the *English Mechanic*, she was taken into Dundee. A large crowd assembled to finally welcome the lifeboat to her new station, where she remained until June 1888, being replaced by the *Samuel Shawcross*. The *English Mechanic* printed reports of the lifeboat's career and subscriptions continued to arrive at the publisher's office towards the boats upkeep. The Boughty Ferry station remains one of the busiest stations around Britain.

### *Building News*

Kelly, publisher of the directories of that name, started the *Building News* in 1852 as a 4d weekly journal aimed at the artisan classes, but by 1862 it was ailing and Edwards was able to purchase it at what he said was a very attractive price. The first issue to carry Edwards' name was published on 16 May 1862, with an article that attacked the wasteful use of money by the Ordnance Survey. Another early issue contained an article, 'The sacrifice to Bacchus' or 'drinking from the cradle to the grave', a direct attack on the English custom of taking something to drink on all occasions. When a child was born the event was celebrated with a little something to drink, as was the birthday, marriage or burial. The 'evil' of these and other examples, although harmless in themselves, was shown in the excesses they induced in 'the lower orders who are not restrained by position and education and the fearful consequences that follow are depicted – the workhouse, madhouse, prison and the gallows.'

Under his control the journal was turned around, once more to become a prosperous and influential publication representing all aspects of the construction industries. Technical articles were blended with architectural history; new building techniques mirrored architectural competitions and construction projects. And all was delivered with Edwards' forthright editorial style. In 1865 he acquired the *Illustrated Builder's News*, a journal aimed predominantly at the poorer building worker and amalgamated the two early in 1866. So as to retain the readers of the former journal he reduced the price of the enlarged *Building News* to 2d. By 1871 it was selling more than 7,000 copies a week. *Building News* remained a progressive magazine, being the first to replace wood block engravings with photogravure illustrations and in 1872 Edwards handed over the editor's chair to the architect Maurice Bingham Adams, who remained editor until 1923 – a partnership of mutual benefit.

Adams instigated the 'Designing Club', which enabled young architects to submit designs for criticism and was also able to prepare many of the paper's illustrations, without contracting these out at additional expense. Adams was to obtain several major commissions from Edwards, including the Shepherd's Bush library, the Acton library and, the Camberwell Polytechnic and Art Gallery. Through Adams, Edwards was to gain an understanding of building design and costs.

In 1926 *Building News* was sold and merged with the *Architect*, to form the *Architect & Building News*.

It was these two publications, *Building News* and the *English Mechanic* that were the basis of Passmore Edwards' subsequent wealth, wealth that he was to later use for the benefit of those that had created it – the working classes.

***The Echo***

The 1867 Reform Act which had been the catalyst for Edwards' election campaign in Truro through the increase in working-class voters, also led to the *Echo* being published. Produced by the publishing firm House of Cassell, the first edition of the *Echo* appeared on 8 December 1868, the first

Top: Building News

Below: *Stamp of the* London Echo

halfpenny evening newspaper in London. Under Arthur Arnold, later Sir Arthur, as editor it was from the start a radical Liberal paper. While the low price was aimed at a working-class readership, and advertisements addressed their needs, the paper included racing news and stock prices from the 11.30am London Stock Exchange report, making the *Echo* a choice for many commuters and as popular with City Gents as artisans.

Technically an evening paper there were several editions throughout the day, the first appearing around noon. Initially the newspaper dealers refused to handle the paper because the low price meant low profit margins. The answer was to sell directly using squads of uniformed boys – who sold their uniforms, but still sold the paper[3] – and half the price of its rivals it soon found a ready readership. Street selling was an old tradition with every public place having a newsboy even before 1855, but it expanded enormously after the appearance of the cheap daily and especially the cheap evening paper. The *Daily Telegraph* was the first to use uniformed boys and in 1869 the *Echo* employed 500 boys wearing *Echo* caps.

Cassell sold the paper to the colourful 'Baron' Grant in 1875 but after only twelve months of ownership, during which it is claimed he lost a significant amount of money, Grant was ready to sell again. This was Edwards' opportunity, purchasing the title and works for £17–18,000, according to Howard Evans, by means of a loan from Edwards' paper supplier.[4]

Edwards, with his constant aim of educating the poor, considered publishing a halfpenny newspaper even before the *Echo* had seen light of day.[5] He threw himself into this new venture, writing most of the leading articles and much of the rest. He supervised everything, selecting the subjects for special articles, controlling the staff both in the printing and literary departments and was rarely absent from his work from 7.30am until the final edition was on the streets.[6] He immediately dropped the morning edition, introduced by Grant, and with his practical knowledge of printing and the paper trade, made economies that almost overnight turned the paper around with a circulation of some 90,000 copies a day.

Shortly after taking over the *Echo* Edwards arranged a dinner for the staff, at which he outlined his plans for the paper and informed them of the high costs of running it. Although the *Echo* sold for a halfpenny it cost more to produce than the *Building News*, which sold at 4d, a total of more than £45,000 per year. Although staff described Edwards as a hard taskmaster he appears to have treated his workers, if not the editorial staff, well. He was benevolent in as much as the annual dinner became a norm at both the *Echo* and later at Strand Newspapers, and in at least one year, 1890, there was a thousand pound New Year's bonus, to be shared amongst the staff of his publications.[7] He also treated the newspaper boys to an annual meal and entertainment.

Howard Evans, who worked as editor of the *Echo* for several years described Edwards as being a very difficult man to work for, and this eventually led to his departure when Edwards expected him to write in support of the striking engineers, whom he thought had little chance of success in their actions. Edwards supported the strikers and on occasions supported them financially as well.

Evans did agree that Edwards had a knack of attracting the right people onto the paper and many of the great journalists of the time had first won their spurs at the *Echo.*[8]

Leading woman journalist, Mary Frances Billington[9] had occasionally written for the *Echo* and Edwards invited her to London to join the staff. She stayed for two years before joining the *Daily Graphic*[10] but said that she gratefully remembered the excellent training her time with the *Echo* gave her. Another woman journalist at the *Echo* was Frances Cobbe. Cobbe had been the *Echo*'s main leader writer under Cassell, leaving when Grant took over, and Edwards invited her to return when he became proprietor.[11] She was both a feminist activist and anti-vivisectionist, founding the National Anti-Vivisection Society, an interest shared by Passmore Edwards, who was later made vice President of one of the London Anti-Vivisection Societies.

Edwards used the *Echo* to push his own issues, whether it was animal or human rights, and the paper took a significant part in the 1880 election campaign that resulted in a large Liberal majority. Copies of Gladstone's speeches were printed as supplements to the paper and circulated in their thousands.[12] In 1883, however, Sir William Harcourt, then Home Secretary, appeared not to have heard of the *Echo* when questioned over a leading article relating to the Government's policy in Ireland that, allegedly, was an incitement to violence.[13]

**Rich man poor man**

Much has been written as to whether the *Echo* was profitable, and Edwards often made contradictory claims.

He once said that John O'Connor, former Irish MP at Westminster, had been telling people at the National Liberal Club that Edwards had made a fortune out of the *Echo*. 'As a matter of fact,' he said, 'I keep the *Echo* out of the profits of my paper appealing to Builders'.[14] Howard Evans realistically said that while Edwards constantly tried to convince the staff that it was only his other three papers, *Building News*, the *English Mechanic* and the *Weekly Times & Echo*, that kept the *Echo* afloat, it was really a gold mine and Edwards' assertions were merely to counter any applications for a raise in salary.[15] Aaron Watson agreed, adding that although his other papers were doing well and permitted him to buy the *Echo*, in the early days of ownership Edwards didn't have the money to lose. H W Massingham, radical journalist and editor of the *Daily Chronicle* wrote that Edwards was undoubtedly one of the kings of the modern newspaper enterprise. 'With profits of £12–15,000 a year from the *Echo*, Edwards was a wealthy man'.[16]

*Sketch of Passmore Edwards from the* Graphic, *10 July 1870*

Edwards gave support to these views when many years later he said that he was taking several thousand a year out of the *Echo,* but in 1893 told his employees, at the annual 'wayzgoose'[17] that for several years he had not taken a penny out of the paper for himself but had used all of the profits to fund his gifts of public buildings.[18]

## The Edwards-Carnegie partnership

Andrew Carnegie, a first generation Scottish American and self-made millionaire, had long dreamt of controlling a newspaper and through it spreading his own republican and radical views. In 1881 the chance arose through a meeting with an old friend, Thomas Graham, and Samuel Storey, proprietor of the *Sunderland Echo* and the *Tyneside Echo* and MP for Sunderland. It was a meeting that was to lead to the formation of the 'Storey-Carnegie syndicate', the biggest newspaper conglomerate of the day. In fact there were several syndicates, but each having Storey and Carnegie as members. With Carnegie's help Graham bought up three Midland newspapers, to form the Midlands News Association whilst Storey brought in his two *Echos* but retained personal control of them. The syndicate obtained several other provincial newspapers, including the *Portsmouth Evening News*, and Hugh Gilzean-Reid added his *North Eastern Daily Gazette* but retained personal control. Storey also purchased the *Northern Daily Mail* and within two years controlled eight daily and ten weekly newspapers, all published in areas with radical sympathies. But the syndicate needed a London daily and they looked to Passmore Edwards' *Echo* to fill this gap.

It was Storey who approached Edwards. Edwards, doubting Storey's seriousness said that he would only part with control of the paper for £70,000. Storey surprised Edwards by agreeing to the price and set about recruiting extra staff – but Edwards had second thoughts and at the last moment it was heard that 'The old buffer has cried off'.[19] Edwards returned the purchase price but forfeited £5,000 deposit, telling Storey that if he chose to go to Court to uphold the contract, he would fight him all the way. Only six weeks later, in August 1883, negotiations had reopened and Edwards eventually sold a two-thirds share of the *Echo* to Storey and Carnegie for £70,000.[20]

Storey took over the management of the *Echo* and appointed Aaron Watson editor. Watson accepted under two conditions – one that he should have entire control of the newspaper, and the other that there should be no interference from Passmore Edwards. Watson said that he had 'seen much of' Edwards and he was 'not at all to my taste'.[21] Edwards had, thought Watson, the sense of the privileges of the man who pays, and described a large chair in Edwards' office, with a seat low to the ground, on which contributors were to sit while Edwards strode about the room criticising the articles they had written. Watson also recounted being called into Edwards' office where, pointing out of the window at the old Gaiety Theatre opposite, he said 'You pretend to know about art. Now I know something about art myself', and went on at length to praise the artistic and architectural merits of the building, which were, apparently, only appreciated by Edwards.

It was during this period that Mervyn Hawkes, an *Echo* journalist, son of a republican journalist, wrote *A Primrose Dame*, although it was not published until after the partnership had ended. Written as a political novel, *A Primrose Dame* was set around a daily newspaper, *The Volcano*. The three members of the syndicate, Edwards, Carnegie and Storey, appear under the names of Paralysis Agitans, Mr Pittsburgh and Silas Holt. Agitans is shown to be a politically timorous and penny-pinching character. Edwards was a shrewd businessman. Having built up a very successful publishing business he knew how to make a newspaper profitable and what may affect that profitability, but was he 'politically timorous'? It is true that he did not speak directly against major issues when he was in Parliament, but he had been very outspoken both during the Crimean War and the Opium wars, and was again later over the South African wars. And he was ready to vote against his own party when he thought that it was the right thing to do.

The partnership was to be a short-lived affair. Whilst the *Echo* had always had republican overtones Edwards was not the republican that Carnegie was and tensions grew amongst the partners. Carnegie also wanted to pull all of the publications into one, which neither Storey nor Edwards would agree to and Edwards, although by then owning the *Weekly Times*, missed the editorial control that he had once held at the *Echo*. In July 1885 Edwards gave the others an ultimatum. Either buy his share or sell him theirs, putting the value of the *Echo* as a whole, which now included the *Weekly Echo*, at £100,000.[22] Their decision was the latter, and led to the dissolution of the syndicate. Carnegie retired from the newspaper business and Edwards, once more master of the *Echo*, immediately dismissed Watson.

Though Kibblewhite became general manager of the *Echo* in 1892,[23] Edwards was to remain in overall control until 1897 when he again sold the controlling interest to a syndicate, which included Thomas Lough, MP for Islington, John Barker of Kensington and Messrs Gilbey who between them put up £75,000. Edwards allowed his share, £25,000 to remain to preserve his interest. Lough, who had founded the *Star*, another ½d evening paper that had been started out as a rival to the *Echo* and which had since taken the lead in presenting the Liberal position, was to play the leading role in directing the policy of the paper, with Edwards surrendering his editorial control altogether. It was also suggested that Wills, the tobacco firm, had a financial interest in the syndicate through one of the partners.[24]

The fortunes of the paper diminished along with the popularity of the Liberal Party, and the paper was sold again, in 1901, to Frederick Pethwick-Lawrence. Originally a Liberal, Frederick Lawrence had been converted to socialism by his future wife, Emmeline Pethwick, and he recruited his radical friends, Ramsay MacDonald and Henry Noel Brailsford to write for the *Echo*, which then became a left-wing newspaper. However, despite subsidies from Henry Wilson, Liberal MP for Sheffield, in 1902, the paper finally folded in August 1905.

### The *Echo* Treats

During the summer of 1894 the *Echo* organised days out for 10,000 London working-class women and children. Eleanor, Edwards' wife, was one of those who took part, taking the children in groups of 200, by train to Chingford where they were to spend the day at Epping Forest. Tables and benches were set up to serve tea to the children, together with amusements and entertainments.

On the 17 August 600 child watercress and flower sellers were taken on the trip in one group. It was described 'as a motley group of all sorts and sizes. Some very neatly and a few picturesquely clad, others were badly clad and without shoes and stockings'. More than one was on crutches and one little one was so paralysed that he could not lift his cake to his mouth, but ate it from the table without the use of his hands.[25]

In the following year Eleanor took part in a charity bazaar, entitled 'An International

Frost Fair' at Kensington town hall early in December. Held in aid of a fund for free breakfasts and winter dinners for destitute children, the Countess of Chesterfield, Lady Peyton and Lady Agnes Cooper were listed among the other stallholders.[26]

### *Weekly Times & Echo*

The *Weekly Times* had been in existence for more than half a century when in 1884 Edwards paid J Hutton, who went on to own the *ABC Railway Guide*, £28,000 for it. At 1d, and published on Sundays, it was a Liberal paper, the editorial profile already matching that of the *Echo*. For a while there was speculation that Edwards intended to bring out a morning paper using the capacity at the *Weekly Times* but nothing came of this. Instead he amalgamated the paper with the ailing *Weekly Echo*, which had begun publication, under Aaron Watson, during the Storey-Carnegie syndicate period.

The *Weekly Echo* was designed at securing a wider public with a broader range of interests than the other penny weeklies, including serialised original fiction with a London connection, often illustrated with line drawings. Aaron Watson said that Edwards was envious of him starting the *Weekly Echo* and as soon as he regained control of the *Echo* he combined the two titles. The *Weekly Echo* had not, however, been as popular as it had set out to be and it was an obvious decision to combine the two titles, which by 1890 was to be advertised as the largest penny weekly newspaper, with five editions every week.[27]Edwards kept the paper at its old address of 332, Strand and subsequently moved the *Echo* there where he was later to establish the Strand Newspaper Company.

Help and assistance to the working classes was provided through regular advice columns. Dr Thomas Allinson, LRCP as the medical editor, published answers to questions sent in by readers. Allinson, a naturopath and vegetarian GP, was struck off the medical register in 1892 for his outspoken opposition to drug based medicines but went on to found the Natural Food Company, and Allinson flour.[28]

In the same way almost free legal advice was provided through a column in the paper. The advice came from a solicitor by the name of Fred Wetherfield, although it was usually only the answer that was published, not the question to which it related, benefiting only the reader who had submitted the question along with a printed token from the newspaper and a 1s postage stamp.

In line with the format of the *English Mechanic* help was also provided through a 'Mutual Aid' column, whereby readers would write in with their queries, to be answered the following week by other readers.

Besides attempting to answer all of life's little questions the paper was not short on political news and comment as well as including general local news and even a serialised novel. Passmore Edwards' direct contribution to the paper is unknown since articles were generally unattributed and much of the 'comment' would have been written by the editor, Kibblewhite, rather than the proprietor, though both shared very similar views.

Edwards tendencies towards the new socialist movement was demonstrated in 1894 when a series of articles on the 'Men of the Movement' appeared. These were by John C Kenworthy, founder of the Croydon Brotherhood Church, and included biographies of George Bernard Shaw, Tom Mann and John Burns. When, in July of that year, an appeal was made by the Independent Labour Party for a fund to support candidates at by elections, the *Times & Echo* joined *Clarion*, the *Labour Leader* and the *Weekly Dispatch* in asking its readers to contribute. A target of £125 from each paper was set. 'It must be war in the House of Commons against Capitalism,' stated the editorial, 'waged by the people's true representatives in the good old English constitutional fashion or – war on the streets!' However subscriptions were slow to arrive, only £6 by the beginning of August and 1 guinea of that coming from Kibblewhite, who said the response was lamentable.[29] Whilst *Clarion* raised their contribution within a few weeks the *Times & Echo* was to raise less than £20 before closing the subscription list. Edwards, whose support for socialism was being commented upon in the competitive press, contributed £25. The *Liberty Review* published an extract of a letter Edwards had written to George Brooks, author of *Industry and Property: A plea for Truth and Honesty in Economics, and for Liberty and Justice in Social Reform*. – 'THE CAPITALIST CLASS ARE THE CORRUPTERS OF CIVILISATION,' he wrote, 'and if they are not first curbed, and then crushed, by the Democratic Party, they will destroy civilisation. I WILL DO MY BEST TO CURB AND CRUSH THEM'.[30] The *Review* pointed out that Edwards was a capitalist, but it was not the men like himself, who created goods and services, employing their capital in providing employment that he was referring to, but the moneyed families, the bankers and the financiers who grew rich on the backs of others but contributed little.

## Betting

Passmore Edwards had a lifelong dislike of betting as he had seen how both gambling and drink had brought destruction to lives. It was customary at that time for the House of Commons to suspend proceedings for Derby Day, so that the Honourable Gentlemen could attend the races, and during the time Edwards was an MP he always voted against the motion, though it was never lost.

In the early 1870s three Manchester morning papers banned betting news from their pages but only the *Manchester Guardian*, with its Liberal middle-class circulation was able to sustain this policy.[31] Edwards quickly dropped the horseracing pre-race odds when he took control of the *Echo* in 1876, though continuing to publish the results and starting prices. This lead, initially, to a dramatic loss in sales but the readership returned because of the high quality and fair journalism. The *Weekly Times & Echo* was also used to attack gambling in all forms and this brought Edwards head to head with the horseracing press.

The *Sporting Life* attacked the *Echo* for hypocrisy, declaring that while it took the moral stance in its editorial, amongst the classified columns lurked advertisements of a most unpleasant character. Referring in particular to an advertisement that read 'Apartments, furnished, wanted by a lady and a gent for occasional use, near Edgware Road', the *Sporting Life* called for Passmore Edwards to 'forbid this sort of thing: If you don't we shall'.[32] When Edwards led a subscription to present Gladstone with an ornamental silver axe as a seventieth Birthday present, *Sporting Life* suggested that Gladstone should use it to cut off Passmore Edwards' head.

In 1894 Edwards was elected to the council of the National Anti-Gambling League and became President the following year. Attacks on Edwards' advertising policies again appeared, this time against the *Weekly Times & Echo*, although by then Edwards had no editorial control. The advertisements objected to were those advertising 'homes for illegitimates' or unwanted children, 'for consideration'. There was wide concern that such children were in fact being sold into a life of misery and were even abandoned or murdered once payment had been received. Kibblewhite refused to discontinue the adverts, but instead required a doctor's reference before publication, and the insertion fee was increased.

**The *Southern Echo***

With the *Echo* now firmly back under his control, the experience gained from the Carnegie-Storey syndicate, and having retired from politics, Edwards looked to expand his newspaper empire outside London. He was to take a controlling interest in the *Salisbury Times* and in December 1885, bought the *Hampshire Independent* an old established weekly suffering dwindling sales and advertising revenue. Edwards bought both the title and the printing works and placed his nephew, Frederick Augustus Edwards, in the position of works manager. It was clearly Edwards' intention to start a Liberal evening newspaper to cover the Southampton area, and it is said that he conceived and practically set the new paper going within twenty four hours. But it was not until 20 August 1888 that the *Southern Echo* appeared on the streets of Southampton, priced one halfpenny.[33] The purpose of the paper and the target readership was made clear. It was to be – 'A high class evening paper for Hants, Wilts and Dorset, containing the latest and fullest information on all matters of local and general interest, of questions affecting the working and industrial classes'.

It was a hands-on approach by Edwards, as editor, and even presiding over a party given to the paper's young news sellers. Between 120 and 140 lads, many of them shoeless, and probably as many homeless, were invited to the Victoria Skating Rink, Southampton, for a meat tea and concert on the Saturday before the paper was launched. The report that appeared in the *Southern Echo* suggested that for these boys the invitation to 'a real good solid meal partakes somewhat of the character of an angel's visit' and the lads were queuing outside the ice rink well before time the meal was to commence, many bringing armloads of newspapers for their Saturday night's business. Grace having been said the cry of 'Meat, meat, meat' went on as long as the supply of ham and beef lasted. Following plum cake and bread and butter the tables were removed and the seats rearranged for the musical entertainment.

Before the concert commenced, Frederick Edwards spoke to the newsboys to remind them of the need for conscientiousness in their work. His comments regarding the money they would earn caused one little urchin to shout 'I got *sumin* in the savings bank' a dozen others following with 'So have I', and a forest of little hands indicating a consensus of opinion that the Penny Bank was the best depository for the few coppers that remained after the demands of 'home' had been met.

The concert continued with songs, monologues, conjuring tricks and gymnastics, and even contained a recital from one of the boys with the encouragement of his mates.

Finally 'God Save the Queen' was sung, and the boys wandered off, some declaring as they left the rink, 'we won't go home till morning'.

The *Southern Echo* was to become a campaigning paper from the start. The *Echo* reporters were sent out into the poor areas of the town to write about the conditions they found, the overcrowded courts, the poverty, drunkenness, disease and vice. Although the fact that Southampton did not have a free library was reported, Edwards did not offer to fund one, though he did, later, donate 1,000 books when a library was established. In politics, the paper declared itself to be decidedly Liberal, but its news and reports would be without bias or partiality, following the example of the best of the London papers, by which Edwards meant the *Echo*, in which 'political preferences and prejudices would be confined to the editorial columns, the news being free from party influence and reports above suspicion'.[34]

The immediate success of the *Southern Echo* caused much concern amongst the board of the *Hampshire Advertiser*, who had planned to start a daily paper but had been beaten to it by Edwards. The answer was either to proceed with their own paper, or attempt to purchase the *Southern Echo* from Edwards. In December 1888 they decided to take the latter option. Just why Edwards would be willing to part with his new venture is not known. Although it was still to show a profit it was at least paying its way. But after enquires by the board Edwards indicated that he would be willing to consider a sale. He had paid £10,000 for the *Hampshire Independent* and £1,200 for the printing plant as well as several hundreds on alterations and in launching the *Southern Echo*. However, he indicated that he would be prepared to sell the lot for £12,000, less the 'book debts'. Negotiations continued for two years, with offer and counter-offer being made. Finally, on 24 April 1891, the deal was agreed. The *Hampshire Advertiser* would purchase the *Hampshire Independent* and *Southern Echo* together with the printing business, which had a mortgage of £3,000, paying Passmore Edwards £9,500. The new owners would continue to recover the book debts on Edwards' behalf until £2,500 had been recovered, after which they were entitled to any that remained. The last issue of the *Southern Echo* to be published 'by F A Edwards for the Proprietor' appeared on 14 July 1891.[35] Since then the *Southern Echo* has continued to be published from the former *Independent* address at Above Bar, Southampton, by Southern Newspapers Ltd.

**The Strand Newspaper Company Ltd**

The Strand Newspaper Company Ltd was registered on Monday 27 November 1893 taking over the business of the *Weekly Times & Echo*, *Building News* and the *English Mechanic*, all published at 332, Strand by Passmore Edwards and his junior partner E J Kibblewhite. Edwards retained nearly eleven-twelfths of the interest in the company, the directors being Edwards, Kibblewhite, who became general manager of the three titles, and his son Harry Passmore Edwards. Both Eleanor and Ada, their daughter, also received shares in the new company. The *Echo* was not included in the new company although Kibblewhite was at that time the general manager.

The company, which also included book-publishing interests, continued to be successful for many years. In August 1892 Edwards handed over the reins at the Strand Newspaper Company, and management of the *Weekly Times & Echo*, *English Mechanic* and *Builders' News*, to Harry. Kibblewhite continued as editor of all of the publications, except for *Building News* – edited by Maurice Adams, but later succeeded Harry as managing director when Harry became chairman, a position he held until he retired in 1924.

In July 1894 the staff travelled by steam launch on the Thames for the annual outing. At the following dinner, Harry Passmore Edwards told the staff that the three papers remained as profitable as ever, even in a time of commercial depression. In response to a toast to the health of Passmore Edwards, Kibblewhite responded, Edwards not being present. He reminded his colleagues of the principles of the *Weekly Times & Echo* – working to the best of its ability to bring about that better time when 'the workers' share of the fruits of the wisely organised industry of the Commonwealth should be an adequate one, and when for mere charity would be substituted brotherly help and mutual kindness'. It was the distinguishing glory of Mr Edwards, he said, that he was one of the very few really beneficent and generous philanthropists. Mr Edwards had not waited until his thousands had grown into hundreds of thousands, or millions, and then flung to the masses mere doles out of his great superfinity; but had hastened at the beginning of his deserved prosperity, and had increasingly continued as that prosperity grew year by year, to donate by far the greater proportion of it to the spread of education, to the relief of the sick and needy and for the encouragement of self reliance and self educating men and women of the masses. It was the curse of the abominable individualistic system under which they all laboured that almost all charity was but a mere ineffectual palliative and was swamped in the great sea of misery that surrounded it. Hereafter it would be remembered, to Mr Passmore Edwards' undying renown that he, among a very few – had the wisdom to select, and the large hearted generosity to make successful and permanent factors in education, the comfort and support of the workers which would materially shorten the transition time between the evil of today and the end tomorrow, and would make the hard times endurable while they were yet with us.[36]

During more than fifty years connection with newspapers Edwards had contributed to all of the political and social controversies of the time. During many of these debates he had been with the struggling minority but had always written and done what he believed to be true and in the public interest, whether popular or not.

# Ten
# Slavery

### *Uncle Tom's Cabin*

When Mrs Harriet Beecher Stowe published *Uncle Tom's Cabin* in 1852 it was met with hostility in some quarters, including in the *Times*. Although declaring support for the anti-slavery movement, the *Times* considered the publication of Mrs Stowe's work, at least, questionable and not at all in the interests of the American slaves.[1] The *Times* was unable to accept that the level of abuse described in the chapters of *Uncles Tom's Cabin* existed on the plantations in the southern states of America. No one would set out to deliberately damage what was a valuable commodity, it argued.

Passmore Edwards published an edition of *Uncle Tom's Cabin* in London but also edited and published *Uncle Tom's Companion*, the true accounts of runaway slaves from the South and their journeys to freedom in the North. He published this, he said, 'to vindicate *Uncle Tom's Cabin* and to refute the unjust criticism of the *Times* and all who think with that paper'.[2]

### Calls for boycott

Although the word 'boycott'[3] was not to enter into public use for another 20 years, Edwards outlined the principle of the boycott in relation to the purchase of goods obtained by the means of slave labour. In 1830 the National Negro Convention had encouraged a boycott of slave-produced products and Edwards later wrote and published a pamphlet on this.[4] The English people, he declared, consumed more products of slave labour than any other country and through this were sustaining and extending slavery. When the price of sugar fell as a result of the demands of free traders for the lowering of tariffs, so the demand for slave labour in Cuba and Brazil increased. A 100% increase in the number of slaves, 65,000 a year, followed the reduction in tariffs on imported sugar from these two countries alone. After describing eyewitness accounts of the treatment of the slaves during transit in vivid detail; boys of age eight to twelve years being the favoured cargo, *they pack more conveniently*; and their life in the plantations, Edwards concluded with a demand that consumers should 'Prefer sacrifice to Sin – *rather not know the taste of sugar than be responsible for the broad black iniquity of slavery*'. It was possible to purchase slave-free sugar and Edwards said that one should purchase only where there was a guarantee of honest production.

As expected Edwards was active in many of the groups and societies that campaigned against slavery. He was member of the Aborigines Protection Society, founded in 1837, an international organisation that sought to improve the wellbeing of the indigenous populations of the colonies by publishing tracts and pamphlets. He was also a member of the Anthropological Society of London and elected a Fellow in 1869.

Edwards was amongst a deputation from the committee of the British and Foreign Anti-Slavery Society that met with Charles F Adams when he visited England in 1863 seeking the Government's support for the Northern States in the American Civil War. He also attended a combined meeting of the London Committee of Correspondence on American Affairs and the Emancipation Society, of which Edwards was the President, addressed by Rev Henry Ward Beecher, brother of the author of *Uncle Tom's Cabin*, seeking support for the Northern States.

The Emancipation Society was founded as a means of countering the sympathy within the country for the Southern, Confederate, States by voicing support for the United States Government in its emancipation policy. The Society was the result of a meeting in London on 11 November 1862 and Passmore Edwards' name appears on a long list of general committee members, along with John Stuart Mill and G J Holyoake.[5]

Ida Wells, an African-American journalist began her anti-lynching campaign after three friends were killed by a lynch mob in Memphis. In 1893 she brought her campaign to England, speaking at packed lecture halls and churches. Passmore Edwards was amongst those that welcomed her to London. With the Duke of Argyll as President and counting the Archbishop of Canterbury, Keir Hardie, Mary Ward and many MPs as members, the London Anti-Lynching Committee was formed, the first of several similar groups in England and America. Passmore Edwards was elected Treasurer, saying that he had already secured donations of £2,000. In September 1894 the Duke took his committee to America to find out the truth about lynching of African-Americans and threatened a boycott of US goods. Edwards was then seventy years old and there is no evidence of him accompanying them. Through Wells' campaign legislation was enacted against the mobs and the number of lynchings began to decline.

# Eleven
# Parliamentary Business

### A Parliamentary Candidate

With Edwards' 'darkest days' behind him and the owner of two successful publications, Edwards was eager to play a more public role in society and to him this meant following Bright and Cobden into Parliament in support of their Radical Liberal principles. His first step towards this goal came in 1865 when Liberals at Bath, where he had often lectured and where his brother Richard was by now a successful businessman and respected member of the community, nominated him as their candidate. He accepted, knowing that he was weak in local influence and not wishing to endanger Liberal interests he offered to stand down if a stronger candidate of his own side could be found.[1]

In August 1868 a letter appeared in the *West Briton* from a 'Cornishman in London', reminding Truro electors that they were represented by one Liberal and one Tory and that these two consistently voted against each other negating Truro's influence in Parliament. The result of the 1867 Reform Act was to add another 700 voters to the electoral role for Truro, mostly skilled working men, and some of these newly enfranchised initiated a petition to choose a second Liberal candidate. Forming the New Liberal Association they invited this 'Cornishman in London', Passmore Edwards, to address them.

A large gathering of electors gave him an enthusiastic welcome when he appeared in Truro on September 7, accompanied by his brother Richard who was acting as his election agent. Ably discussing the chief political issues of the time he praised the standing Liberal Member, Captain Vivian, assuring them that he was not there to cause disunity and would do nothing to jeopardise Vivian's position as a Member for the Borough. He had only one object in view; the country, and the country would be best served with Gladstone as the Prime Minister. Recognising that prior to the Reform Act the two parties in Truro were evenly balanced he said that bringing forward a second Liberal Candidate could be justified, only if a majority of the new electors were of the Liberal persuasion. The question was – were the majority of the new electors Liberal? If so, and a majority requested that he should serve them, he would do so, and would fight their battle as well as he could. He asked that the older electors and those recently enfranchised should work together with that single aim, for if they did not it would be the Tories that returned two Members.

A resolution was passed unanimously, 'That he is in every respect a fit and proper person to represent the Liberal interests of the Borough in Parliament, in conjunction with their present esteemed and valuable member the Honourable Captain Vivian'. Edwards responded with a letter to the *West Briton* addressed 'To the electors of Truro' simply stating that 'having been invited by several hundred of the electors of your borough to become a candidate for their suffrages to represent them in Parliament, I cheerfully comply with their request'.[2]

The meeting was followed up with further correspondence in the *West Briton* praising Edwards. 'Others may speak from observations – he from personal experience. He knows our wants for he has felt them; he has toiled as we have toiled and suffered as we have suffered. He has fought the uphill battle of life, he has been driven back, beaten down, but he rose again, and at last, after many struggles, by hard work and honourable conduct gained his present position. Our wrongs are his wrongs – our cause his cause. He is devoted heart and soul to our interests; let us one and all give him a hearty support and prove that if principle and patriotism are driven from every other class they are still to be found in the hearts of Cornish working men'.[3]

The *Royal Cornwall Gazette*, a Tory paper, was not so supportive, the editor, a Mr Quin, wrote and published several mischievous 'letters' about Edwards. Richard Cobden at that time was being portrayed by the Tory press as a 'donkey' and Quin followed this lead likening Edwards to 'Bottom' from *A Midsummer Night's Dream*, with an ass's head 'roaring' and 'braying'.

The Tory Member of Parliament was Frederick Williams, Cornish banker and copper merchant. The Williams family was very influential in the area, as were many of the Tory supporters and he had polled 29 more votes than Captain Vivian in the last contested election, in 1865. The ballot box was not introduced in to England until 1872 and prior to this employers and landowners were able to influence their employees and tenants by sending representatives to the public polling stations. It was not uncommon for bank owners to remind customers that they had a loan outstanding prior to polling. And with no limit on election expenses, more affluent candidates were known to bribe would-be voters with drink or employment during the election campaign.

Described as the workingmen's candidate, Passmore Edwards made several public speeches during the election campaign and set out his political creed in a notice published in the *West Briton*. Declaring his loyalty and unfaltering support for Gladstone his election address was the most visionary of the 1868 election.[4] He said that he favoured voting through the ballot box; would place the means of education within the reach of every child; rigidly enforce economy in every department of government; maintain the Cobdenite policy of non-intervention and, wherever possible, substitute arbitration for war as a means of settling international disputes. He would abolish the purchase system in the army and navy; put an end to the game laws; open up the universities to candidates of every religion; endeavour to make the colonies self-supporting; and abolish the death penalty. There were other social reforms that claimed his attention such as improved dwellings for the working classes; the introduction of courts of arbitration to prevent strikes; the cultivation of waste land; a revision of the licensing system and the protection of funds of all legally constituted societies. They were principles that he would continue to uphold throughout his life, although he was eventually to abandon his total loyalty to Gladstone over support for Irish Home Rule. He concluded by speaking out against those that sought to bribe, or intimidate their way into Parliament.[5]

Edwards addressed more than 3,000 people in Truro's Green Market a week before polling day. The crowd was very violent and attacked Quin who had to be escorted to the Red Lion Hotel amid threats. Edwards, having endeavoured in vain to allay the passions he had raised, assisted in protecting him.[6] Whilst Edwards openly attacked Williams and the Tory party he showed support for his fellow Liberal candidate, Captain Vivian, even ceasing his campaign for a short while when Vivian hurt his foot and needed to go to London for treatment. But Edwards was disappointed that Vivian's supporters did not show him the same consideration. The old Liberals would have preferred a county gent as their candidate and were just as concerned about Edwards' lack of pedigree as the Tories. Edwards suggested that they colluded to keep him out – a fact that was admitted by a Liberal voter in a subsequent letter to the *West Briton*.

For some time prior to polling day rumours of intimidation and undue pressure by Tory party supporters on behalf of their candidate were rife. On polling day the results seemed to indicate the accuracy of these rumours. Many of the new electors and some of the old that had promised their support for the two Liberals voted for the Conservative candidate. As a contrast to today, the results of the poll were given throughout the day from the four polling stations. From the first Williams took the lead with Vivian close and Edwards trailing. At the close of poll, at 4pm, the results were Williams, 731 votes; Vivian, 683 votes; and Edwards 406 votes. At that time, where a constituency returned two Members, each voter had two votes. These could be given to any two candidates but only one could be given to a single candidate. Where voters chose only one candidate this was known as 'plumping' and Edwards had called for there to be no 'plumping' amongst the Liberal voters. The results showed that his plea went unanswered. It was later said that amongst the 400 signing the original resolution supporting his candidature only about 230 recorded their vote in his favour.

As the clock moved towards the close of the polling stations the atmosphere in the borough, previously quiet and orderly, began to be disturbed. Large crowds gathered at the Red Lion and the Royal, the candidates' headquarters. The main centre of the disturbance was at the Red Lion where a number of Tory supporters displayed placards with the poll results and threw cigar stubs and fireworks down onto the waiting crowd. This led to a return of fire from the crowd, which had swelled, filling and blocking Boscawen Street. The firework volley continued unabated for more than an hour, together with stones and other missiles until not a pain of glass remained in the windows of the hotel, nor the police station. At the Royal Hotel, where Edwards was, there was minor damage.

At 7pm, the time for the results to be announced, Edwards was the first to arrive at the Green Market, together with a group of his supporters, to be greeted with loud and prolonged cheering. Captain Vivian arrived shortly after, similarly escorted and similarly greeted by the crowd that filled the market place. Frederick Williams, the successful Tory candidate failed to appear, merely sending a message that owing to the excited state of the crowd he was afraid to leave the Red Lion Hotel. Even when the Mayor, the

Town Clerk and two magistrates visited him to give assurance as to his safety, Williams refused to budge. During the wait the crowd kept up a constant call for 'Mr Edwards', Captain Vivian', 'Mr Bright', and 'Gladstone', interspersed with 'where's the dummy?' 'He's learning his speech!' After a delay of twenty minutes the Mayor came forward to announce the result and declare the absent Williams and Captain Vivian duly elected to represent Truro.

In his acceptance speech Vivian acknowledged Edwards' campaign, which he described as one of 'perfect purity and perfect honour'. He held a high opinion of Edwards' talents and honour and asked that the crowd remember that and not do anything that would tarnish that reputation. Edwards responded to say that though defeated he was not dishonoured; bent but not broken. He said that he could honestly say that he did not feel as defeated as he thought he would and that he would rather be in his position, with 400 votes, than in the position of Williams, with his 700 votes. When he came to Truro he had preached purity of election and had not deviated from that principle. He had no employment to offer, no inducements to hold out, and had not offered any man a single farthing. He claimed that pressure had been brought on voters to support the Tory candidate and quoted two examples that had been brought to his attention. One, a man in humble circumstances and the other in a respectable position but both put under unfair pressure to break their promise of voting for him.

When Captain Vivian called for a vote of thanks for the Mayor in conducting the poll, Edwards stepped forward and begged to be permitted to second the motion, 'in the unavoidable absence of Mr Williams'. This was met with laughter and cheers. The crowds then began to disperse and by 10 o'clock the town was quiet.

Edwards was convinced that his loss of votes was due to dirty tricks by Tory supporters, saying 'I know and can prove and hundreds can demonstrate that political opinion was not unbiased in Truro, and that men did not vote with freedom. Inducements were held out, employment was offered, bank and loan society influences were used and in many instances intimidation was resorted to obtain the desired end.'[7] But he did not lodge a formal complaint.

Whether Edwards failed because the old Liberals distrusted someone who was not 'of their sort'; or, as thought by Edwards, because of bribery and intimidation; or whether his views were just too radical, we cannot be certain. However, the Parliament elected that November, with Gladstone as Prime Minister and an overwhelming majority of Liberal members, saw an almost universal rejection of workingmen's candidates, those connected with the Reform League and Liberals with extreme views.[8] He was later to state that he had been beaten by both Whigs and Tories.[9]

Though Edwards wrote that he made no other attempt to enter Parliament until he fought the Salisbury election of 1880, he was reported as having been invited to do so on many occasions.

Following the death of the Member for Liskeard, Sir Arthur Buller, in 1869, Edwards was one of several Liberals to address the electors there but later withdrew,[10] and in 1871 he informed the Liberals in Truro that he was willing stand for the borough again, but his offer was not taken up.

The Southwark Liberal Association were next to consider Edwards as a prospective candidate and invited him to address the general committee in January 1879. One of five candidates, Edwards offered to retire in favour of Professor Thorold Rogers if the committee thought to select him.[11] Was this a selfless act to ensure the best candidate was chosen, or Edwards assessing the competition and not wanting to enter a race he was unlikely to win? A few weeks later the *Plymouth & Cornish Advertiser* announced that he had been invited to address the electors at St Ives, although Edwards declared that the report had not been authorised by him,[12] and at the same time it was reported that he been approached by Liberals in Darlington.

A west country newspaper dismissed the London radicals in March 1861 as 'all lesser men and not men of station and property and it was unlikely that the public will follow them'.[13] By 1880 Edwards, who had earlier been described as a *small poet*, was now, undeniably, a man of both station and property.

### The Salisbury Election

Edwards expressed surprise as to why, in 1880, he was chosen by the Liberals to contest the Salisbury seat. One of the candidates was Thomas Hughes, the author of *Tom Brown's Schooldays*, who was an experienced Member of Parliament. However, Hughes had upset the local traders by championing the Co-operative movement and this led to his failure to be reselected. Edwards, who was also a strong supporter of the movement, kept quiet on the subject.

As with Truro in 1868, Salisbury then returned two MPs and the Liberals fielded two candidates, Edwards and W Grenfell. Edwards often made dramatic use of statistics when delivering his speeches. In a speech in Salisbury in March 1880, he referred to the increases in expenditure by the last Conservative Government and asked the crowd whether they knew what a million pounds meant.[14] He then went on to describe just what the alleged eight million pound budget deficit could provide. First there were 80 churches at £5,000 each, and 80 chapels at £5,000 each. Also 2,400 schools at £2,500 each; 80 colleges at £5,000 each; 60 bath and washhouses at £5,000; 500,000 blankets at ten shillings; 200,000 tons of coal at 20 shillings a ton; education for 100,000 children and payment for school books allowing £10 each; 100,000 suits of workmen's clothes at 40 shillings each, 100,000 pairs of boots at 10s; 40 infirmaries at £10,000 each; 80 reformatories at £5,000; 400 lifeboats and lifeboat stations; 80 public parks at £5,000 each; 4,000 cottages at £100 each with furniture for £40 more; 20 museums for science and art at £10,000 each; 100 drinking fountains at £200; 40 free libraries at £5,000; and pensions of £20 a year for the remaining 12 years of 1,000 old people's lives. And on went the list, £200,000 to be distributed amongst the benevolent societies, £200,000 to the British & Foreign Bible

*John Passmore Edwards, MP for Salisbury*

Society; four million pounds of beef together with 20 million loafs of bread, 2,500 pounds of tea at 2s 6d a pound, and 20 million pounds of sugar to sweeten it with, and at each point he gave a brief and often amusing anecdote, often including a reference to his own poor upbringing. Fortunately no one seemed to be keeping count of Edwards' shopping list as it amounted to far more than the £8 million he suggested.

A decade later, having failed to make the contribution he wanted in Parliament he set out to provide just a few of the items on that shopping list, free libraries, schools, museums, infirmaries, public parks and drinking fountains.

Opponents accused him of being an atheist, religion being a strong element of politics at the time – an allegation that he strongly denied. 'If there was one thing more contrary to the truth than another, that was'. He said that wherever he went 'he bowed in submission not only to the law, but also to the great Law-giver that presided over all'. He saw a Deity 'not only in every blade of grass that waved, not only in every sunbeam that gleamed through space, but in every atom of matter.' In his autobiography he adds that he 'believed, with Shakespeare, that a Divinity shaped our ends and "Heaven have a hand in all"'. Whilst he did not profess to any single congregation he was clearly a God-fearing man and his grandson's view that he was a Unitarian is probably not far from the mark. It is certainly the only group he expressed an interest in subscribing to and although often solicited for help with building and restoring churches and chapels, he only gave to the Wesleyan chapel in his own village, where he helped towards clearing the deficit in the building fund and the funding of the St Day Church School Room, in memory of his uncle. The Rev E W Matthews, the Secretary of the British & Foreign Sailors Society, considered Edwards as belonging to the 'universal church of believing and doing souls' and his life's work supports that position.

When polling ended it was Edwards and Grenfell who had been elected, defeating the two Tory candidates, Dutton and Kenning. But this time it was the Tory, Kenning, who called foul play and lodged an appeal against the election result on the grounds of bribery and undue influence. At the same time Edwards was subject to a concerted attack by the Tory paper, the *South Wilts Express*, with letter after letter, most anonymous, maligning and misrepresenting him. The petitioners, though prolonging their thin case as long as possible by padding, were given short shrift by the presiding Judge, Mr Justice Pollack. On the fourth day he dismissed the petition with costs against the petitioners. Even so, Edwards and Grenfell, were required to pay their own lawyers costs, the sum of £500.

### The House of Waste

At Truro Edwards said that he had only one object in view, but it was a great one for his country and he believed that the object would be best served by making Mr Gladstone Prime Minister, believing that he would not do anything whatever to jeopardise a single vote that might be recorded in favour of Mr Gladstone in the House of Commons. 'He should at all times sacrifice himself to his party'. The much fought for seat in Parliament, however, did not bring Edwards the satisfaction he had hoped for. He was disparaging about the parliamentary system, and many of those that sat there. Many who had seemed so enthusiastic in their election campaigns took things easy once elected, using their time for self-advancement rather than for public benefit. The chief duty of the backbencher appeared to be to wait for the division bell and to vote along party lines as directed – no matter what his level of knowledge of the facts of the debate.

Edwards never made a major speech in Parliament. Many of those that did speak, he said, would waste the precious time of the House promoting themselves, their business interests or the aristocratic society to which they either belonged or aspired to join. Though MPs did not receive a salary at that time money was to be earned through lobbyists, supporting the interests of others and through lectureships, committees and commissions. Edwards was to suggest that after the 1885 election half the Irish MPs in the House earned a living from their work in the House.[15]

He called it the 'House of Waste' and his critics said that he would roam the corridors of an evening, turning down the gaslight in unoccupied rooms. Probably an exaggeration but Edwards complained of those who treated things bought with the public purse as if they had been paid for personally.

Edwards' contribution to the working of Parliament was through committee work and in challenging Ministers over issues of civil liberty. He was later to suggest that the nation owed more to committee work than generally supposed. Although a few men, the acknowledged leaders, received publicity and praise, it was the less well known men who did the work, unseen in committee. Unfortunately, *Hansard* did not at that time record the workings of the Parliamentary Committees so we do not know just how active he was. In 1881, speaking of his opposition to the Coercion Bill, we do know he said that he would do his best to amend it in Committee and he was also a member of several other committees, including one considering the North British Railways Bill in 1885.

On 30 June 1880, Edwards asked the Home Secretary, Sir W Harcourt, whether he was aware of Catherine Connoly who had been sentenced to 21 days imprisonment without the option of a fine, for smuggling a quarter of an ounce of tobacco to her husband who was being held on remand. The penalty had been handed out by a magistrate in Clerkenwell well known for the severity of his sentences. The Home Secretary was not, at that time aware of the case but promised to look into the matter. Three days later Catherine Connoly was released.

A month later Edwards again asked the Home Secretary about the case of a youth who had been convicted of stealing a rosebud from a garden in Cambridge and sentenced to three months imprisonment. The Home Secretary replied that although the youth had been previously convicted of smashing a plate glass window he agreed that his sentence did appear too harsh and he would communicate his opinion to the Magistrate.

He also added his name to several bills successfully presented to Parliament, including a Hares and Rabbits Bill, amendment of the Cruelty to Animals Act and a bill to strengthen the rights of leaseholders. Edwards represented the working man, a fact that upset at least one Salisbury elector. Written on the back of an election circular just a few days after the election, Edwards received a note from one elector who declared that he did not consider that Edwards represented him. 'As a body' the people of Salisbury had voted entirely the other way. Edwards' support, he said, came from the back-courts and slums, and the '£7 suffrage', the lowest classes, a fact he found most distasteful. Edwards' response was only to say that the Tories would have been happy to receive such support but it was time to put such recriminations aside and get on with the job that the electors had chosen them to do.[16]

In March 1884 when Edwards voted against the Liberal Government over its Egyptian policy the constituency officials demanded an explanation. Edwards' response was a letter to the chairman stating that as a consequence of their dissatisfaction to his actions in the House, he would stand down. A deputation was immediately dispatched to London and whatever was said Edwards withdrew his resignation. The truce was, however, short lived and the following year Edwards confirmed that he would not seek re-election.

On 14 August 1885 Passmore Edwards sat in the cross party benches as Black Rod commenced the proceedings which were to bring the 1880 Parliament, and Edwards parliamentary career, to an end.

**The Irish Question**

Edwards said that he was 'for the integrity and independence of the British Empire' and would not give up one inch of land, or, as the French representative said to Bismark, one stone of a fortress. He would do all he possibly could to benefit Ireland, but he could not think for one moment of the decomposition of the British Empire.[17] There was, he said one law underlying European civilisation. Nations, instead of breaking to pieces were gradually concentrating – coming closer and closer together, and were growing stronger. France had once consisted of several smaller countries, Germany consisted of about 300 different nationalities and principalities and Italy had previously been divided into seven or eight different provinces. Great Britain had once been seven nations, which in the course of time reduced to four: England, Ireland, Scotland and Wales.

Rather than separatism he believed that it was possible to introduce Municipal Home Rule for Ireland, giving the Irish the local government that existed within England. For one thing there was far more work presented to Parliament than could possibly be dealt with and it should be possible for arrangements to be made that allowed Ireland to decide whether to dig canals or extend fisheries or any of the other local arrangements about which the people of Ireland knew far more than those in London.

In 1881 Gladstone introduced the Protection of Person and Property Bill as emergency legislation, a Coercion Bill, to control the situation in Ireland. The Irish Land League were campaigning for improvements in the position of tenant farmers and ultimately for a redistribution of land from landlords to tenants, especially from English absentee landlords. The Land League demanded 'the 3 Fs', Fair Rent, Fixture of tenancy and Freedom for the tenant to sell their interest in land. Most Irish tenants had few rights. They had no right to a written lease and when a rental agreement, usually a 12-month period, expired, they could be evicted with no compensation for any improvements made. Adverse weather, poor harvests and low world food prices worsened the situation for the Irish tenant farmers leading to an outbreak of violence, with rent strikes and attacks on landlords and their agents. Gladstone's Bill, suspending *Habeas Corpus* – introducing imprisonment without trial by jury, and secret inquisitions – was intended to restore law and order.

Edwards saw the need for legislation but considered that the Bill went too far, voting in Committee against inclusion of clauses that he considered unduly stringent and would loose the Liberal Party support. He considered that a Land Act, to rectify the inequity that existed in Ireland should be introduced at the same time not later. Though he succumbed to the Whips' pressure and did not vote against the Closure Bill in 1882, he voted to remove treason from the list of offences to be tried by a judge without a jury, under the Government's proposals for a Prevention of Crime in Ireland Bill.

**The Rochester Election**

Edwards lack of speeches in the House did not seem to deter other constituencies from wishing to have him represent them. Berkshire considered inviting him to stand against John Walker, the owner of the *Times*, as did Leicester and more than ten other constituencies. In October 1885 he was sounded out by the Plymouth Liberals with a view to representing them but declined saying that he had no thought of re-entering Parliament and that journalism was absorbing his attention. It was the withdrawal of the Liberal sitting member for Rochester, Sir Arthur Otway, three weeks before the 1885 election that persuaded Edwards to reconsider his position and he was rushed in to fill the breach.

A meeting of the Liberal 300 in Rochester confirmed Edwards as their candidate on Friday 6 November and he arrived in Rochester the following afternoon and commenced house-to-house canvassing. Posters announcing a hastily arranged meeting, to be held that evening at the Corn Exchange, were put up at 4pm but the room was still full to overflowing. Not having a prepared speech he merely stood before them and announced 'such as I am – here you have me'.[18] He remarked on how he had gone to Salisbury with only 48 hours notice and arrivied knowing nobody, yet he had won the trust of the electorate to the extent that he polled the largest majority the city had ever seen. This, he said, would hold well for Rochester. He then answered questions from the floor. He was more prepared on the Monday evening when he addressed an overcrowded meeting at the Corn Exchange and set out the principles that he brought to Rochester. He was in favour of a reform of local government and this to extend, 'in the spirit of generosity and justice', to Ireland. He stated that he was in favour of further advances in Free Trade and wanted changes to the taxation system that 'bear lightly on those whose lot it is to labour'; he was in favour of Land Reform and in reform within the House to prevent the obstruction of the parliamentary process for selfish or party political advantage. Whilst he gave, he said, ungrudging but independent support to the Gladstone Government he considered their policy on Egypt to be mistaken. He also explained his position with regard to Ireland. He was to develop these points during a series of well-attended public meetings during the following days. Generally he was well received by the voters but the rumours previously spread at Salisbury that he was 'an atheist, Republican and a destroyer of the church' were again circulated in the area, against which Edwards quickly defended himself, as he had done at Salisbury five years earlier. Such accusations were, he said 'a great thumping lie'. He had voted to allow Bradlaugh, the secularist, to take his seat in the House, not as a vote for Bradlaugh but as a vote for the people of Northampton, to send who they chose to Parliament. Edwards told them that many years ago the Society of Friends published the *Peace Advocate* in Rochester but they handed it over to him, and he then published it at his own expense. Since that time he had been indissolubly connected with Christian institutions throughout the country. 'Would they have associated themselves with him if he had been a destroyer of the church?' he asked. 'Would Salisbury have elected him if he had been a destroyer of the church?' Neither was he a republican and had never even uttered or written a word in favour of it.

Although his campaigning continued to attract large crowds Edwards was at a serious disadvantage in being able to canvass for only two weeks prior to the election, and the rumours spread about him added to his difficulties. When the poll was held, on 24 November it was Colonel Hughes-Hallett who was triumphant, with a majority of 241. The 1884 and 1885 Reform Acts extended the vote to agricultural workers for the first time and redistributed seats in favour of the larger towns, meaning that both Salisbury and Rochester lost seats and became single member constituencies. Rochester had returned two Liberals from 1857 up until 1880, when one had been lost. Now the single seat had gone to the Conservatives. Though Edwards defeat came as a surprise to the Liberals in Rochester, they also lost votes throughout the country; the Liberal majority of the previous Parliament being slashed to 86, and they relied on the Irish Nationalists to form a government. There was also talk of foul play on behalf of Hughes-Hallett, though unlike at Salisbury previously, no action was taken. Within the week Passmore Edwards and his wife had left Rochester for London. His departure was to bring an end, once and for all, to his parliamentary ambitions.

As Ann Widdecombe remarked in 2009 when she retired as a Member of Parliament: there was more potential in addressing an issue through the media than through Parliament. A television documentary she appeared in attracted an audience of four million while the subject in Parliament would have attracted an audience of no more than forty. Passmore Edwards had regained full control of the *Echo*. Did he consider that through the pages of the *Echo* or the *Weekly Times & Echo* his voice was more likely to be heard than at Westminster, where the Whips ensured that the party line was adhered to? He certainly had much more to say, and do, about the social issues of the day.

# Twelve
# Creating a Legacy

Throughout his earlier life Edwards had a reputation for philanthropy; his name appearing time and time again on lists of responders to disaster appeals and appeals in support of good causes – but it was following his departure from Parliament that began the chapter of his life for which he is most well known.[1]

He said:

> There is a time for everything; a time to sow, and a time to reap; a time to gather, and a time to distribute. Having gathered, I determined to put into act what I had long nurtured in thought, and use certain means at my disposal for the general good.

Edwards considered the means by which he should redistribute his wealth, discounting the setting up of 'public funds to be administered by others' as Carnegie had eventually done, as he thought that they may not use his money as '*economically*' as he would himself. One thought lay uppermost in his mind. Since his wealth had been brought about by the labour of others, it was reasonable and just that those who had contributed to his wealth should now benefit from it, and this could be done best by promoting and supporting schemes that added to the general well being of the working classes.

His election manifesto at Truro in 1868[2] had included, among a long list of pledges, 'to place the means of education within the reach of every child in the kingdom'. The 1870 Education Act provided the means to an elementary education and 'Board Schools' but Edwards looked beyond this. For many the opportunity to continue in education, or even to read anything more than a hymn book or the bible, was denied them. He had campaigned in support of William Ewart and the Free Libraries Act in 1850 and it was the provision of libraries, and the opportunities for self-advancement they offered that was to form the mainstay of his legacy. With only one or two exceptions, there does not seem to have been a master plan, Edwards undertaking what he termed a 'survey of need' and then responding to opportunities and circumstances as they presented themselves. And with his gift there was usually a lasting involvement with those he helped.

## Andrew Carnegie and the Gospel of Wealth

Carnegie, the son of a handloom weaver, went as a boy with his family from their home in Scotland to settle in Pennsylvania.[3] Initially finding work with a telegraph company and then a railroad, he invested in the emerging steel industry and by the late 1880s was the second richest man in the world.[4] In 1889 he wrote his essay on philanthropy, called *The Gospel of Wealth*.[5] Passmore Edwards shared Carnegie's view that it was the duty of the self-made rich to redistribute their wealth whilst still living, rather than to leave it to either heirs or others, who may not have the desire or ability to properly manage it. Edwards was later referred to as the 'Cornish Carnegie' and while Carnegie acknowledged his debt to Edwards, dubbing him 'St Passmore', Carnegie's views were well established before Edwards began his philanthropy.

## The Blackwater Literary Institute

Edwards was already giving large numbers of books to existing libraries and institutes and in 1889 the vicar of Mithian, the parish in which Blackwater is situated, wrote to Passmore Edwards. He had rented a two-roomed cottage, which he had opened as a reading room for the men of the village, and asked whether Edwards would kindly donate some suitable books for this purpose. Passmore Edwards responded to say that not only would he supply 500 books, he would be pleased to supply the building as well, if the village could provide a suitable site.

On Thursday 7 August 1890 the Reverend Rogers officially opened the first of over 70 buildings to be funded by Passmore Edwards.

Based on his simple principle of self help for the workingman it was always a condition of his gifts that the community receiving them should act as trustees and maintain and protect the building for future generations. There was also usually a requirement that the community should contribute to the costs either by supplying the land or completing the furnishings. At Blackwater the community struggled to make their contribution. The land on which the Institute still stands was offered by Lord Falmouth but the cost of furnishings, just £40, was eventually met by Edwards. And he remained a member of the Institute, paying his two guinea annual membership until he died.

John Symons, Edwards' former school friend, and his son Frank built the Institute, a simple single-storey building in local stone with granite quoins to the front and a Delabole dry slate roof, costing £250. Originally there were just two rooms, divided by a wooden partition that could be drawn back to provide one large room for concerts and other entertainment but an additional room was later added at the rear of the Institute. Edwards opened this extension in June 1893, on his first visit to Blackwater for many years, following which the usual midsummer tea was held in a nearby field. For nearly thirty years Edwards had provided an annual tea for the old folk in the area, which on one occasion included a monster 140-pound plum cake. While Edwards met and talked with many who had not seen since his youth, his wife and daughter helped pour the tea and looked after the elderly villagers.

Although in his autobiography, Edwards gives an extract from his speech at the Institute's opening ceremony, the *West Briton*[6] reported that Edwards was unable to attend, his letter arriving only on the morning of the opening day and the honour falling to the Rev Rogers. Edwards, presumably, had written a speech for the occasion and this had remained with his papers, to be quoted again by J J McDonald[7] in 1900 and R S Best in the 1980s.

Newspaper reports give details of social events and concerts held in the Blackwater Institute in those early years but the accounts show that the management committee struggled to make it pay its way. Up until 1910, Edwards' annual membership subscription of two guineas, together with an equal subscription from Mr Strauss, MP for Camborne and the proprietor of the Pen Pol Tin Smelting Works, represented more than a quarter of the Institute's annual income. Despite being given as a community building for all of the residents, especially the younger villagers, over the years the Institute became more of a private snooker club for the men of the village. The original books that formed the library, which included 150 given by Richard Passmore Edwards in 1891, were sold off after being judged old fashioned and a batch of second-hand novels were purchased from a book supplier in Truro, by the pound weight. The snooker club gave rise to a number of successful snooker players, but the maintenance of the fabric of the building was neglected, regular meetings of the management committee ceased and by the millennium the club had all but closed.

*The opening of the Blackwater Institute, 1890*

Unfortunately the condition of the building deteriorated rapidly and by 2007, even with the best efforts of Charlie Palmer, the last elected chairman, who had personally funded emergency repairs, it was semi-derelict with vandalised windows, slates missing and rot affecting both floors and walls. Thankfully, in January 2008, a group of residents was formed to restore the Institute and to reopen it as a village hall.

But when the group researched the records it appeared that the deed of gift for the land from the Tregothnan Estate had never been completed by the original trustees, probably due to the death of the 6th Viscount Falmouth in 1899. They were advised that the land and the building had reverted to the Estate. Although the Estate was reluctant to complete the deed of gift a new 125-year lease was offered at a nominal rent. At the time of writing the project to reopen the Institute as a community building 'where every single person in the village might find a hearty welcome',[8] as Edwards' intended, was progressing slowly, with the hope that the building may be, at least in part, in use for the centenary of Edwards' death in 2011.

*Blackwater, showing the Institute*

**Free Libraries**

Passmore Edwards claimed only to have 'done a little in the press' to support William Ewart, author of the Free Libraries Act,[9] but an article in the *Morning Chronicle*[10] in September 1849 on the lack of free libraries in England, was most likely by Edwards. He stated that there were only three in England, compared to France (107) and America (over 100), and that 'there was no reason why libraries should not be universal – in every town, many, in every village, one.'

This call was to be repeated in May 1890 when he unveiled a drinking fountain he had funded in Victoria Park, London. In the speech that followed he announced that he intended to open a library in every village and had set aside £50,000 for this purpose. Although he funded far fewer libraries than this optimistic target, they cost him much more.

Ewart's first Free Libraries Bill was introduced into the House of Commons in February 1850. It proposed that Town Councils should be authorised to levy a rate of no more than one half penny in the pound for the erection or purchase of property to be used as a library for the free use of all classes. No provision was allowed for the purchase of books, these were to be donated by the more wealthy members of the community or purchased by public subscription. The bill was opposed by those who considered that the half penny rate would materially affect the landed interest, who were already too heavily burdened to endure such an imposition for mere intellectual gratification.[11] By the time the Bill had been accepted by Parliament it had been amended to apply to only those boroughs with a population of more than 10,000 and only then with the support of more than two thirds of ratepayers voting in a referendum. But it was a start and it was to be followed by several amendments so that by 1855 the rate had been increased to 1d in the pound and borough councils could use the money, if sufficient, to purchase books. Even so, the establishment of free libraries was slow, even in London and the provincial towns and cities. While Salford had established a free library in 1850, and Manchester and Liverpool quickly followed suit, the numbers in London were small, with many ratepayers, who were the wealthier residents, arguing that the working classes were already educated enough.

# Thirteen
# Family Memorials

Passmore Edwards' name more often than not appears above the door of the buildings he funded, but he preferred to dedicate them to those he admired, and on a few occasions to the memory of his family members.

Most of this latter group are in Cornwall, the first being the convalescent home at Perranporth, erected to the memory of his mother, Susan.

### The Cornwall Convalescent Home

In his autobiography *A Few Footprints*, Passmore Edwards wrote, 'Next to the demand for hospitals I learnt that more convalescent home accommodation was necessary.'

On 6 April 1892 the weekly board meeting of the Royal Cornwall Infirmary considered a letter from Passmore Edwards offering to endow the Infirmary with a Convalescent Home he was building at Perranporth, on the north coast just eight miles from Truro. His offer was to provide both the building and the freehold site.[1]

The Board of the Infirmary accepted the offer immediately and started an appeal for donations towards the future maintenance of the home. Lord Falmouth drew up the appeal and headed the subscription list with a donation of £25 and an annual subscription of £5 5s. Edwards transferred railway stocks valued at £3,000 as an endowment.

He was invited to join the board of governors for the home, becoming Vice President, along with J C Williams MP and Viscount Falmouth. Dr William Whitworth was invited to be the honorary medical officer to the home, a position which he accepted, pointing out there were now to be three convalescent homes within the area of his practice and 'However willing I am to give my services to any or all of them it is hardly in my power to supply medicines gratuitously ... I suggest the home be furnished with a small supply of medicines and a small charge made to those requiring medicines, or alternatively, if supplied medicines from my own surgery, then patients should pay the cost price.'

The next step was the appointment of a matron. The post was advertised at a salary of £30 per annum and was to be taken up straight away. Only one candidate was asked to come and meet the committee, Miss Isabella Rimmington, who was appointed and asked to go to Perranporth, take up residence at one of the hotels and, together with Miss Burgess, matron of the City Infirmary, supervise the furnishing and staffing of the home which was now nearing completion. The governors paid her travelling expenses of £3 to the interview.

It was Harry, Passmore Edwards' son, who laid the foundation stone in March 1891, and Eleanor, Passmore Edwards' wife, cut the ribbon to open the home on 1 August in 1892.[2] Eleanor became personally involved in furnishing the home spending some time in Perranporth as it was being built and their daughter, Ada, chose the pictures that were hung in the rooms, several of which were said to be valuable. Although Passmore Edwards was present he chose not to make a speech, merely saying that his wife's act of declaring the home open spoke for itself.

Passmore Edwards continued his involvement with the hospital and was to become one of the Infirmary's most generous benefactors. This resulted in him becoming the first honorary freeman of the City of Truro in 1893, an occasion that saw thousands of local children lining the streets to welcome him. As well as the endowment to the home, Edwards paid an annual subscription of ten guineas and his wife two guineas. At the time a one-guinea subscription would entitle the subscriber to place two patients in the home for a period of up to two weeks.

The home, built on land purchased from the Enys estate, was designed and built by John Symons and his son, Frank, who were also responsible for the woodwork and some of the furniture. Built mainly of local stone, it has many similarities with the Blackwater Institute and comprised on the ground floor, a library, a reading room, a day room and dining room with a kitchen at the rear. The main entrance in the eastern wing of the building lead into a spacious vestibule divided from the lobby by a screen filled with cathedral tinted glass. The reading room and library was in the front of the building as were the dining room and day room. Occupying prominent positions on the walls were portraits of Harry Passmore Edwards, Bishop Wilkinson, and Mr Arthur Laverton, ex-Mayor of Truro. Other rooms on the ground floor included the matron's room and other offices.

A wide staircase lead to the first floor where there was accommodation for 20 male

*Convalescent Home for the Royal Cornwall Infirmary, Perranporth*

patients in seven bedrooms, with hot and cold running water (rare in those days), linen closets, and electric bells. A large bathroom was also located on this floor. On the second floor a room was set aside for 'private devotion' at the suggestion of Bishop Wilkinson. A feature of the home was a 16-foot-wide balcony running between the east and west wings with commanding views of the sea.

The home made a slow start with only 55 patients being admitted in the first 12 months, from 29 parishes, and the average number occupying the 20 available beds was only 4.4 patients, with an average stay of 24 days. In the following year 89 patients were admitted and by 1900 the number had risen to 114 with the average stay remaining at 24 days.

Miss Rimmington proved a very popular and satisfactory matron but the committee found it necessary to admonish her as she was constantly using her influence to keep patients longer than necessary.[3] Conditions in the home were far better than those experienced by the typical patient in their own homes and she was averse to sending them home to such conditions. Many of the cottages were old and in disrepair and had only one bedroom, which sometimes was divided by a wooden partition half the height of the room. There was usually only one small window, no ceiling, no proper outlet for foul air and no fireplace.[4]

In May 1895, the committee introduced a 4-week admittance limit and told Miss Rimmington that this must be strictly adhered to. However, the matron was not so easily persuaded. In July 1894, Passmore Edwards' daughter, Ada, came to stay with her for a month and Passmore Edwards himself stayed for a week in August 1904, after which he left a cheque for £10. Miss Rimmington continued as matron until 1916, when she retired after 24 years service.

It was not until after the First World War that provision was made for female patients. When T L Dorrington, a jeweller and former Mayor of Truro, died in December 1911 he left shares in Lloyds Bank and the residue of his estate to the Infirmary for the establishment and maintenance of a convalescent home for women. But it was not until 1914 that plans drawn up by Cornelius, for a seven-bed home, were approved and work on the building commenced. However, with the outbreak of war in August 1914, the Passmore Edwards Home closed, to be made ready for convalescent soldiers and sailors. The military made little use of the home and after an enquiry from the Girls' Friendly Society both the Passmore Edwards Home and the now completed Dorrington House were used as accommodation for girls working in the munitions factory at Perranporth. Five beds at the Epiphany Convalescent Home at St Agnes were placed at the disposal of the Infirmary during this period to replace the facilities at Perranporth.

When the homes were handed back to the Infirmary in 1919, they were renovated and reopened under a new medical officer, Dr Barker and new matron, Miss Jordan.

The two homes were taken into the National Health Service in 1948 and continued in use until closed in the 1960s. Both homes were then sold off and converted to residential apartments, the Passmore Edwards Home being now known as Nampara Court.

## The hand that rocked the cradle

Passmore Edwards' relationship with his mother is striking. As a boy, it is to his mother that he went when he had difficulty in understanding words he came across in the books he bought. As a man, it is to the 'memory of my beloved mother' that he dedicated his first major public building, the Perranporth Convalescent Home, and many years later it was the memory of his mother that caused him to break down with emotion after laying the foundation stone to a library dedicated to her memory. Finally on his deathbed his thoughts were again with his mother, a mother who had 'ever lived in vision before his eyes'.[5]

His father was the route to those early experiences of life, the effects of alcohol on the working man, the hell and damnation sermons, the lectures at the local literary and scientific institutes, and the source of reading matter through the *Penny Magazine*, raising in him an interest in the social and moral issues of his time. But it is his mother, Susan, 'Blessed be her name and memory',[6] that he attributed the development of his character and the means by which he will later address those issues.

In *A Few Footprints* Edwards wrote that his mother rarely went to chapel, 'her household duties being as numerous and as necessary on Sundays as on other days'. She was a quiet and busy woman, with four children to look after and probably with involvement in the beer house and brewery, who 'put her religion into her life'. Essentially a peacemaker he never heard her cause a family argument, say anything against a neighbour or give offence to anyone.

The most illuminating evidence of the esteem with which Edwards held his mother comes from an article published in the *Public Good* in 1850. The article is entitled 'They who rock the cradle rule the world', and sets out Edwards' views on the relative positions of man and woman in Society but goes on to express his dreams of his own potential position in that Society, a position he owes to his mother. 'Man is more influential in some positions, woman is more influential in others,' he states; adding, 'I have no sympathy with a great deal of sentimentalism and refined flattery which is frequently spoken at public meetings with reference to woman's influence, I think she is more degraded than elevated thereby. I look upon man as one and I look upon woman as one. They are both grand units equally intrinsically valuable as human beings, equally important to the existence and well being of society and equally responsible to their fellows and to God'. But it is clear that the position in which he considers woman to be more influential is as a homemaker and he praises the role of woman as a mother. 'Home and mother, what significant things do these words express. They have not hitherto been appreciated but they will be esteemed of mighty importance in the future.'

Edwards, clearly, had his own mother, and his own childhood, in his thoughts when he wrote:

> Cast your eyes again on that gentle looking woman. She is by her own fireside; she has her child on her knee, to whom she sweetly talks, tenderly kisses and warmly presses to her bosom.

This is as much his autobiography as the early chapters of *A Few Footprints*, and is far more revealing.

> Her sunny smiles, her gentle upbraidings, her songs, her pretty stories, her warm embrace, soon become assimilated with the moral being of her child. By anxious watching, by patience and persuasion the child becomes a counterpart of his mother, step by step he grows into virtue and knowledge; his physical frame gets stronger and his mind grows correspondingly. Years pass away and the child expands into boyhood and his feet are planted in the way of knowledge and goodness. He is still obedient to his mother's teachings – he still feels a pleasure in performing her will – he catches inspiration from her benignant looks and consolation from her perpetual anxiousness and inexhaustible love. Other years pass away and boyhood ripens into manhood. Even now the mother is considered and consulted in every important act of life. The noble courageous independent minded man, does not forget the lessons of wisdom he received when young; he cannot, and he would not if he could, erase from his memory and his being the impressions, sentiments and instructions given him by his mother. At one time he obeyed her will, and acted according to her wishes, because she desired it; now he walks in the same pathway, strives after the same objects and aspires to dignity of character, and usefulness of life because it is right. Now he stands among millions of his fellow men with a noble and incorruptible heart, with a cultivated intellect with an enterprising spirit, with an energetic will, with heroism of soul and with measureless sympathies. His heart beats in unison with the generous impulses and magnanimous action of the great and good of all ages. He looks around upon a rich and luxuriant universe and sees that it is fitted to nourish and foster the human soul. He looks at his fellow man and finds that every one of them is capable of a lofty and enduring destiny. But also, evil meets his eye almost wherever he looks. But he is not to be dismayed by the difficulties and discouraging appearances. He sees that wrong can be vanquished and he buckles on his armour to do battle with it – He who a few short years since was a lisping prattler on his mother's knee is now a poet, a prophet and the favourite of his country. He not only writes essays, but histories, – he speaks and moves society to its very foundation – he rises in the senate house and with contemplation sitting on his brow and with generous flashing of his eyes he pours forth a stream of eloquence which electrifies and recaptures – he vindicates liberty and puts to shame its enemies, worthy man of worthy mother.

Susan would have followed her sons' lives closely, ever ready with a word of advice, although we do not know to what extent Edwards confided in his mother. It was Susan, alone, who travelled to London in 1852, when Edwards was about to become overwhelmed by his early publishing endeavours, although Edwards did his best to keep his financial problems from his family. There was still no direct railway link from West Cornwall to London at that time so the journey would not have been straightforward. However, both William and Susan travel to Hayle to see James and his family and to Bath, to see Richard and their oldest son, William.

But it is in Bath, at the home of her son Richard that Susan died in 1870, having moved there after the death of her husband six years earlier. Passmore Edwards had by then regained his finances and position, paid off his creditors and had recently married. He had also taken on the responsibilities of parenthood himself.

**Newton Abbot Free Library**

The most notable building in Newton Abbott is the combined free library and science and technical school and recent redevelopment in the town has done nothing but enhance its position.

Passmore Edwards was a member of the Cornish Lodge in London and at one dinner he found himself seated opposite a member of the Newton Abbot Urban Council, Mr H T Parker. During their conversation Edwards remarked that his mother had been born in Newton Abbot and he would like to be able to do something for the town in her memory. Initially he suggested he provide a hospital, but as one already existed he offered to provide a library, if the Council first adopted the Free Libraries Act. Parker took the offer back to the local Masonic Lodge and it was then taken before the Urban Council and a public meeting was held.

The offer came as a great but welcome surprise to the townsfolk and after an open lecture by the librarian of the Plymouth library on the advantages of a free library, the vote on adopting the Public Libraries Act was carried unanimously.

A proposal was made to construct a larger building to accommodate both the library and a replacement for the existing science and art schools and it was agreed that a technical college should be constructed alongside the library, although Passmore Edwards insisted that, unlike at Falmouth, internally they should be arranged as separate buildings.

An opportunity was taken to address concerns over a dangerous corner at the junction of Market Street and Bank Street. After acquiring the site by compulsory purchase, the dilapidated buildings were demolished, the roads realigned and the new buildings erected on the remaining land.

Silvanus Trevail, who had designed the Truro library and school for Passmore Edwards, with which it shares similarities, was appointed architect and the contract to build was awarded to Henry Goss of Torquay. The costs were to be £3,543 for the technical schools, of which the County Council gave £2,700, and £2,290 for the library funded by Passmore Edwards.

The day chosen to lay the foundation stone was set for Thursday 26 June 1902, the date of the Coronation of King Edward VII, following the death of Victoria in 1901. The day was to start with the firing of a cannon, ringing of bells, a short religious service, bands, processions, public luncheon, tea for the children, old English sports at the recreation ground, dancing, and a host of other entertainments. However, on the Tuesday preceding Coronation day, a telegram was received that the King had undergone an operation in order to save his life and that, consequently, the Coronation had to be postponed. Rejoicing subsided into prayer for the King's recovery, the street decorations were dismantled, the ceremonies and entertainments postponed.[7]

The townsfolk waited until the beginning of October for their day of celebration, when the town was again gaily decorated with bunting and banners that proclaimed 'Welcome to Mr Passmore Edwards', and 'Success to the Free Library and Technical Schools'.

Even the wet and miserable weather failed to deter the crowd that witnessed the solid granite block being carefully lowered into its place; loud cheering breaking out as Edwards declared the stone for the library 'well and truly laid'. Lord Morley, chairman of Devon County Council then laid the foundation stone of the technical schools, and the dignitaries retired to the Alexandra Hall for luncheon. Passmore Edwards' vegetarian leanings were no doubt challenged by the menu, which included pheasants, game pies, chicken, duck, turkey, sirloin of beef, hams, tongue, veal and ham pie, spiced beef, trifles, tipsy cake, charlotte russe, cream, jellies and fruit tarts.

Following the luncheon there were the usual toasts and responses. Edwards responded to a toast to 'the health of our honoured guest, the generous donor of our Free Library', by saying that had he known that he was to receive such an undeserved welcome he should have thought twice before coming; he might have gone to his doctor and asked to be relieved. He went on to say: 'I can assure you that so pleasant as it may be to you to cheer me it is not so pleasant to me because I do not think that I deserve it. I do not see that I have done anything worthy of this splendid public recognition. I will only try to deserve it a little more in the future.' Passmore Edwards was in his eightieth year! He went on to talk about the Boer War, which had recently ended and the need to build up the nation's commerce and industry. Comparing England to Germany and America, which he said had made significant progress in introducing both primary and secondary education, Edwards said that towns like Newton Abbot

*Newton Abbot Free Library and Technical Schools*

were redressing the balance. After saying how pleased he was to visit Newton Abbot that day he said 'I remember my poor mother ....' but was overcome with emotion and could not continue. 'Ladies and gentlemen,' he finally said, 'I thank you most heartily for the reception you have given me' and sat down, to loud applause.[8]

And so the toasts and speeches continued, to the 'County Council', the 'architect', 'the builder', and finally 'the guests', bringing the ceremonies to a close. Passmore Edwards, although nearly 80 years old, had travelled alone to Newton Abbot from London that morning on the 5.30am train and he returned that afternoon, leaving Newton Abbot station at 4.52pm.

Following the delayed foundation stone ceremony all did not proceed as plan. Work continued, slowly, for some time before it was found that the builder would be unable to complete his contract and another builder was engaged to complete the work, and the clock turret, originally planned to surmount the building, was omitted. Further delays occurred following the death of Councillor Charles Vicary, who had worked so diligently to secure the success of the project and, in 1903, Silvanus Trevail shot himself while travelling home to Cornwall on the train from London. Trevail's practice was taken over by his only assistant, Alfred Cornelius, who completed the library and technical school; the opening taking place in August 1904.

The disappointing weather at the time of the foundation stone ceremonies had not deterred the people of Newton Abbot from planning celebrations to mark the completion and opening of the library and technical schools. At 11 o'clock members of the Urban Council were assembled at the council offices ready to drive to the station to meet Passmore Edwards, General Sir Redvers Buller, who was to open the library, Viscount Ebrington, who was to open the technical schools, and the other distinguished visitors taking part in the day's proceedings. Almost at the last moment it was announced that Passmore Edwards had telegraphed the chairman to say 'Since writing you I have passed nearly a fortnight in Cornwall and intended to return today, stopping

Above left: *Terracotta bust in Newton Abbot Library*

Above right: *Decorated streets welcomed Passmore Edwards to lay the foundation stone of the new library* at Newton to be present at the opening of the library and technical schools; but circumstances have arisen to upset the arrangement and to prevent my being with you, which I greatly regret, and can now only cordially wish the new composite institution a prosperous and useful future'.

It is recorded in the history of the Perranporth Convalescent Home, built by Passmore Edwards in memory of his mother, that he had in fact spent that time in Cornwall in the home. The procession was to travel from the railway station to the library passing the house in Wolborough Street where Susan Passmore had been born. Did the 'circumstances' that prevented Edwards from attending relate to his health, or was it that the day would once again stir such deep memories? Everyone had been anticipating that Edwards would be present at the opening of the building he had given to the town and genuine regret and disappointment was expressed.

A bust of Passmore Edwards, presented to the library committee by Hexter Humpherson & Co of the Watcombe Pottery was displayed at the luncheon and afterwards was placed in the newly opened library. In 2010 it was looking down on visitors mounting the stairs to the local studies library on the first floor, and no doubt Passmore Edwards looked down also, satisfied that the library he had given remained one of the busiest adult and community learning centres in the county.

When Mrs Lillian Ridler retired as head librarian at Newton Abbot in 1976, she had spent her entire working life at the library. Starting as a library assistant in 1933 she reached the position of head librarian in 1947 and remained in charge for another twenty-nine years. She had seen both the museum and the school close and the beginning of the dispute over ownership of the building in 1974, when local government reorganisation transferred the responsibility for library provision to the Devon County Council, a dispute that was to rumble on for another seven years.

Devon County Council has, however, treated the building with the respect that it deserves. It remains both a public library and centre for adult education, and recent highways improvements have opened up the views towards Silvanus Trevail's last commission. This wonderful building remains a memorial to an otherwise unknown woman, wife and mother, Susan Passmore. In December 2009 Devon County Council approved plans for a major, £2.3 million, restoration and extension of the library, to produce the first of Devon's new generation of public libraries, creating a hub for the community. In order to carry out the work the library closed in August 2010 but will reopen in 2011, the centenary year of the death of its benefactor.

**Hayle Institute**

Edwards had been involved with the Hayle Institute even before it was formed. The employees of Harvey's foundry established a Mechanics' Institute in 1840 but they could not persuade their employer to provide them with premises. In May 1846 Edwards gave a series of lectures, under the banner of the 'Pleasures and advantages of knowledge', in aid of establishing a literary and scientific institute in the town.[9] The lectures covered the whole gamut of Edwards beliefs, the first being on 'Human Progression', the second on the 'Principles of Permanent and Universal Peace'; the third on the 'Inefficiency and wrongfulness of capital Punishment'; the fourth on the

'Truths and Tendencies of the principal Moral Movements of the age'; the fifth on 'Knowledge' and the sixth on 'Moral Greatness of the Temperance Reformation'. The lectures were given at the Mount Pleasant chapel, where his brother, Richard, was Sunday School Superintendent and 'resulted in a healthy toned excitement in the district as never existed before and which must contribute to the moral and mental elevation of the people'.

Eventually an institute was opened in Foundry Square, in the old railway station, and this provided a billiard room, reading room and library, to which Edwards donated a hundred books.

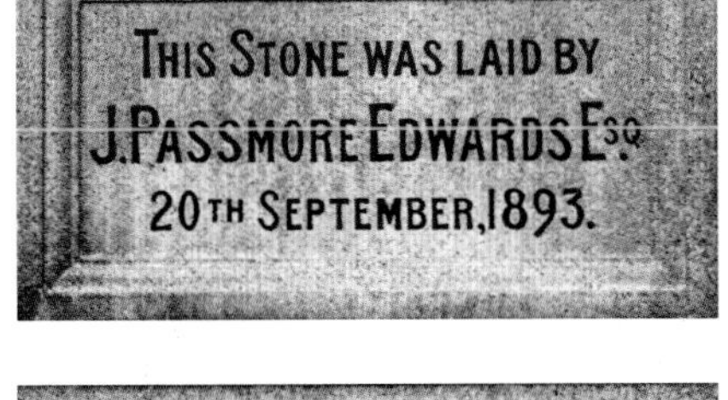


Above: *The Passmore Edwards Institute, Hayle*

Below: *Foundation stones, Hayle Institute*

The new technical institute was the first of several commissions for Edwards by the Cornish architect, Silvanus Trevail and was built by John and Frank Symons. The site chosen was on made up ground and this, together with the ambitious design prepared by Trevail brought the cost of the institute to £3,000, rather more than Edwards was expecting to pay. The institute at Blackwater had cost him only £250.

The day chosen to lay the foundation stone, 23 September 1893, was declared a holiday and streets and premises were gaily decorated, the festivities going on throughout the day and with an evening tea, a promenade concert and finishing with fireworks.

A procession nearly a mile long made its way from Copperhouse to the site, under evergreen decorated triumphal arches, bearing banners – 'Be Just and Fear Not' – the motto of the *Echo*, 'Welcome', 'Success to the Institute', 'Long life and happiness', and the names of Edwards four publications – the *Echo*, *Building News*, the *English Mechanic* and the *Weekly Times & Echo.*[10]

Before laying the foundation stone Edwards was presented with an illuminated address, thanking him, on behalf of the town, for the gift of the Institute, and after the proceedings were complete they all retired to the Public Hall for lunch. Both Eleanor Edwards and their son, Harry, attended but their daughter, Ada, was not amongst the party.

During the customary speeches Passmore Edwards said that he was no stranger to Hayle having for some years visited his mother and father who then lived nearby at Phillack, where his father superintended a farm and flourmill on behalf of Messers Sandys, Carn & Vivian. It was to the memory of his father that he dedicated the Institute. His three brothers also lived in Copperhouse for some time and, although Edwards did not mention the fact, James had emigrated to Australia more than 15 years previously, but his wife's family still ran a butcher's shop in Hayle.

It was to be another three years before Eleanor officially opened the Institute although it was Passmore Edwards who responded to the vote of thanks, on his wife's behalf.

The Institute was erected to provide education and technical training for local men at a time when Hayle was suffering from a decline in the mining industry, a decline from which Hayle has yet to recover. Trevail's building, sombre and dignified[11] lacks the elegance of many of his later designs for Passmore Edwards, though what it lacked in looks it made up for in functionality. Edwards said that he was glad to see that it was constructed of Cornish granite, which was one guarantee that it would last for many years and probably for ages. The science laboratories, classrooms and library have long since gone but the Institute still retains a pivotal position within the community. Ongoing maintenance by an enthusiastic management committee will ensure that Edwards' guarantee is upheld.

### The Miners' and Mechanics' Institute, St Agnes

A literary institute had been established in St Agnes in 1841 but its fortunes varied over the years as interests waxed and waned. In 1889 a letter was received from Passmore Edwards offering to supply 200 books for the Institute's reading room and from this began a period of communication between Edwards and Dr William Whitford, the Institute's honorary secretary, which culminated in an offer to build a library and Reading Room in the village, in memory of his elder brother, William. The offer came via John Symons, Edwards' old school friend and builder of the Blackwater Institute.

The day after Edwards was granted the freedom of the Borough of Truro, he was in St Agnes, to lay the foundation stone of the Miners' and Mechanics' Institute. As at Truro the bands played, flags and bunting decorated the village and children lined the street as Edwards was led to the site. In his speech he spoke of his inseparable connection with St Agnes and of his youthful memories of the village. It was to St Agnes that he came to sell soft fruit or to run errands for his mother and it was in the graveyard nearby where a little brother and a little sister of his lay. He went on to say that in his gift to St Agnes he was realising a dream; that it gave him more satisfaction and joy to make public gifts than it could possibly give to those who accepted them.[12]

It is usual that a time capsule is placed in a cavity in foundation stones and in the case of St Agnes a bottle containing silver coins, a newspaper and a programme for the day's ceremony was placed under the stone. However, a week later the *Western Morning News* reported that the bottle and its contents had been stolen. Although a £5 reward was offered the identity of the culprit remained unknown and a replacement bottle was later placed under the stone.

Edwards and his family returned to St Agnes in April 1894 when Harry performed the opening ceremony, using a silver key, and both Harry and his father were made honorary members of the Institute in recognition.

His gift to St Agnes also shows his involvement with the Royal Cornwall Infirmary and the Convalescent Home he had built at Perranporth. The document signed by the original trustees of the Institute included the condition that if the building ceased to be

*The Miners' & Mechanics' Institute, St Agnes, Cornwall*

used as an institute then it should be sold and the money given to support the Infirmary. If the community failed to make good use of his gift then they would not benefit from its demise.

Despite falling membership at the turn of the century, due first to emigration and then the Great War, the Institute remained open and had 100 members in 1919. The use of the Institute for 'sports', rather than literary pursuits, increased with an emphasis on billiards and table tennis tables were placed in the reading room. Eventually the books and newspapers were moved to a small room at the rear of the Institute and the area in the former reading room used for the playing of cards. By the end of the Second World War a second billiard table had been purchased and soon after this the library was sold off, for the sum of £6.

By 1963 the Institute's financial situation was dire. As a means of raising additional income a 'one armed bandit' was installed and within just a few years the income from this had put it back on firm financial grounds. Later the Charity Commission were to remind the Institute's trustees of the need to widen the benefits the Institute to the people of St Agnes, and the Institute was restructured and extended to provide both a social club and rooms that could be used by village organisations.

After closing for almost two years the Institute reopened in September 2009 as a place for the local and wider community to use for events, functions and regular classes, fulfilling Edwards' original wish. Now known as 'MMI', over £900,000 has been spent completely updating the Grade II Listed building, increasing access and providing learning opportunities for both the local community and visitors.

**William Edwards**

There is less known about William, the oldest of the surviving Edwards' brothers, than the other two, although he is the only one mentioned to any extent in *A Few Footprints*.[13] Edwards recounts that William, then about 14 years old, suffered so much from what he describes as indigestion that a doctor was called who recommended William should be bled. This involved a band being fixed around the arm above the elbow and a half-inch incision made along the chosen vein. The blood was caught in a bowl held for that purpose. It was Passmore Edwards' fate to be chosen to hold the bowl and he recounts how, when the bowl was half full, he fainted. Though Edwards soon recovered, the same could not be said of William who appears to have remained ill for some time and for many years after felt languid and depressed at the same time of the year. Edwards believed that bleeding, a common treatment for all and sundry, impaired his health rather than improved it and probably contributed to his shortened life.

Beyond this we know, from the 1851 census, that William became a carpenter, like his father, and followed his brother Richard to Bath, where in 1861 he was described as a carpenter and bird fancier. By the time of the 1871 census he had become a photographer and the 1881 census finds him at Walton on Thames, a 'retired artist', described as paralysed. Within 12 months he was dead.

**St Day School & Meeting House**

In the early 1800s St Day was a thriving town at the centre of the richest mining district in the world. By the 1870s both copper mining and the town were in decline and today St Day is a small residential village. Still central to the life of the village is one of the earliest of the Passmore Edwards bequests. Passmore Edwards had already given a number of books in 1890, to form the nucleus of a library in the village, and in 1892, when fundraising began to find the £250 needed to restore the church schoolroom, the Rev J J Murley wrote to Edwards for his assistance. Edwards immediately replied to say that he would fund the erection of a new building in the memory of his uncle, John Edwards.

At the suggestion of Edwards, John Symons was instructed to produce the plans and by Christmas two foundation stones had been laid, the first by local landowner Michael Williams and the second by E D Anderson on behalf of the Freemasons. By April of the following year the building was not only complete but Edwards had instructed Symons to repair the old mission room adjacent to the new schoolroom. Edwards visited the village on 4 May 1893, probably for the first time in more than fifty years, to open the schoolroom. After a short service of dedication in the church the party of dignitaries processed to the schoolroom where Edwards was given the key with which to perform the opening. Afterwards he said that village schools, like those in Blackwater and St Day, though comparatively unimportant individually, were by number a significant factor in the educational system; and it was cheering to see the interest they evoked in that somewhat deserted part of Cornwall.

The new building was constructed of locally quarried stone with granite and St Day brick dressings, gothic style windows with hood mouldings, lead lights and cathedral glass. Directly inside the entrance there was a lobby with side doors opening into the main room 48 feet by 30 feet. A raised platform was installed at the far end so that the building could be used for entertainment. The old schoolroom had also almost entirely been rebuilt by John and Frank Symons and refitted with red pine to match the new room.

In 1955 the new minister at the Holy Trinity church closed the building after an inspection suggested that 'the spire and pillars have been defying the accepted laws of science for a number of years during which time the likelihood of structur-

*The Sunday School and Meeting Room at St Day, Cornwall. Now used as the parish church*

al failure has been worsened'.[14] The report stated that the walls were constructed of a poor quality and decomposing granite, and the brick columns were crumbling and bending under the weight of a shifting and poorly-constructed roof; predicting that the whole lot could come tumbling down on the congregation when the organ was played at full volume.

Church services were moved to the schoolroom, a temporary altar was erected, and, since Cornish miners had emigrated to the four corners of the world, a world-wide appeal was launched to raise the £10,000 needed to convert the building into a church.

One of the features of the new church is the altar, removed from the old church but reduced in size and mounted on three granite steps. Hidden windows built into the ceiling space above the altar provide natural illumination and seating is arranged at the front and around both sides. In the northwest corner there is a shrine with a small statue of Our Lady with the Christ Child mounted on the wall.

Curiously the old church is still standing, although the roof was demolished using dynamite in 1985, and it is now maintained by the Old St Day Church Preservation Society.

**Uncle John**

Uncle John is the only relative outside his immediate family that Passmore Edwards makes reference to. One of five children John went to live in St Day where he married and became a grocer like his father. At Blackwater he was superintendent of the Sunday School and so soon became associated with the Sunday School at St Day, and later, the Anglican church as well; going to church in the mornings and chapel in the evenings.[15] John died in 1882, after more than 50 years service to the village, and is buried in the churchyard.

**Chacewater Literary Institute**

After providing an institute and library for Blackwater he was asked to do the same for Chacewater, a neighbouring village, and he did so in the memory of his younger brother, James, who had gone to Australia with his family and died there within a few years of arriving.

When Edwards laid the foundation stone, in September 1893, he said that Chacewater held a special place in his memory. His father had brought him to Chacewater more than fifty years before to the literary society and it was there that he heard his first talk, by Henry Sewell Stokes, on 'The Pleasures and Advantages of Knowledge'. He said that he considered it a privilege to be enabled to erect buildings for the general good and a greater privilege that the memory of those near and dear to him should be connected with useful institutions built near to their native village.

Edwards opened the Institute during one of his grand tours in April 1894 accompanied by his wife Eleanor and children, Ada and Harry, during which he also laid the foundation stones at the Falmouth and Camborne libraries, opened the Mithian Institute and met a deputation at Redruth to discuss his offer to build a library there; whilst his wife opened the Falmouth Cottage hospital, and his son, Harry, opened the St Agnes Institute.

The Chacewater Literary Institute had formed many years earlier and, as a boy, Edwards had joined the reading society and as a young man, had delivered lectures there. The new building replaced a smaller building rented from Lord Falmouth at a peppercorn rent of 3s a year. It is an almost replica of the Miners' and Mechanics' Institute at St Agnes, both designed and built by John Symons and his son, Frank.

During the lunch in the Oddfellows Hall that preceded the opening, Edwards said that many of his memories of his childhood days clustered around the village of Chacewater, which was as dear to him almost as much as London itself. 'It was here that he came to Sunday school; it was here that he had his first *custas*. Not only did he have his first *custas* there, this was the village in which he first tumbled neck and heels in love'. Just what *custas* was, or is, is not explained but he went on to say – 'Some of you are inquiring as to what the meaning of *custas* is. If you had as many of them as I had, you would remember it forever'. Edwards concluded that 'Both the *custas* and love were very warm things'.[16]

Outside the Institute a large crowd had gathered. It seemed as if all of Chacewater had turned out to witness the event together with several hundred from the surrounding villages. Handed the key by Frank Symons, Edwards declared the Institute open and 'welcome to all'. He joked about the extent of the undue flattery expressed, saying that it would lead to a trifling weakness of his moral backbone and thought that it perhaps gave him more pleasure to use his money in this way. He commented: 'Oh that he was as wealthy as some Cornishmen, Oh what he would endeavour to do for Cornwall. He had done little compared with what some gentlemen could do, though they had the heads and hearts, if they did not remain in Parliament to waste their sweetness on the desert air.' Seconding the vote of thanks, John Charles Williams, MP for Truro, nephew of Frederick Williams the successful candidate at the 1868 election, and heir to the Caerhays estate, could have had little doubt that he was included amongst those to whom Edwards referred.

By 1990 the Institute had fallen into disrepair and was unused. Although a campaign to save the building for village use was started, the village already had other halls and rooms available and the money required could not be raised. Under the terms of the original deed of gift the building reverted to the Tregothnan Estate and was sold by the estate, and tastefully converted into a pair of houses.

*The former Chacewater Literary Istitute*

### James Henry Edwards

Unlike his brothers, Richard and John, James was not a teetotaller. In a commercial directory for 1862 he is listed as 'Grocer and Ale & Porter Merchant, Copperhouse'. He had left Blackwater with his parents to live at Phillack and there met the butcher's daughter, Jane Runnalls. After they married in 1850, they lived at Copperhouse where they started the grocery shop and where they had nine children. Later he was to try his hand as a commercial traveller, the 1871 census showing James, Jane and three children in Brixton, London, although by the time of the birth of their son, John, Jane at least was back in Copperhouse.

In the autumn of 1875 James and his family embarked on the *Somersetshire* for the three-month journey to Australia, disembarking in Victoria in January 1876. The passage would have cost him around £100, a significant investment.

He again found work as a commercial traveller but his health failed and after a long illness James died from tuberculosis in 1880. The family prospered, however, and their descendants are still to be found in Victoria today.

**Redruth Library**

Edwards chose James Hicks, the Redruth architect and member of the Urban District Council, to design the Redruth library and John and Frank Symons of Blackwater constructed it.

The District Council decided that they should only use Edwards' offer of £2,000 to construct the library and invest the bequest from Octavia Allen Ferris, a further £2,000, to provide for ongoing maintenance. However, Edwards' offer was not sufficient to meet all of the building costs and some of the Ferris bequest was used for incidental works such as the boundary wall, and only £1,200 invested to aid the running costs. A penny rate raised £94 per annum but the interest on the invested money brought this up to £130 per annum.[17] The librarian was paid just £54 per annum but with free house rent, coal and gas.

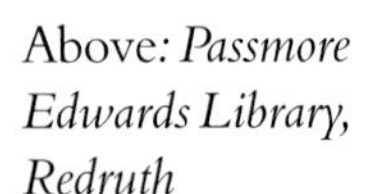

Above: *Passmore Edwards Library, Redruth*

Below: *Bust of Passmore Edwards by G A Frampton in Redruth Library*

More than 7,000 gathered to witness Edwards lay the foundation stone in September 1894. Joking that he had heard there was rivalry amongst the Cornish towns as to which town could raise the largest number of spectators, he hoped that there would be equal rivalry as to which town would make the best use of the buildings he was providing, and considered offering a prize to the library that had the largest number of visitors and readers within a given period. By the end of the decade he was expressing concerns about the under utilisation of some of his libraries in Cornwall and wondered whether he should have spent less in Cornwall and more in London. All twenty of the Passmore Edwards buldings in Cornwall have survived, and only one of the eight libraies he funded – Launceston – is no longer used as a library.

On Wednesday 30 May 1895, after the opening of Camborne library, Passmore Edwards returned to Redruth, to open the library, which he dedicated to the name of his younger brother, Richard. It was the fourth ceremony he attended that week, laying the foundation stone to the Liskeard Cottage hospital on Monday, the foundation stone for the Newlyn Art Gallery on Tuesday, and the opening of both the Camborne and Redruth libraries on Wednesday. On Thursday he was to open the Truro library. Not that this was the end of Passmore Edwards' week as he was due back in London on Friday, where he was due to open another library.

In his speech he referred to his memories of Redruth, walking there as a boy on a hot summer day to sell strawberries at the market, and returning home with a light or heavy heart, depending upon the amount of money taken. Had he thought then, that fifty or more years later he would bring to Redruth something more lasting than strawberries and receive such good wishes as had been showered on him that week, he would have walked with a more elastic step and sold his strawberries with a lighter heart.

As was usual in Cornwall a day's holiday was declared, and in the afternoon sports were organised on the recreation ground, and in the evening the people of Redruth celebrated with a carnival, fireworks, bands and a procession of floats.

The library has undergone a number of reorganisations over the years and has extended into the former Redruth College building, adjacent, which had previously been home to the YMCA and used as a telephone exchange.

**Richard – the other Passmore Edwards**

Three years younger than John, the life of Richard, who had also been given his mother's name – Passmore, was overshadowed by that of his famous sibling. But having shared the same experiences in early life it is not surprising that they shared similar beliefs as adults. Richard no doubt had the same basic education at the same local dame school and would have worked alongside his brothers in helping in the brewery and beer house. Like John Passmore Edwards, Richard was averse to alcoholic drink, remaining teetotal for most of his life. He also accompanied his father to chapel on Sunday and, as his brother before him, subsequently took his place as a Sunday School teacher, but at a chapel in Chacewater. He found a position as a commercial traveller with a firm of wholesale grocers in Truro and was well known in and around the city. When the family left Blackwater to go to live in Phillack, the Chacewater Sunday School presented Richard with an illuminated testimonial, which was later framed and hung in a prominent position in the family home.

In Phillack, Richard opened a grocery shop, like his brother James but probably continued to work as a traveller. In around 1844, while aboard the *Herald*, which regularly sailed from Hayle to Bristol, he met a temperance speaker and signed the pledge. He was associated with the Mount Pleasant chapel in Hayle serving as a Sunday School teacher and finally taking over as superintendent in 1848.

In 1850 Passmore Edwards started his first venture into publishing, with the *Public Good*. He said that he worked entirely on his own; acting as editor, publisher, and advertising agent, and for a while at least both lived and worked in the one rented room in Paternoster Row. But disturbed by the continual noise within a short while he had taken lodgings in Islington. Richard shared these lodgings when he joined his brother in London, both of them being described as writers on the 1851 census. Richard wrote articles on temperance and vegetarianism and also some poetry, all of which appeared in the *Public Good*, but their time together was of short duration.

How he came to meet his future wife, Elizabeth Ellen Biss, is not clear but in August 1852 they married in Bath, where Richard was to take over his father-in-law's cheese business. Richard and Elizabeth had three children; Charles, Frederic Augustus and Eva, but no grandchildren appeared to take the family name forward. Richard became a member of the Council and campaigned for the adoption of the Free Libraries Act and was instrumental in the founding of the first free library in Bath. Like his brother he was an accomplished public speaker but preferred deeds to words and quietly went about doing good where he saw a need. And there were few public issues with which he was not involved, being a Governor of the King Edward VI School in the city and introducing Christmas treats for the children in the workhouse. But it was his involvement in the Temperance movement that maintained his interest throughout his life. He became a member of the Western Temperance League, served a term as President and remained as a Vice President for the rest of his life. He was also for many years a member of the committee of the National Temperance League and of the Middlesex Band of Hope Union.

It was at the Guildhall in Bath that in January 1858 Passmore Edwards delivered his lecture, 'The Triple Curse', denouncing the Opium Wars; Bath was also where he made his first unsuccessful steps towards a career in politics. When he was considered as a candidate to represent Bath at Westminster in 1865, three years before he stood for Truro, Richard was amongst his supporters. Like his elder brother Richard was a Radical Liberal, campaigning against the Corn Laws as a young man and later supporting Gladstone, but he never sought a political career for himself. During the American Civil War, Richard became involved in the anti-slavery movement and, always attempting to do what was right when he saw an opportunity, he organised the collection and dispatch of clothing to be distributed amongst the liberated slaves.

After their father died in 1863 their mother went to live with Richard and his family in Bath and it was there that she died in 1870.

Richard became a moderately wealthy man, though not as wealthy as John, but he suffered from what was then termed Bright's disease, an inflammation of the kidneys. Retiring in 1881 he moved with his family to live in Hammersmith, where he again became actively involved in local affairs and was elected to the Hammersmith Vestry, the equivalent of the town council, serving until the year of his death. His support for education and free libraries led him to campaign for the founding of the first free library in Hammersmith, the Ravenscourt library, of which he was a governor, and he was campaigning for a branch library in Shepherd's Bush when his health worsened. Passmore Edwards was to fund the building of the Shepherd's Bush library, which opened in 1896 and closed only in 2009, the library service being transferred to a modern building. The Ravenscourt library was destroyed by bombing during the Second World War. Passmore Edwards also funded the installation of a drinking fountain on Hammersmith Broadway in memory of Richard but this was later moved to Ravenscourt where, unfortunately, it too was destroyed during the same bombing raid. In Cornwall, Edwards dedicated the Redruth library to Richard when he opened it in 1895.

By November 1893 Richard had taken to his sick bed. In his final months he had hoped to revisit Blackwater whilst attending the opening of one of his brother's institutes. Whether this was to be the Miners' and Mechanics' at St Agnes, dedicated to the memory of his eldest brother, William, the Chacewater Institute, dedicated to his younger brother James, or Hayle, for the opening of the Institute dedicated to his father, is not known but it was not to be. Though he regained his health sufficiently to spend a few days at Folkestone his recovery was short lived and he passed away on 19 February 1894.

At his funeral the Rev Mottram, a lifelong friend, read lines from a poem written by Richard just a few weeks before he died –

*Far out beyond life's earthly bounds*
*A rest awaits for me.*
*So let there be no murmuring sounds*
*When I go out to sea.*

# Fourteen
# The Cornwall Libraries

Octavius Allen Ferris, born in Truro in 1805, became headmaster of a Manchester Boarding School before retiring to London. When he died in 1892 he left a sum of nearly £2,000 each to five towns in Cornwall for the provision of free libraries. In Penzance plans were drawn up and the present library was opened in 1893. In Truro there was already a lending library in existence, operating from the public rooms, which the bequest helped to maintain and extend, whilst in Camborne, Redruth and Falmouth the authorities were at first disposed to look upon the bequest as a white elephant.

After establishing the Blackwater Institute and the Perranporth Convalescent Home, Passmore Edwards offered to match the Ferris bequest at each of the four towns where free libraries were still to be founded, provided that they adopted the Free Library Acts. To Penzance, he offered 1,000 books. In January 1895 Edwards presided over the Annual Dinner for Cornishmen in London. Here he met Lord Mount Edgcumbe, the Lord Lieutenant of Cornwall, and asked him to pass on an offer to provide libraries at St Ives, Helston, Penryn, St Austell, Liskeard, Bodmin and Launceston if they too would adopt the Free Libraries Act and undertake to maintain the libraries out of the public rates.

### Camborne Free Library

An early library existed in Camborne within the Camborne Literary Institute, which was founded in 1829, to which Edwards had given 250 books in 1899 and subsequently been elected a life member. The decision to build a free library was taken as the Local Government Board for Camborne was due to be replaced by the Camborne Urban District Council, under the 1894 Local

*Camborne Library*

Government Act. At this time the population was almost 15,000 with a rateable value of just over £40,000. A penny rate raised approximately £160 per annum.

There had been a lot of debate in the town about building a library, even after the Ferris bequest, and it was Joseph Grenville Edwards, a Camborne accountant and the son of John Edwards, Passmore Edwards' uncle, who first suggested asking Passmore Edwards for assistance.

It was a family affair when, on Tuesday 9 April 1894, Mr and Mrs Passmore Edwards, accompanied by Harry and Ada, were in Camborne to lay the foundation stone for the new library. The whole town and district turned out to welcome them, with processions of Friendly Societies, local board, fire brigade, volunteers; bands playing and church-bells ringing.

Designed by Silvanus Trevail, the library was built by John Symons & Sons on an awkward shaped piece of land immediately facing the main approach to the railway station. At the junction point of five streets it would be the most prominent building seen by those arriving in the town by rail. The board purchased the leases of the four tenements that had occupied the site, and Arthur Basset, owner of the nearby Tehidy estates, granted a 999-year lease at a nominal rent provided that the building was used as a library. Trevail met the challenge of the shape of the site producing an asymmetrical structure with a square tower. Built of pink elvan with granite and Bath stone dressings the library is topped with a Delabole slate roof. The dimensions of the principal rooms were: – newsroom, 40 feet by 20 feet; lending library, 32 feet by 20 feet; porch, 10 feet by 5 feet; hall, 24 feet by 12 feet; borrowers lobby, 20 feet by 10 feet; periodical room and reference library, 41 feet 6 inches by 20 feet; general committee room 20 feet by 19 feet; a book repairing room, and a librarian's room, 20 feet by 12 feet. A caretaker's flat included in the original plans was never built.

By the time of the opening in May 1895 the library had 2,900 books ready for issue, the reference room held a valuable collection of books, mainly provided by gifts from private individuals and libraries within the town, and the reading room was stocked with daily and weekly newspapers and weekly and monthly magazines and periodicals. Part of the Ferris bequest, of £1,947 1s 11d, was used for furnishings and books, the remainder being invested to fund the ongoing maintenance of the building. When, at the opening ceremony Edwards found that he had only sent 600 books instead of the 1,000 offered he said that he had thought that the 600 represented the second consignment that should have taken his donation over the number offered. Now he knew of his mistake he would insure that another 500 were dispatched.

*Camborne Library in 2010*

The first librarian was Jacob Laity of Fore Street, Beacon. By trade Jacob was a boot and shoemaker who kept a shop in his back garden where the villagers brought their shoes for repair, but he was described as a 'knowledgeable man' and he served as librarian for fourteen years, until 1909.

Although the library had been built and stocked at no cost to the ratepayers, providing the library service was a different matter as a downturn in mining meant a reduced income for the new council. As a result the library committee was allocated less than the product of the 1d rate and the interest earned on the Ferris bequest was not used to supplement the amount allocated. Mr Laity was expected to serve as both librarian and caretaker and the library was opened only during the evenings on weekdays and all day Saturday.

Nevertheless, during the first year 2,000 readers registered for tickets with 45,000 issues being made from a stock that had risen to nearly 5,000 volumes. Like many libraries of the time the reference library depended upon gifts and donations and around the turn of the century the room was used by the Camborne Urban District Council, initially as office accommodation and then as a committee room, to the concern of Passmore Edwards. By 1931, however, 1,200 reference books had been acquired together with numerous objects 'relating to art, history, science and industry'. This included the bust of Richard Trevithick, the Cornish engineer, presented by Passmore Edwards in 1903 and which remains in the library today.

The museum was not established until 1913, when Mr James Thomas, a local postman and amateur antiquarian, donated his extensive collection of local 'finds'. The outbreak of the Great War prevented further progress and it was not until the conclusion of the Second World War that a curator was appointed to give separate attention to this element of the library.

The period between the wars saw a steady growth in the Camborne library with the addition of the entire circulating library from the Tehidy Working Men's Club in 1929 and a grant from the Carnegie trustees of £420 spread over three years from 1927, conditional on the Council increasing its support to the full one penny rate, which by then raised £320 per year.

*Bust of Richard Trevithick at Camborne Library*

In 1932 a statue of Richard Trevithick was unveiled at the front of the library facing towards Beacon Hill, where Trevithick's locomotive had travelled 'up Camborne Hill, coming down' nearly 130 years earlier.

A setback occurred in 1933 when the reference library room was taken to house the magistrates' court and it was not until 1948 that it was refurbished and reopened for its original purpose. The end of the Second World War also brought a refurbishment of the library and for the first time a separate juvenile section, reopening on 4 September

1951. Almost 100,000 issues per year were then being made. Further refurbishments have taken place over the years and the library, now under the control of the Cornwall Council, remains open to serve the people of Camborne.

**Falmouth Free Library**

In 1893 Edwards agreed to provide a cottage hospital in Falmouth (see Chapter 16) and as a consequence was presented with the honorary freedom of the Borough of Falmouth in September of that year. During the celebratory dinner that followed, he said that as Cornwall was mainly surrounded by the sea, he should like to build a lighthouse at the Manacles. The Council decided that they would rather have a library.

Following the adoption of the Free Libraries Act by the Falmouth Council early in 1894 and the formation of a library committee, under the chairmanship of Alderman Thomas Webber, Passmore Edwards confirmed an offer of £2,000 to match the Ferris bequest.

The authority decided upon a building that would house new municipal offices and a science and technical school as well as the library and the architect W H Tresidder was appointed to join F J Bellamy, the borough surveyor, to produce the design. Application to the Department of Science & Art in London, resulted in a grant of £420 towards the School leaving the Town Council to raise the remaining £2,000 a loan of £1,800 being negotiated with the Falmouth Lodge of the Oddfellows, sanctioned by the Local Government Board.

The Town Council provided a site in the centre of the town, previously used as a pig market, and the contract was awarded to a local builder, Mr Carkeek. *Building News* on 13 April 1894 reported that

> the front would be in Plymouth limestone, with Cornish granite dressings, and the remainder in local stone. Great care has been bestowed on the plans with the object of getting the maximum of accommodation and light. The fine entrance hall, staircase, and newspaper-room will form attractive features, and ample space has been given for the lending and reference libraries, above which are three commodious, well-lighted rooms for technical instruction, for which there is a great and growing want in Falmouth. One wing of the building will be devoted to municipal offices, with council chamber and anteroom.

A look at the contract specification shows some interesting facts. Apart from Bridgewater bricks and Plymouth limestone, materials were sourced locally, 'Mabe' granite and 'Kergilliack' sand being specified, both being villages on the edge of Falmouth, and local stone, for the rear elevations, was quarried at the town quarry, just a couple of hundred yards from the site. A damp course was provided to the walls by means of a ¾ inch thick layer of clean fine ashes and gas tar, presumably both found locally whilst the ground floor joists were required to be 'old ships oak'.

The specification also called for six foot deep foundations but as excavations commenced it was discovered that the site was an filled-in creek and a steam crane had to be brought in to clear the debris as the contractors took the wood-lined trenches down to twenty two feet to solid rock. There had been a lot of opposition to the project from certain ratepayers and the extra costs of the foundations were another opportunity for them to attack the Council's decisions. At a Ratepayer's Association meeting, attended by only eleven members, a motion was passed calling on the Council to hold a public meeting, in an attempt to stop the building of the municipal buildings element of the project.[1] But since no members of the public had raised objections when the plans had been on display the Council chose to disregard the ratepayers' concerns.

On 13 April 1894, the same day as his wife opened the Falmouth Cottage Hospital, Passmore Edwards laid the foundation stone of the library, standing on the granite block to make his speech. But the following winter was severe and building work on the new library building almost came to a halt on several occasions. By February 1895 it was reported to the Town Council that 'The whole of the Municipal end was raised to the level of first floor, and a large portion of the building, including the portico, was built to the height of the cornice, a great part of which was in position'.

Even then opposition to the building continued. Complaints over the cost of the foundation stone ceremony were dismissed by Webber saying that the costs had been shared with the hospital committee, the Councillors had all contributed and the total remainder to be paid by the Council was only £10 13s. After continuing remarks that Passmore Edwards was only giving the money so that his name would be displayed above the door, Edwards entered the fray. Writing to the *Falmouth Packet* in March 1895 he said that 'I have never even suggested that any Institution I have provided should bear my name', and 'I am sorry that any hostile feeling should have arisen in connection with the use of my name, and if its permanent removal will provide public harmony, the competent authority is at liberty, as far as I am concerned, to remove it'.

The library committee had agreed to provide a temporary library in rented premises in Arwenack Street and Alderman Webber opened the reading room at the beginning of April 1894, and the lending library a week later. As usual Passmore Edwards donated 1,000 books and these, plus 100 books from other donors, were transferred to the temporary premises, and insured at the Royal Exchange in the sum of £350. As the permanent library was delayed the temporary library was very popular, with 604 borrower tickets being issued that year and 1,200 books a month being issued at a rate of between 50 and 150 a day.

*The opening of Falmouth Free Library in 1896*

Passmore Edwards was unable to visit Cornwall again until the summer of 1896 but the schoolrooms were handed over to the technical instruction committee as soon as they were ready. When Carkeek handed over the buildings to the Coun-

cil, apart from the additional costs of the deeper foundations, they had been completed within the original estimate.

On 1 May 1896 Mr and Mrs Passmore Edwards arrived at Truro on the 12:20 train but continued to Falmouth by road where they joined Frederick Horniman, tea dealer and Liberal MP for Penryn and Falmouth. At Falmouth the dignitaries, which as usual included the mayors of all eleven Cornish towns, processed along Market Street, led by the Artillery Volunteers and the band of the Rifle Volunteers, halting at the Polytechnic to visit the annual Misericordia Society[2] Bazaar before continuing to the Moor. Here Passmore Edwards was given a silver key with which to open the library. The Mayor went on to open the municipal building and Mr Bowles, the secretary of the Technical Instruction Committee the schoolrooms. After inspecting the rooms, the party finally appeared on the balcony to receive the cheers of the assembled townsfolk. Mr Horniman then crossed the Moor to open the new fire station before the party reassembled for lunch at the adjacent town hall.

In Passmore Edwards' lunchtime speech he said that many people were in the habit of calling him a grand old man – but his wife told him that he would be a fine old man. 'He had,' he said, 'a great dislike to being called an old man. When he came to Cornwall at the beginning of the week he felt like a young man but he had had so many lunches and dinners he would return to London an old man.' He was seventy-three.

Today the Falmouth Town Council occupies only the upper floor of the Municipal Building, the lower floor being given over entirely to the library. The technical and arts school was a continued success but not in that building. First the technical school moved to a new location, formally the old grammar school, now the site of the Marine School, and the Arts School led to the founding of the Falmouth College of Art. The remainder of the first floor and the adjacent extension is utilised by the award-winning Falmouth Art Gallery opened in 1978 and extended in 1994.

*The Falmouth Free Library, Municipal Building and Falmouth Art Gallery*

### Truro Free Library

Edwards referred to the existing Truro library as being 'cabin'd, cribb'd and contain'd in the public rooms building'.[3] His offer to Truro, of matching the Ferris bequest to provide a free library in the borough, came with an added bonus in the form of an oil painting of Edwards. This was by G F Watts and is a copy of the painting exhibited at the Royal Academy and now part of the National Portrait Gallery collection. The painting, which Edwards said he gave to the people of Truro and not to the Council, is nevertheless hung amongst other Truro worthies in the council chamber.

Building the new library commenced in May 1895 under the eye of Silvanus Trevail, both architect and Mayor, and in early May 1896 the crowds that gathered to witness the opening exceeded even those that attended when Edwards was presented with the freedom of the Borough. Led by the Mayor of Truro and the mayors of most of the Cornish towns, all adorned in their robes and chains of office, a procession made its way to the new building in Pydar Street, where Edwards declared the library open. The library was dedicated to Henry Sewell Stokes, the Truro lawyer who had been Edwards' first employer. Stokes became the Clerk to the County Council when it formed in 1894

*The Free Library, Truro*

but was also known as 'The Cornish Poet'. He died in 1895, a month after construction of the library commenced.

In his reply to the vote of thanks Edwards said that some men had 'no objection in writing their names in characters of blood and fire over war blasted provinces, or over bombarded and broken cities', but he preferred to write his name, 'if I write it at all, in characters of light over my native county and over London where I have lived and laboured'. His original intention was to open three buildings in Cornwall; the Institute at Blackwater – his place of birth; the Convalescent Home at Perranporth – in memory of his mother; and the Institute at Hayle – in memory of his father. However, the three grew to seven, which he called his 'Seven Cornish Sisters in Stone' and as other places pleaded for an equality of treatment, the seven increased to twelve and then to nineteen, 'and with which number his work in Cornwall would be accomplished'. Did he not remember that it was he that had extended his offer of providing the additional libraries following his meeting with Lord Mount Edgcumbe?

Truro library still imposes itself on the street scene in this tiny Cornish city. When the adjacent technical school was closed in the late 1970s the library service took over the whole of the building. A few years ago the County Council proposed selling off the building for retail use but fortunately this idea was abandoned. Since then the library has been extensively restored and modernised internally and as the Truro community library is the flagship of the Cornwall Libraries Service.

**St Ives Free Library**

After Eleanor opened the Hayle Institute, and after the obligatory luncheon and speeches, they made their way, together with the obligatory procession of Cornwall's mayors and aldermen, around the bay to St Ives. Here they were met by the Mayor and Corporation, and the thousands lining the gaily-decorated streets. Passmore Edwards was there to lay the foundation stone for the St Ives free library, which he did, in the name of 'one and all'.

The Borough of St Ives had been swift in accepting Passmore Edwards' offer of a public library and adopting the Free Library Act, but finding a suitable site was not so easy. Initially, a site was chosen near the Western pier, via which local road stone was exported, but there was concern that building a library there would restrict the pier's use.[3] Thomas Bolitho, MP for the Western Division of Cornwall, offered an alternative site as a gift, the site on which the library was finally built and where it still has pride of place in this busy little Cornish seaside town.

Silvanus Trevail thought that he would gain the commission for the library but instead Passmore Edwards instructed his friend John Symons to design and build it, Frank Symons preparing the plans and borrowing features from Trevail and James Hicks' work. By January 1897 the library was complete and handed over to the Corporation but it was not until April that the official opening took place. Passmore Edwards was invited to carry out the opening ceremony but replied that he could not travel all the way to St Ives for just one building and so the honour of opening the library fell to Bolitho.

The front elevations are of pink Elvan stone on a granite-dressed plinth and with

Bath stone dressing. The other walls are of local stone with brick dressing. There is a noticeable influence from Trevail, whilst the corner castellated turret is similar to Hicks' design for the Redruth library.

Internally, the ground floor was given over to the newspaper and periodical room, lending library and borrowers' lobby and a boys' reading-room. A reference library shared the first floor with a committee room, the librarian's room and the caretaker's apartment. Ladies not wishing to use the main library rooms could also use the committee room.

The choice of building material, though resulting in a much more pleasant design than the more sombre Institute at Hayle meant that the library has needed renovation over the years and following transfer to the Cornwall County Council the library has seen several changes. As recently as 2006 refurbishment and extension of the library has taken place to prepare it for another century of service to the residents of St Ives. Now home to the St Ives art collection and the St Ives Trust Archive, the renovated library provides the Internet connection and other services required of a library in the twenty first century.

When James Brown, librarian of Clerkenwell public library visited Cornwall on holiday in 1900 he was tempted to pay a visit to some of the public libraries in West Cornwall, including the St Ives library. He found that in all the libraries he visited there were rooms not being used for library purposes. The reason, according to Brown, was that the buildings were larger than required to meet the needs of the town's population, and more expensive to maintain than the limited product of a penny rate, ranging from £60 to £150 per annum, produced.[4] However, the difficulties experienced in those early years were overcome and as library provision has developed the larger buildings have ensured that space has not been a limiting factor and all but the Launceston public library remain in the Passmore Edwards buildings.

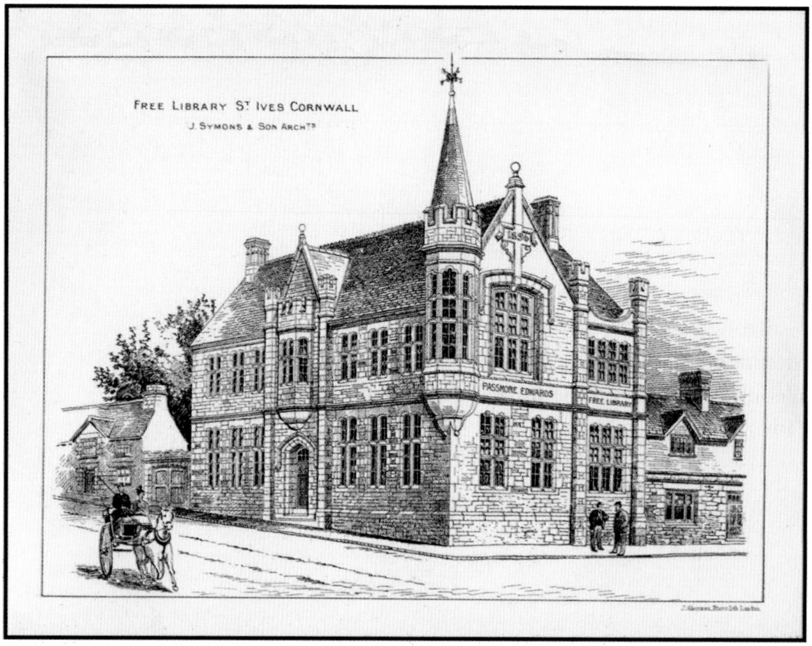

*This drawing of the free library at St Ives shows an open setting very different to the cramped street scene today*

### Penryn

When Lord Mount Edgcumbe wrote to Penryn Town Council they met to discuss Passmore Edwards' offer. The product of a penny rate within the town was only £30, and though they considered this insufficient to maintain a public library they agreed to hold a public meeting.[5]

By August, seven months after the offer had been received the matter was raised at the quarterly meeting of the Council and the Mayor admitted that he and the Town Clerk had been nominated to meet Passmore Edwards to discuss their difficulties but had failed to do anything about the matter, saying that everyone was well aware that the town could not afford to maintain such an institution. The Clerk added that it was difficult to meet with Edwards. One of the Councillors, Mr Curgenven, said that Penryn had acted discourteously towards Passmore Edwards by not even responding. There were other needs in the town: the Local Government Board had written to the Council asking them to build a contagious infection hospital; Edwards may have been willing to help them with that, or by supporting the school, which was in great difficulty.

**St Austell**

In St Austell, Passmore Edwards' offer caused similar heated debate throughout both the urban and rural districts, the subject taking centre stage in the *St Austell Star*. Perhaps Edwards was naive in treating a small town like St Austell in the same way as one of the East London boroughs, with their densely populated residential areas, with which he was more familiar. Whereas a London borough could find little difficulty in supporting a library from a penny rate, and indeed some supported several, in St Austell a penny rate would only provide £40 a year, insufficient to maintain and staff a library.

But there was much support for the scheme with the *Star*'s 'Watchman' waxing lyrically on the values of free libraries and several others speaking out in favour, including 'A book lover' who reminded readers that whilst there were a number of small private libraries in existence in the town, these were not generally accessible to women, being housed in men's clubs.

A suggestion was made that the rural district could join with the town, raising between them £170 per year, but many from the 'country' areas argued that they would be paying three quarters of the cost but have to walk as much as five miles each way to visit 'their library'.

The Urban District Council was in a position to adopt the Free Libraries Act without reference to the ratepayers but the Rural District Council could only do so following a poll of all ratepayers. The subject of the free library was, therefore, the only item on the agenda at the annual meeting of the Rural District Council held on 19 April at Carlease. There had been several separate unofficial meetings in areas of the district and it was clear that feelings were high. According to the *Star*, 'much misleading and malicious misinformation had been spread'. At the annual meeting, no one stood to support the library whilst one after another opposed. The general impression given was that the town's folk were expecting the 'country' to pay for their library.

The rural authority had already asked Edwards whether the offer could be extended to the whole district, Edwards merely replying that he wished to provide for the most and it was for them to decide how it was to be used. The option expressed at the Urban District meeting, that there could be a main library on the edge of the town with a small branch within the most populated area of the district, was not even raised.

A proposal was made that the rural authority did not adopt the Free Libraries Act and this was accepted without dissent. Although the Urban District Council made some representations to Edwards for possible amendments to his offer, the matter was dropped. St Austell was to wait more than sixty years before a public library was built. Prior to that the library operated from a room below the White Hart pub.

**Liskeard**

Work on the Liskeard library commenced in February 1896, within the former garden to Stuart House. During the excavations workers found a well-defined silver lead lode, two feet wide and seven foot from the surface and it was reported that 'some fine stones were taken from it before being sealed over'.

Edwards laid the foundation stone on April 1896, the same day as he opened the Cottage Hospital he had given to the town. It was another of Edwards' triumphal processions, escorted by mayors, aldermen and Town Councillors, as he visited Liskeard, Bodmin, Hayle, St Ives, Falmouth, and Truro laying foundation stones or performing openings wherever he went.

The building being directly on to the pavement, complaints were received during construction about obstruction, and some members of the Council raised concern about finding the £200 required to complete the furnishing of the library. But all this was forgotten when, on a dry and sunny October morning the residents of Liskeard joined in the celebrations as Passmore Edwards dedicated the library to the memory of Charles Buller, former MP for the district.

Designed and built by John Symons and his son, Frank, the library was constructed in Polyphant stone with Bath stone dressings. Although it was a building that the people of Liskeard could be proud of, keeping the doors open was a different matter. The Council allocated only £14 for a part-time librarian and the ground floor was let to the Cornish Bank to help with running costs. In addition, the Town Clerk and rating office

*The Charles Buller Memorial Library, Liskeard*

were housed at the library until 1950 and the National Provincial Bank also operated from the premises until 1954 when library provision was taken over by the County Council.[6] Under the control of the County Council the library prospered and today provides the services of a modern public library. In the year 2000 a mural, depicting events from Liskeard's history was unveiled at the library. The work, by local artist June Cole covers 25 feet by 13 feet and is displayed in the stairwell to the library.

In 1905 Leonard Courtney, MP for Liskeard from 1876-1885, unveiled a bust of Charles Buller presented to the library by Passmore Edwards. The bust has since been removed from the library and in 2010 was in the public hall.

Above: *Bust of Charles Buller presented to the library by Passmore Edwards*

**The William Molesworth Free Library and Science & Art School, Bodmin**

At the opening of the Bodmin library on Monday 24 May 1897 Edwards said that he would have liked to see Molesworth's name inscribed on the building but although he mentioned it to one or two people, it was not taken up. This seems surprising, as he would only have needed to ask Trevail to include it in the plans to ensure that his wishes were carried out. Especially – as had happened at falmouth – as Edwards had been accused of only offering to fund the library so that his name would appear above the door.

He was glad to see that the building included a technical school as well as a library. He said that each year England spent as much on tobacco as it did on bread, showing that we had the means and the power but not always the will and judgement to direct them to the right channels. Without directly saying that people should not smoke, the *Echo* voiced an anti-smoking campaign throughout Edwards' ownership; he said that he hoped the day would come when less was spent on smoking and more on libraries.

One of the institutions opened in the Jubilee Year of Queen Victoria and opened by the Right Hon Leonard H Courtney MP the Bodmin library was erected on the site of Hugo's Temperance Hotel and Grocery, bought for £100 from Lord Robartes. As with other libraries of the time books for loan were catalogued and listed on an index. Once the borrower had chosen from the list he ordered the books at the hatch in the borrowers' lobby on the ground floor. The librarian's assistant would then collect the books from the shelving in the lending department. Also on the ground floor were the newspaper and magazine room, the librar-

Below: *Opening of Bodmin Library, 1897*

Originally including an Arts and Science School, the Passmore Edwards Free Library, Bodmin

ian's room and a room for the younger boys still at school. The first floor held the committee room, periodicals room and the ladies' room. There was also a reference library and museum holding 'artifacts of interest from within the parish and beyond'. The ladies room and the periodicals room, which were divided by a removable partition, were let to the technical instruction committee for science and art schools, at £10 per annum.

Bodmin had taken over the role of county town from Launceston in 1836 but was conscious of a gradual move of administrative functions to Truro, with its new cathedral, city status granted in 1877 and seat of the Cornwall County Council when formed in 1894. The Borough Council, therefore, wanted a library to rival the one designed by Trevail at Truro.[7] Apart from the Bath stone dressings the construction materials were locally sourced, with walls using stone coming from Robartes' Margate Wood quarry on a Luxulyan granite plinth and with a Delabole slate roof. While the standard of design and construction at the Passmore Edwards buildings was usually excellent, problems soon began to appear at the Bodmin library. By December the Town Clerk needed to write to Trevail referring to walls and ceilings 'which had fallen down', and to defective Bath stone on the south-west window. Sampson Trehane, the builder, undertook to make good these defects but there was further damage reported when the mullion 'fell away' later that month.[8] A few weeks later the library committee was required to approve repairs to the roof and in the following September repairs were needed to the mullions on the north end window. Again, in 1900, the borough surveyor reported that the southwest Bath Stone window had been gradually giving way with the pressure of the weight of the wall above. The lintel had broken in four places and the transom and mullion had also broken. He recommended that the window should be taken down and replaced to prevent further settlement and damage. By the end of 1900 a petition had been signed by 147 library users calling for the repairs to be put in hand.

There had been complaints twenty years earlier over Trevail's apparent lack of supervision of his many School Board commissions[9] and in Bodmin the Town Clerk looked to Trevail to rectify the problems occurring at the library. The arguments continued for years but in the end the Town Clerk won the case.

During the 1970s serious problems with the structure of the building were again discovered by the County Architect, the County Council having taken over control of the library in 1953. Serious cracks in the west wall were detected and the partial collapse of the ceiling to the first floor storeroom highlighted an ongoing problem of leaks from the roof through defective lead flashings and valley timbers. In addition one corner of the building was discovered to have sunk considerably over the years, opening up cracks in the stonework and causing surface water to drain towards the foundation.[10]

Further roofing repairs were carried out in the 1980s to replace decayed timber due to dry rot and some of the lead valleys and gutters. By 1989 cracks in the rear south wall lead to it being removed in its entirety and rebuilt with a modern, rendered, cavity block, and the original wood windows replaced with UPVC.

Finally, the building surveyor reported to the County Architect that 'as a result of considerable expenditure over the last few years' the building was in a reasonable condition. However, 'The front wall is subject to movement, possibly outwards and may eventually require very extensive remedial work. The soft wall and ornamental parapet stonework is subject to steady weather damage. A hard frost after a wet period may involve some expense'. It is to the County Council's credit that they have not abandoned the building and sought a less problematic structure elsewhere in the town.

Today the library is in full use. Although Passmore Edwards still looks down on those entering the library from his position high above the entrance lobby, today's users come not only to borrow from the extensive stock available at the library or through the inter-library borrowing scheme. While the ground floor is given over almost entirely to the lending library the first floor is now home to a suite of computers giving access to the Internet.

**Launceston Free Library**

In February 1898 the Mayor of Launceston received a letter from Passmore Edwards asking what progress had been made towards building the library.

> I do not know what progress you have made in the free library question for Launceston but I regret to learn that several of the free libraries I have provided in Cornwall are in a somewhat languished condition.
>
> At Liskeard the ground floor of the library building has been let to the town post office to assist in paying the expenses of maintenance. At Bodmin only a ¼ of the rooms provided are utilised and very few books have been supplied, and at Camborne they have closed the newsroom. If this is the condition of things where local opinion was practically unanimous and where a majority of the population

were apparently in favour of the free library system it is more likely to be the case in Launceston where much less zeal has been shown. It is now more than three years since I proposed to provide a library building for your town and from the first only a hesitating half hearted, or rather third hearted, feeling has shown itself in favour of the scheme. From some cause or another there is an evident lack of disposition in Launceston for a Free Library to be maintained at public expense. Experience has taught me, and particularly in Cornwall, that it is easier to erect an institutional building than to adequately maintain it. I think therefore I am justified in asking that some reasonable assurance be given if I provide the building that it shall answer its intended purpose; and unless this assurance is given I must reluctantly withdraw my offer to Launceston. If you ask what assurance I require my answer is, if I undertake to erect a building for £2,000 that the district shall provide a site and promise £500 towards equipment and books for the time of the opening of the institution.

Yours faithfully JPE

In reply the Mayor said that the County Council had promised to fully equip the upper floor for science and art schools but asked Edwards to reconsider the £500 to be found by the town; Edwards had originally accepted that £200 of the promised £2,000 could be used for furnishing leaving only £300 for the town to find. The penny rate would bring in £60 and to this would be added rent of £20 for use of the school from the County Council. Two local gentlemen had offered £5 a year for 10 years and others would no doubt also contribute.

This brought an almost immediate response.

*The Adams Memorial Library, Launceston*

> Your letter was somewhat reassuring though you have not complied with the reasonable condition indicated in my last letter. I have no desire to back out of any promise I have made but I shall not like to provide another public building in Cornwall with such lack of zeal and smallness of practical result as seen in some other places in the county. Had I known a few years since what I know now, I should have spent less money in Cornwall and more in London. My wish is to benefit the largest number of my countrymen and experience has taught me that but few comparatively are benefited in Cornwall by what I have done there. But I will hope for the best. I cannot consent to reduce the cost of the building to £1,500. When I consented that £200 of the £2,000 should be devoted to equipment and books the conditions were different. The new site will entail more cost in the construction and one half of the building is to be devoted to arts and science. You will need to spend at least £2,000. Get on with it!
>
> Time passes and life is short, or at all events, for some of us, and I want to do the most in the least time and to get the maximum of good for the minimum of expenditure.

Problems at Launceston had arisen from the beginning. Passmore Edwards appointed Trevail as architect without reference to the Council and left it to him to tell them. This he did by inserting a public notice in the local paper, immediately establishing a difficult relationship with the Council and a stream of offers of potential sites.[11] Each site needed checking, surveying and sketches produced to put to the Council. And each Councillor on the building committee had his favoured site and wanted to put his penny worth in to the library design. To save costs Trevail's proposed bell tower was deleted and the library restricted to the ground floor, the upper floor to be given over to technical education.

The final gift from Passmore Edwards to the people of Cornwall, the last of the nineteen stepping-stones stretching the length of Cornwall, as many stones as there were letters in Edwards' name, opened in April 1900. Set into the front of the building, in terracotta, were the words Passmore Edwards Institute at first floor level, to represent the art and science school and Adams Memorial representing the library. John Couch Adams, the mathematician and astronomer, joint discoverer of the planet Neptune, was born near Launceston. Edwards had previously wanted to build a lighthouse in memory of Adams but had to be content with the library and a marble bust of Adams presented to the library.

*Bust of John Couch Adams, Launceston Library*

At the luncheon following the opening of the library the town clerk quoted Edwards, from a previous opening ceremony as saying that by diligent and hard work he had become custodian of a certain number of sovereigns. Most of these sovereigns came from the working man and his desire was that the money should find its way back to the source from whence it came.[12]

It is a very attractive building of terracotta and local Polyphant stone. Trevail used terracotta in several of his buildings and secretly received a commission from the supplier, Henry Dennis, the owner of the Ruabon Clay works.[13] On the ground floor three rooms housed the library, newspaper room and magazine room whilst on the first floor there were four rooms to be used for arts and science classes. Accommodation for the caretaker was provided in the basement.

Sadly, the last of the Passmore Edwards libraries to open in Cornwall was also the first to close. In April 1971, concerned with increasing maintenance costs, the County Council moved the library service to a new building in Bounsall's Lane. The Adams memorial building has since been converted into residential apartments.

**A love of Cornwall**

Although Edwards voiced his concerns about the use of his buildings in Cornwall and lived in London for most of his adult life he never lost his love for either the county or the people. He had witnessed the hardship caused by depression in the mining areas when he was a young man and was very aware that the ores that gave Cornwall wealth and employment could not last forever. On many occasions when speaking in Cornwall, he approached the subject of a Cornwall without mining and how the county could develop the other natural resources that made it special to him and to all who live or have lived there.

When in Falmouth to receive the freedom of the Borough he stayed at the Falmouth Hotel on the sea front. At the ceremony he remarked that he had walked around Pendennis Castle grounds earlier in the day and it occurred to him that Falmouth might become one of the most attractive watering places in England. They had, he said, enchanting sea and landscapes all around them, with unsurpassed climate advantages. The Cornish were an interesting people and if 'great landlords gauged their duties as they were inclined to extract their rights', it would become easier to develop the rich resources of the district.[14] Earlier that year, in June, Edwards had visited Truro to receive the freedom of the City, the first person to be so honoured. During his speech there he had said that the time would come when copper and tin would be so far down that it would not pay to bring it to the surface. 'Prepare for that day,' he told them. Cornwall had, he believed, certain advantages that were better than any tin or copper under the surface. These advantages were on the surface for all to see. The glory of Cornwall would, he said, by and by attract Londoners who will come to spend the winter in Cornwall and spend money. Referring to the banquet they had just been served, and in particular the fresh fruit, he said that Cornwall's capacity to grow fruit was almost exhaustless and potentially could make Cornwall even more prosperous than it had been from mining.[15]

Edwards referred to the demise of tin mining again when laying the foundation stone for the Newlyn Art Gallery. He said that while artists were forming a colony in Newlyn, Cornishmen were, in greater proportion than those from any English county populating the new colonies in other lands. His gift of the art gallery was to ensure the success of the art colony in Cornwall. 'As the mines of Cornwall were drying up under the soil, he wanted the world at large to know more of the scenic wealth of Cornwall on the soil'.

# Fifteen
# London Public Libraries

In London the provision of public libraries was no better than elsewhere. There were a number of subscription and commercial libraries, both serving the middle and upper class subscribers, libraries set up by working-class reformers, such as the library of the London Working Men's Association, and literary institutes, but few libraries had been created under the Free Libraries Acts. The local authorities found a large amount of opposition to them adopting the Acts, the first step towards creating a free library. It was first necessary that a group of ratepayers requisition the local authority, at that time the Vestry, to hold a poll. Only if a majority of voters voted in favour of adopting the Free Libraries Acts could the Vestry proceed and it would often take several years before a positive outcome was achieved. The requirement for a penny rate was not popular amongst many ratepayers, usually more affluent and educated persons who saw little need for greater education amongst the working classes.

### Whitechapel

The first of the Passmore Edwards libraries to be built in London, and the first rate supported library in the East End, was the Whitechapel library. Canon Samuel Barnett, and his wife Henrietta, had moved to St Jude's parish, Whitechapel, in the 1870s, an area of appalling poverty, poor housing conditions and overcrowding; mostly involving Jewish immigrants from Eastern Europe. The Barnetts set about with missionary zeal to improve the conditions of their parishioners. Like Edwards, Canon Barnett believed that 'the social problem is at root an educational one'[1] and that free libraries were a means of educating the adult masses. Barnett campaigned for adoption of the Free Libraries Acts in the parish after it had been rejected in 1878. However, in 1889 a poll voted by nearly 4 to 1 in favour.[2] At the first meeting of the Library Commissioners, in January 1890, Barnett reported that he had collected promises of £4,500 towards the library and arrangements were made to choose an architect. A suitable site was obtained on the High Street, the busiest part of Whitechapel, and construction began, the foundation stone being laid by the Lord Mayor in July 1891.

When the vicar of St Paul's, Dock St, offered his entire collection of relics, fossils and works of art, some very rare and valuable, as a nucleus of a museum, 'if proper accommodation could be provided', the architects were asked to amend the design.[3] The library, designed by Edward and William Potts, and Arthur Hennings, set the pat-

tern for East End libraries, which, though by different architects, are similar in their domestic scale and the general seventeenth-century asymmetry.[4]

The building was almost complete when Canon Barnett invited Passmore Edwards to view it, hoping to obtain a donation that would close the shortfall on the required funds. Edwards was sufficiently impressed to later write 'I cheerfully comply with your request and relieve you of the difficulty which presses upon you by paying the entire cost of the building ... I do this not merely from a sense of duty, but because I think it is a distinguishing privilege to assist in lightening and brightening the lot of our East End

Top: *The Whitechapel Library, the East End's first Free Library, 1892*

Below left: *Memorial to Isaac Rosenberg, one of many who gained an education at the Whitechapel Library.*

Below right: *The last days of the Whitechapel Library*

fellow citizens'. Included was a cheque for £6,454 to which he added the offer of a thousand books.

By May 1892 the reading room was open and the official opening of the library by Lord Rosebery took place in October. In the week prior to the opening more that 2,500 were using the reading room daily with another 1,264 on the Sunday.[5] Hundreds of other books were to be donated even before the library opened, including a copy of the Koran. During the first year more than 2,500 residents registered as members and for many the Whitechapel library – soon to be known as the 'University in the Ghetto' – promoted by its librarian, Morley Dainow, was the only means of getting an education. Members in those early years included First World War poet Isaac Rosenberg who perished on the Somme, Jacob Epstein, the sculptor responsible for the work representing St Michael at Coventry cathedral, and historian Jacob Bronowski, creator of the TV series, the Ascent of Man. Playwright Bernard Kops wrote about the Whitechapel library – 'the door of the library was the door into me'.[6]

From the beginning Hebrew books and papers were provided, the library later holding the largest collection of Jewish books in any public library. By 1910 a Hebrew-speaking assistant, Mr Bogdin, was appointed to manage the collection of books in Hebrew, Yiddish and Russian, a collection that remained in the library for 70 years. Loans peaked in 1937 at 18,000 volumes but in 1970 Indian language books were added to the catalogue for the first time and soon outnumbered Hebrew and Yiddish issues. Always at the forefront, as the immigrant population changed, so did the library's membership and the library was the first to stock Somali texts.[7]

The Whitechapel library, like several in London, was damaged during the air raids of the Second World War, the upper floor being completely burnt out and not reopened until 1955. It also stands not far from the site of the Brick Lane restaurant bombing of 1999 and the Tube bombers target at Aldgate in 2005. Though escaping these threats to its existence the building could not escape the march of progress and closed its doors in August 2005, the library moving to a new building in front of Sainsbury's – *The Idea Store*.

**Bethnal Green and Islington**

There were calls for a free library in Islington from as early as 1855 without success and campaigns in 1874 and 1887 both failed to receive the required support of the ratepayers. In August 1896 Passmore Edwards wrote to Thomas Lough, MP for West Islington, offering to give £10,000 to the parish if the Libraries Acts were adopted.[8] The result of the poll was that only 11,000 were in favour of the library whereas over 14,000 voted against.

A similar situation arose in Bethnal Green where a poll in 1875 resulted in a rejection by 727 votes for and 1,215 against adopting the Acts.[9] The Bethnal Green supporters decided to start their own library with, apparently, great success; by 1889 they had a stock of 39,000 books. A further call for the Vestry to adopt the Free Library Acts was made in 1891 and this was supported by an offer from Passmore Edwards of £15,000 to build a library. However, even this was not sufficient to persuade the ratepayers who voted 3,098 to 2,996, against the move.

Edwards offered to donate 1,000 books to any London borough that adopted the Free Libraries Act and funded the building of thirteen public libraries in London before he died in 1911.

**Haggerston Free Library**

The areas of Haggerston and Hoxton, collectively known as Shoreditch were, at the end of the nineteenth century a seething mass of people crammed into slums. Poverty and overcrowding affected almost the entire district and there were few buildings or institutions of an educational character. In March 1891 the overseers of the then parish of St Leonard received a requisition signed by nineteen ratepayers requiring them to take a poll, in order to adopt the Free Libraries Act. Later that month, 3,154 ratepayers voted for and 2,076 voted against, but only for a maximum of a ¾d rate.[10]

In Haggerston the overseers decided to convert a building for library use rather than build a new one and chose the offices of the Independent Gas Company in Kingsland Road, with a large garden at the rear and a house adjoining, at a price of £4,250. Although a loan was arranged from the Prudential Assurance Company Passmore Edwards came forward and offered £5,000 to cover both the purchase and conversion work, and gave 1,000 books.

As soon as the newsroom and the reading room were ready they were opened for public use, although it was to be another four months before the lending and reference libraries were ready and the building could be formally opened. This took place on 10 May 1893, the Duke of Devonshire given the honour of doing so.

The library was an immediate success; so much so that a temporary reader's shelter was constructed in the rear garden, such was the demand. It opened with 6,460 books in the lending library and 2,346 in the reference library, and 160 newspapers and periodicals in the reading room; 51,000 books were issued in the first twelve months. It was soon decided that an extension was needed and this was designed by Maurice Adams, Passmore Edwards providing the £2,000 needed. The extended library was opened on 17 October 1896, and named the Passmore Edwards Library.

In 1975 the library closed its doors for the last time and after standing unused for some time was converted into residential apartments.

*The former Haggerston Branch Library, Hackney*

*The Hoxton Free Library, Pitfield Street*

**Hoxton Free Library**

Finding a suitable site for the second Shoreditch library was not so simple and a temporary library opened in Great Eastern Street with 5,000 books. The Baths and Washhouses Committee was also looking for a site on which to build and it was decided to combine the two, choosing a site in Pitfield Street with Henry T Hare preparing the plans.

Passmore Edwards laid the foundation stones for both the extension to the Haggerston library and the Hoxton library on the same day. When the library was opened in 1898 it bore the name the Passmore Edwards Public Library, Edwards having given £4,450 towards the total cost of £20,000.

In recognition of the gift of the two libraries, the Borough of Shoreditch commissioned George Frampton ARA, to produce a marble bust of Edwards. Frampton had already exhibited a bronze bust of Edwards at the Royal Academy and the marble bust unveiled to mark the first anniversary of the Hoxton library was identical. Frampton produced a second marble bust of Edwards, which he presented to Eleanor and which graced the Edwards family home for many years. Copies were also placed in the Redruth and Bodmin libraries in Cornwall.

The Hoxton library suffered extensive damage during the Blitz in 1943 and remained closed for thirteen years. When Hackney Council opened a new library in Hoxton Street in 1995, the Pitfield Street library closed for good. For a while the building became home to the English National Opera Company (ENO) and it was here in 2003 that researcher Knighton Berry went to enquire about the marble bust of Edwards that had stood for many years on the main staircase to the upper floors. The bust was nowhere to be found but his enquiry produced sufficient interest in Teresa Deacon,

Administrator at the ENO, to continue searching amongst the disused rooms at the former library. On a later visit Teresa was able to take Knighton to the old boiler room in which amongst the broken furniture stored there lay the lost bust, badly chipped and covered in grime. With the permission of the London Borough of Hackney and the ENO he was able to retrieve the bust, have it cleaned and repaired by the ceramics department of the West Dean College in West Sussex and have it transported, through the Tate, to St Ives, in Cornwall, where on 31 May 2007 he presented it to the Cornwall County Council. Today the bust stands once more in its proper place, in a Passmore Edwards library.

Following the departure of the ENO the library found a new use in 2007, as the Courtyard Theatre, providing two performance areas and rehearsal space, whilst the upper floors have been converted to office and residential accommodation.

**Passmore Edwards and the St Bride Library of Printing**

The St Bride library was an integral part of the St Bride Foundation formed in 1891 through a union of several local London parish charities with the aim of providing 'social, cultural and educational facilities within Fleet Street and the surrounding areas'.

After the foundation opened a printing school in 1894 for young apprentices in the printing trades and the managers they worked under, they decided to create a reference library to support the school. The governors were fortunate in being able to purchase the library of William Blades, the printer and bibliographer who had died in 1890, and this formed the basis of the technical reference library. However, they were also in need of modern works on printing, paper making, stereotyping, binding and other allied trades and so approached Passmore Edwards[11] for assistance. He responded within days to say he would 'cheerfully comply with your request' offering £500; £400 for works already published and £100 set aside for technical books published in the future.

Sir Walter Besant, the novelist and historian, opened the two libraries, the William Blades library and the Passmore Edwards library in November 1895. At the same time, William Blades' widow and Eleanor Edwards unveiled terracotta medallion portraits of the two men fixed above the doorways to the libraries.

When the Printing School moved to Southwark to form the nucleus of the London School of Printing (and Kindred Trades) in 1922, later to become the London College of Communication, the technical reference library remained at the Institute, and was formally renamed the St Bride Printing Library in 1952.

The Corporation of London took over management of the library in 1966, offering both the library and foundation financial stability but this support was withdrawn in 2004 and management and owner-

*Readers enjoy the Passmore Edwards Collection at St Bride's Library*

ship of the collections was returned to the St Bride Foundation.

The library remains open to the public as the world's foremost printing and graphic arts library, with its collection of early printed books, typefaces, rare newspapers and an archive covering the history of printing. The original Institute building included a swimming pool which has since been converted to form the Bridewell Theatre, whilst other rooms have been transformed into lecture rooms, exhibition space and meeting rooms, one of which is called the Passmore Edwards Room. A bust of Samuel Richardson, the novelist, was presented to the library by Edwards and remains in place today, looking down on visitors as they enter the library.

**Shepherd's Bush Public Library**

Passmore Edwards' brother, Richard, was instrumental in persuading the Hammersmith Vestry to take up an offer from the Metropolitan Board of Works for use of Ravenscourt Park Mansion as a library and museum, the first free library in the district. When the Ecclesiastical Commissioners subsequently offered a gift of a piece of land in Uxbridge Road, Shepherd's Bush, Passmore Edwards offered to give 'substantial' assistance in building another library, providing that he was assured that the authority could afford to maintain it. This was achieved by calling on the ratepayers to accept a further half penny rate.

Richard had originally asked his brother to help with providing an additional library but Edwards had declined, saying that he would leave the west of London to take care of itself and concentrate on the east of London. After Richard's death he was approached again, by a vestryman unaware of the previous request, and Edwards initially declined but after further thought decided that there were sufficient working men in the area to benefit from his help.

Edwards provided £5,000 towards the £6,000 the library cost to build and furnish and the residents of the area showed their appreciation in the welcome they gave to Lord Rosebery, the Prime Minister, and Edwards when the library was opened in July 1896, and dedicated to the memory of Leigh Hunt and Charles Keene, both associated with Hammersmith. The Uxbridge Road was decorated with flags, bunting and rustic flower baskets, whilst a handsome maroon and cream banner across the road announced the 'Welcome' to the visitors. Both private and commercial property was

Bottom left: *Shepherd's Bush Library, 2009*

Below right: *Medallions of Leigh Hunt and Charles Keene at Shepherd's Bush Library*

similarly decorated with banners, flags and floral arrangements.

Designed by Maurice Adams, the library is in Eng-lish Renaissance style constructed of red brick with Portland stone cornices and mullions. The front gable carries a life size sculpture representing the 'Shepherd in the Bush'.

Edwards returned to the library on two occasions, in 1896 and 1897, to witness the unveiling of bronze portraits of Charles Keene and Leigh Hunt, after whom he had dedicated the library. The medallion of Keene, an artist and Punch cartoonist, was subscribed for by about sixty of his friends, and unveiled by Edwards, whereas Hunt's medallion, installed on the foyer wall adjacent to that of Keene was commissioned by Edwards himself. Hunt was a poet and journalist and both he and Keene lived in Hammersmith.

In 2009 the Hammersmith and Fulham Borough Council closed the library after moving the library service to a new building in Wood lane. At the time of writing the Council were proposing to sell the Passmore Edwards building but were grappling with the restrictions set by covenants in the original deed of gift. There was also a strong interest amongst the local community to prevent its loss as a public building.

**Dulwich Public Library**

Although Islington had declined to promote the free library movement the parish of Camberwell, with a population greater than Edinburgh, embraced it, and was rewarded by Edwards' generosity in funding three public libraries in addition to the contribution he made to establish the Camberwell College of Art and the South London Art Gallery.

After establishing a Central library and a branch library at Knatchbull Road, Minet, chief librarian Edward Foskett planned to build libraries at both Dulwich and Nunhead and wrote to Passmore Edwards for assistance. His response was that he would donate £2,500 for a library at Nunhead or £3,000 towards a library at Dulwich, preferring the latter as he knew the area better.[12] Edwards had lived at Camberwell Grove for a while when he first moved to London as a young man, leaving when the house was demolished to make way for an extension of the railway into London.

The governors of Dulwich College were willing to donate the land required but were legally unable to do so and it took an amendment of the Free Libraries Act to allow this to proceed. Built to a design by Charles Barry & Son, the foundation stone was finally laid by the actor Sir Henry Irving on 24 October 1896 and it was opened a year later by Lord Halsbury, the Chancellor, and dedicated to the memory of Edward

*The Dulwich Free Library*

Alleyn, the founder of the Dulwich College. By this time Edwards had increased the amount he had given for the library to £5,000.

During the 1940 air raids a bomb landed on the north-west corner of the library causing considerable damage but as part of the post war rebuilding an extension was added which included a public hall. Today, the Dulwich library, one of a diminishing number of Passmore Edwards libraries in London still in use, is thriving. Disabled access has been cleverly fitted into the internal structure of the library giving access to the computer suite and the public hall. To the rear of the library the gardens are well maintained and provide a pleasant relaxation from the passing traffic.

**Nunhead Free Library**

Though initially indicating otherwise, in February 1896 Edwards wrote to Foskett with an offer to build the Nunhead library as well as the library at Dulwich, and laid the foundation stone in April of that year. Speaking in response to the thanks given to him Edwards said Camberwell, had increased enormously in population since he lived there and was now one of the most populated parts of London. Having expanded so it was now displaying unusual municipal spirit, by competing with other metropolitan parishes and leaving most of them behind. If there was to be competition what could be better than in the promotion of the public good. He referred to man as being a fighting animal but this didn't mean that he must be engaged in murderous struggles on the battlefield. How much better if these struggles were in order to provide public buildings. Edwards later said that although he had provided many public libraries it would be one competition that he would be happy to lose, with others taking up the challenge.

Designed by R P Whellock, the Nunhead library is amongst only four Passmore Edwards libraries in London that remain in use in 2010.

**Wells Street Library, North Camberwell**

Passmore Edwards was again persuaded to contribute to a multi-purpose building when he funded a branch library for the northern part of Camberwell, the third library he was to provide in the borough.

The North Camberwell Radical Club started a campaign for a library in the area in September 1896 but it was not until 1898 that a temporary library was opened in Neate Street. In a response to an appeal, Lord Llangattock offered a site in Wells Way, then occupied by two houses, on a 999-year lease at a peppercorn rent. The value of the offer was put at £3,000 and the Vestry gladly accepted, deciding to meet the needs for both

*The Passmore Edwards Free Library, Nunhead*

public bathhouses and a library by the construction of a combined building.

With a promise of £3,000 from Passmore Edwards for the library, Maurice Adams was given the difficult task of designing the library, whilst the Borough Engineer, William Oxtoby, independently designed the adjoining baths and washhouse. The result is an attractive building in red brick and Portland and Hopton Wood stone dressings under a Brosley tile roof. Internally, the library was conventionally arranged, with newspaper reading room, reference library and lending library, together with the normal offices, book rooms and stores. The public baths and washhouse included two swimming pools – a 75-feet-long first-class pool and a 65-feet-long second-class pool – a laundry and fifty slipper baths.

When Lady Llangattock opened the buildings on 18 May 1903, she reminded the guests that nearly two years previously she and Passmore Edwards had met at Wells Way to lay the foundation stone. On that occasion the heavens had opened with heavy rain adding a thunderous applause to the ceremony. She had remarked that 'What begins in rain ends in sunshine' and so it had with the beautiful and useful building there ready to serve the residents of North Camberwell.[13]

The catalogue of books in 1903 contained more than 3,600 works, with 400 suitable for juveniles but it was not until 1925 that a separate junior library was opened, utilising one of the basement storerooms. In 1927 this room was decorated with painted murals by Guy Millar, one of the South London Artists, showing local historical scenes and scenes from Peter Pan and well-known nursery rhymes.

*North Camberwell Public Library*

The library survived the Blitz whilst the surrounding area was very heavily damaged and at the end of the war the area was cleared for the creation of the Burgess Park. After the war the children's services were expanded with story hour, including short film clips, painting and essay competitions and, by 1960, a chess club. The writing competition in 1960 attracted 1,827 entries. Although the building survived the bombing it could not escape the march of progress, the public baths closing in 1981 and the library just ten years later.

During the post-war clearance of the area a tiled mural of the Camberwell Blue, a rare butterfly first spotted in Camberwell in 1748, was rescued from a nearby paper works and relocated on the end wall of the library.

A boxing club now uses the former bathhouse, but the library building, though previously used as offices by Groundwork London, in 2010 was empty. At the centre of a £4 million redevelopment of the surrounding Park the building is, however, listed and safe from demolition.

**Edmonton Public Library**

Passmore Edwards chose Mary Ward to lay the foundation stone of the public library at Edmonton. This was in April 1897 at the same time that he was in negotiations with her over building the Settlement in Bloomsbury. Immediately after the short ceremony the procession returned to a public meeting in the town hall. In describing the ceremony that had just taken place, she prophesied the time when 'generations of English people, both in and around London and in the remote towns of beautiful Cornwall, would still be entering the spiritual kingdom of knowledge and imagination, the Passmore Edwards Free Library'. Designed by Maurice Adams, the library was dedicated to the memory of John Keats and Charles Lamb, both associated with Edmonton, and she said it was pleasing to think that one day an Edmonton boy, through visiting the library they had just seen commenced, would produce a novel or a poem, or write a history, that would stir the English minds.

At the opening, undertaken by Dr Richard Garrett of the British Museum, in the following November, Passmore Edwards said that the people, mostly working men, now had a library and books but lacked the time to read. Hundreds of working men from Edmonton and other outlying districts of London had to travel into London daily – a journey that would take, on average, two and a half to three hours, each morning and evening. Referring to the engineers strike currently taking place, the engineers wanting an eight hour day, Edwards said that matters were made worse by the lack of workmen's

*The Passmore Edwards Free Library, Edmonton*

trains, resulting in long waits at the London stations. Edwards offered a weekly subscription towards the engineer's strike fund[14] and also subscribed to help other groups of workers take industrial action, including giving £50 towards a strike of bus drivers in London, organised by the socialist Tom Mann.[15] It was Edwards' support of strikes that led to Howard Evans resigning his position at the *Echo*, considering that Edwards, with his editorial support for strike action was giving false hope to the workers.

The Edmonton Local Board of Health had adopted the Free Libraries Acts in 1891 and opened a small temporary library in the Edmonton town hall in 1893. The Passmore Edwards library, in Fore Street, replaced that first temporary library but it was nearly forty years before branch libraries were built, at Bush Hill Park in 1923, Houndsfield Road in 1937, and Weir Hall, in 1938. In 1931 a new lending library was added to the rear of the Passmore Edwards building, which then became known as the Central library, and a further branch, at Ridge Avenue was opened in 1963.

In 1991 the Central library closed its doors for the last time, on the opening of the Edmonton Green library. For some time the old library was used by the Sikh community but in more recent years it has become a mosque, where visitors continue to enter the *spiritual kingdom*.

### Charles Lamb & John Keats

One reason why Passmore Edwards provided a library at Edmonton was that both Keats and Lamb had lived there, and after the library opened Edwards contacted the Library Commissioners to say that he would like to present the library with bronze reliefs of the two great men. The medallions, by George Frampton ARA, were fixed in the entrance of the library and unveiled by the author and positivist Frederick Harrison in May 1899. These have since been relocated to Community House, in Fore Street, Edmonton.

*Medallions of John Keats and Charles Lamb, Edmonton Free Library*

In 1833 the essayist and poet Charles Lamb moved to live at a cottage close to where the Edmonton library was later built but died a year later from an infection of a minor injury sustained after a fall in a nearby street. The poet Keats also lived for a short time in a house close to where the library was built, and this association was enough for Edwards to want to dedicate the library to their memories.

### St George in the East Public Library

Although the parish of St George in the East was one of the poorest in the East End the product of a penny rate amounted to £800 per annum, but this was not, in the view of

the Vestry, sufficient to pay for the construction of a free library. Passmore Edwards responded to an appeal for assistance by saying that he was so involved in building libraries elsewhere that he couldn't help, but added that if they started a public subscription fund then he would reconsider their request as soon as he could. An offer from one of the Vestry Members to start the fund off with £1,000, 'provided there was no lending library', was met with scorn from Edwards, who considered it unwise to leave out a lending library. The Commissioner removed the condition but reduced his offer to £500, and Edwards came back with an offer of £5,000 and a thousand books. The selected site, in Cable Street next to the Vestry, was owned by the Earl of Winterton, who offered to sell for £3,000, but donated £200 of the price to the library fund. Other donations received included £180 from the local breweries, which was surprising since one of Edwards' aims in creating free libraries was to provide working-men with an alternative to the public house during their limited recreational hours.

Edwards suggested that Maurice Adams should be commissioned to design the library and the drawings were exhibited at the Royal Academy and appeared in *Building News* on the 21 May 1897, the day before Lord Russell, the Lord Chief Justice, opened the library.

*The St George in the East Library was destroyd by bombing during the Second World War*

The main feature of Adams' design was the reading room, which had a steel octagonal roof, nine metres wide, rising over a series of arches and equally spaced piers. The room, however, was square, with newspaper stands along two walls and grille-fronted bookcases on the others. The reference room occupied the whole of the first floor, which had three projecting oriel windows overlooking Cable Street. The library was in red brick to first floor level and finished with stucco above whilst he facade was in Portland stone with monolithic columns flanking the doorway and with an arched pediment above. Above the columns were two seated statues representing 'Literature' and 'Art' sculptured by Nathaniel Hitch in Portland stone, and commissioned by Passmore Edwards as an additional gift to the residents of the parish.

Sadly, incendiary bombs destroyed the library during the 1941 Blitz and the shell, in an unsafe condition, was pulled down. A temporary library was built in St George in the East churchyard and this remained in use until the late 1960s when a new library was built in Watney Market.

**Borough Road Library, Southwark**

In August 1895 a letter appeared in the *Daily Chronicle*, written by Passmore Edwards offering £5,000 for a public library in the Parish of St George the Martyr, if the parish adopted the Library Acts. By the following April the poll had been held and a committee constituted. A site in Borough Road was chosen and possession of the land was obtained in time for it to be used as a temporary grandstand along the route of the Queen's procession during her Diamond Jubilee celebrations. This enterprising development added nearly another £2,000 to the library fund.

Edwards laid the foundation stone in December 1897 and returned in February 1899 when James Bryce MP opened the library. The architects were C J Phipps and Bloomfield Jackson and their design was constructed in red brick with terracotta dressings. The west end gable includes a memorial to Queen Victoria in low relief, whilst over the entrance is a figure representative of art, science, literature and music, and above that the tree of knowledge, crowned by 'Wisdom' and the arms of the City of London.

Passmore Edwards again returned to the library on 19 October 1900, to see Millicent Fawcett, widow of Henry Fawcett, Gladstone's Post Master General, unveil life-size bronze portraits of Sir William Molesworth and Sir Austen Henry Layard. Both medallions were by George Frampton ARA and paid for by Passmore Edwards.

Molesworth, a fellow Cornishman, had been MP for East Cornwall when only

*The Passmore Edwards Library, Borough Road, Southwark*

Above: *Relief in bronze of Sir William Molesworth at Borough Road Library, Southwark*

Below: *'Truth' from the gable of Borough Road Library*

twenty-two, was co-founder of the radical *London Review* and later represented the Borough of Southwark, becoming the first Commissioner of Public Works. Finally, when appointed Colonial Secretary, Molesworth brought public attention to the abuses in connection with the transport of criminals and maladministration in the Colonial Office. After Molesworth died in 1855, Layard was elected to the Southwark seat but had a varied career as traveller, art historian, draughtsman, collector, author, archaeologist and diplomat.

Edwards originally wanted Leonard Courtney, the Liberal Cornish MP, to unveil the medallions but the Library Commissioners rejected the idea, fearing that Courtney's unpopular, anti-Boer War stance, combined with Edwards' outspoken views on the war, would result in demonstrations and violence.

Unfortunately the Layard medallion was stolen in 1988, and probably melted down for scrap but although the library closed in 1992 the Molesworth medallion remains in the foyer where it was placed in 1900. The library building continues to serve the community as a nursery for children of staff and students of the London South Bank University. The nursery provides 47 places for children between the ages of six months and five years of age and is funded by the university and the payment of nursery fees by the parents. In 2010, the building also included office accommodation for the British Youth Opera, which provides emerging singers, musicians and technical trainees with professional rehearsal and performance opportunities.

**Plashet Library**

The East Ham Local Board rejected calls for a public poll to adopt the Free Library Acts in 1893, but after the formation of the Urban District Council in 1894 J H Bethell, later Lord Bethell, raised the issue again, this time successfully. The population was at that time more than 50,000 and the product of a penny rate, at £670, was enough to support more than one library. Initially making use of a converted house, the first library was opened in North Woolwich and Bethell then turned to Passmore Edwards for help in establishing a library at Plashet.

Edwards chose Herbert Gladstone, the youngest son of the Prime Minister William Gladstone to open the Plashet free library. Designed by Silvanus Trevail in the Tudor

Renaissance style, with the use of Ruabon red facing bricks – no doubt resulting in extra profits for Trevail – the library opened in October 1899. It had cost Edwards £4,000 plus the cost of the 1,000 books he added towards the 8,000 on the shelves when the library opened.[16] Bethell also provided 1,000 scientific and technical books and in the first year over 3,000 residents registered as members.

In 1903 the East Ham Improvement Act empowered the Council to spend a 1½d rate on its libraries and with assistance from Andrew Carnegie two further libraries were opened, at Manor Park in 1905, and in 1908, adjoining the town hall in High Street South.

*The former Plashet Library, now Newham Registry Office*

**Mark's Story**

From the time Mark was born in February 1963 until the summer heat wave of 1976, he lived in a terraced house in Plashet Grove, just a short walk from the Passmore Edwards library, with the park sprawling out behind it. Mark's dad was an avid reader and he would take his son with him on his weekly visit to the library, returning home with several books after each visit. Shortly after his fifth birthday he was given a dictionary inscribed with the words 'To my son Mark, may this dictionary help you to become worldly wise, with love from Dad, Christmas 1967'. In the same way as Passmore Edwards had been directed to consult the dictionary by his mother when he was a lad, Mark was prompted by his dad to take that dictionary with him when he went to the library, using it for reference whenever he came across a new word he couldn't understand.

The library opened up a world of possibilities for a young, inquisitive boy and Mark developed an early interest in history, geography and music through the huge collection of reference books available. By the age of six, Mark could name the capital city of virtually every country in the world 'as a result of spending time in that beautiful building'. During the school holidays he attended the children's book clubs and art workshops held at the library and around the time the space race was heating in the late 1960s, the library came into its own as Mark plundered the shelves to find out more about NASA and the solar system.

The library's influence on Mark's life is clear. Today, Mark is the editor of a highly respected industry publication that he co-founded several years ago, as well as being a published author. Mark cherishes the memories of 'lazy, golden days spent inside those walls, when I cared for nothing more than discovering the next piece of the knowledge puzzle ... and maybe a game of football in the park afterwards!' The dictionary, equally cherished, was presented to his own first child when she reached the age of five.

The Plashet library closed in 1993 when a new library was opened in nearby Green Street, one of the main shopping streets in Newham and more convenient for users, and the Newham Registry Office now occupies the former Passmore Edwards library building.

**Elizabeth Fry**

Born in 1870, the Quaker Elizabeth Fry was a prison worker, social reformer and philanthropist. For more than twenty years she lived at the White House at Plashet Grove, East Ham, and so it was appropriate that in 1903 her great nephew Mr Sydney Buxton, MP, unveiled a bust of Fry at the East Ham Town Hall. Sculpted by Henry A Peagram RA, the marble bust, one of the thirty busts and memorial plaques commissioned by Edwards, is now to be seen at the Newham library.

**Limehouse Public Library**

In Limehouse a poll was taken to adopt the Free Library Acts after a requisition by twenty-two working men resident in the district. The poll resulted in a 2,000 majority in favour and a board of Library Commissioners were elected to find both a site and the capital required to build it. In January 1900 the Commissioners wrote to both Passmore Edwards and Canon Barnett for assistance. Edwards initially offered to give £6,000 but within days had written to withdraw the offer, saying that he could not promise to substantially assist 'whilst this wretched war with the Transvaal Republic is waged'. The Commissioners decided to continue with their plans and arranged for a loan, meanwhile writing to Carnegie for support.[17] Whether or not Edwards knew about the appeal to Carnegie, he subsequently agreed to pay £5,000 towards the building and laid the foundation stone, at 2.30pm on 19 October 1900.

Edwards declined to give a speech after laying the stone. The first reason he gave was that after leaving Limehouse he was due to lay the foundation stone of the Bow library and at 8pm that evening he was due to unveil the memorials to Charles Keene and Leigh Hunt at the Shepherd's Bush library.

The second reason, he said, was that '*it was difficult to make bricks without straw*' – he could not make a speech without facts to speak upon. He had walked the two miles from Whitechapel to Limehouse that afternoon and said he had been struck by the absence of anything of any architectural character to relieve the monotony. But he had noticed the number of men standing about the streets with nothing to do. The library would be for these men, where they could find recreation different to lounging about.

Designed and built in Commercial Road, by Sabey & Son of Islington, the library was opened a year later by the first Mayor of Stepney, Edward Mann. Edwards was unable to attend the ceremony.

The library was originally fitted with gas lighting but, so as not to spoil the internal decoration, the wiring for electric lighting was also installed for when it became available. In the library's entrance the Brockwell Collection, an exhibition of species of fish caught in the nearby River Lee between 1876 and 1881, was put on display.

There were proposals to extend the library in 1927 with arrangements made for a loan of £15,000, three times the amount given by Edwards to build the library and the library subsequently closed in 1928, and did not reopen until 1931. The wait was well worthwhile; it had been extended at the rear to include a children's library and reading room, both claimed to be the largest in East London, as well as a lecture hall with seating for 256 people. After the formation of the Borough of Tower Hamlets this lecture hall was also used for weekly feature films, with free entry.

In 1987 the Wapping Neighbourhood Committee commissioned local artist Claire Smith to design and execute a mural for the library. Painted in the style of William Blake the mural is called Limehouse Reach, a huge fresco stretching right across the rear wall of the library.

The following year a statue of Clement Attlee, MP for Limehouse from 1922 to 1950 and Prime Minister between 1945 and 1951, was erected outside the library and unveiled by Harold Wilson.

Although talk of closing the library in 1997 initially came to nothing the library's days were numbered and it eventually closed in June 2004. In 2010 the Grade 2 listed building remains empty and neglected.

**Bow Library**

The Parishes of Bromley and Bow initially proposed combining to provide a central library and a branch library in each Parish but as soon as an agreement appeared to have been reached, negotiations broke down.[18] Bromley had already opened a branch library at Brunswick Road in 1895, Passmore Edwards performing the ceremony but not contributing to the costs other than by giving his customary 1,000 books, and it was mainly due to the inability of the Bow Vestrymen to agree amongst themselves that lead to the breakdown and the decision to go it alone. In November 1898 the Clerk to the Bow Vestry, Robert Logan, wrote to Edwards to ask for his assistance and telling him that a deputation of twelve men had been appointed, led by the Bishop of Stepney, to wait upon him. This did not entirely meet with Edwards' approval as he responded to say

*Limehouse Library in 2007*

that whenever possible he avoided deputations, of even one or two, and respectfully declined what he described as 'the formidable deferential interview you propose'. He was pretty well acquainted with the conditions and wards of the district and it would save time and trouble if the Clerk sent a written statement instead of a deputation a dozen strong 'which I should fear to face'.

Mr Logan drafted a lighthearted response saying 'the deputation would not have been formidable' but would have been 'the mildest mannered lot that ever scuttled a ship of cut-throats'. However, the actual response was formal and set out the conditions in the district as requested, pointing out the poverty that existed and the district's inability to build a library by itself because of the high rates that were already levied. When Edwards responded to suggest that the district could not afford to have a branch library, at 126 Brunswick Road, and the central library that they now proposed, Logan was quick to correct him, pointing out that the Brunswick Road library was in the parish of Bromley-by-Bow, not Bow, and it was because they could only afford to open one library, they had planned to construct it right in the centre of the parish at Roman Road. Edwards was forced to admit that he had confused the two parishes but still said that he was unable to promise any help.

The Rev E Schnadhurst, the chairman of the library committee, decided to call on Edwards to plead their case and was successful, writing a note to the clerk to the library committee to say that he had spent two hours with Edwards and 'nothing could be more favourable'. After Schnadhurst's meeting Logan was able to write to Edwards thanking him for his offer of £4,000.

Designed by S B Russell, who also designed the Plaistow library and the West Ham museum, the Bow library was constructed on a salt glazed brick base with redbrick elevations and Portland Stone dressings. There were the usual arrangements for reading room, reference and lending library, with shelving for 12,000 books, but a feature of the library was the heating arrangements, with hot water piped under the road from the public baths and wash house opposite.

Once the date for laying the foundation stone was agreed with Edwards, Russell wrote to the Vestry Clerk to outline the usual procedure. 'Mr Passmore Edwards,' he wrote, 'will be received by a deputation in, say, the Boardroom of the Baths and will be introduced to the chairman and other persons to whom he will have to refer in his address. He will then be conducted to the platform at the foundation stone, where, optionally, the procedure may be opened by prayer by some clergyman. An address of welcome to Mr Passmore Edwards should then be read or spoken by the chairman, eulogising him and his work generally. Mr Passmore Edwards will return thanks for the welcome and then after being presented with a trowel by myself will proceed to lay the

*The Roman Road Library, Bow. Now known as Vernon Hall*

stone. The builder will then present a mallet and level and Mr Passmore Edwards will declare the stone laid. A vote of thanks will then be asked for by some good speaker to Mr Passmore Edwards and can be endorsed by another speaker. Mr Passmore Edwards will acknowledge the vote (he usually added that he did not deserve the praise they were giving him). Some light refreshments should be provided for visitors after the ceremony'. The date set for the ceremony was Friday 19 October 1900 at 4 o'clock, after laying the foundation stone at Limehouse at 2.30. Edwards again resisted giving a long speech. In addition to the two foundation stone ceremonies that afternoon, he had been in West Ham the day before, where he reopened the West Ham Polytechnic and attended the opening of the adjacent West Ham museum, which he had funded, and had witnessed the unveiling of a bronze bust of him at the museum. And the next day, he said, he was due to attend a similar ceremony elsewhere.

Whilst the foundation stones for the Limehouse and Bow libraries were laid on the same day, they also opened on the same day, 6 November 1901, but this time it was Bow that took precedence, the ceremony being undertaken by the Mayor of Bow, at five o'clock. During his speech, Edwards said that east London put north and west London to shame, as throughout Islington, St Pancras, Marylebone and Paddington, not a single public library had been erected. Though he did not say so, this was in spite of Edwards offer to build a library in Islington in 1896.

Plans to extend the Bow library were proposed in 1926 but it was not until 1939 that work commenced, only to cease when the war started and instead a public air raid shelter was built on the site. Bomb damage occurred in 1940 but the library was only closed for a few weeks, and building recommenced in 1949, the extension finally opening in February 1950.

However, 1962 marked the end of the library service at the Roman Road premises, when a new library and community centre was opened in Stafford Road and the Passmore Edwards building was converted into a public hall, called Vernon Hall. This library was itself replaced with the formation of the present library, the Idea Store, in 2002, situated just behind the original Passmore Edwards building. The Bow vestrymen had set out to locate a library at the heart of the community and the Idea Store and Vernon Hall are just that, situated as they are just off the popular Roman Road market.

**Plaistow Library**

This branch library was designed so that it could be managed by a minimum number of staff, as the sum available from the rates was very small. The design produced by S B Russell appears to have been based on his design for the West Ham museum, producing one large room, sixty foot square under a domed and barrelled roof. The exterior is in red brick and Bath Stone. When it opened in 1903, the lending library was in the centre, with space for 12,000 books, separated from the newspaper and reading areas by a glass screen, eight feet high, and which gave a single attendant a clear view of the whole of the library. The flexibility of the building has allowed the layout to be adapted to meet different needs over the years and has, perhaps, contributed to it remaining open today.

Edwards chose Andrew Carnegie to open the Plaistow library in 1903. Carnegie said

that it was the first time that he had been asked to open a library to which he had not contributed even one penny. Any disagreements he may have had with Edwards over the *Echo* had clearly been forgotten as he praised his former colleague. Perhaps a little tongue in cheek he dubbed him 'St Passmore' and said that if he had been born a hundred years earlier he would certainly been canonised.

**Acton Free Library**

Acton, now a suburb of west London and about five miles from the centre, was just a village until its enclosure in 1859 released land for building mainly working-class housing as London expanded.[19] The population of 2,500 in 1851 rose to more than 24,000 by 1891.

A literary institute, with a reading room and small library, opened in 1857 and as the suburb grew other small libraries opened in the Working Men's Clubs. In 1888 the Institute was flooded during a storm, all of the 1,400 books were lost and the Institute never reopened.

The Local Administrative Board discussed the provision of a free library and set up a committee but the local ratepayers, already concerned about the costs of developing a sewerage and drainage scheme, formed a Ratepayers Protection Association. When the Local board held the required referendum over adopting the Free Library Act, the vote was lost, 788 for and 1,145 against.

It was not until 1897, after further changes in local government and the formation of the Acton Urban District Council, that interest in providing a free library was renewed. Amendments to the Free Libraries Act, in 1892, had removed the need for a referendum and on 4 January 1898, the Libraries Act was adopted.[20]

*Passmore Edwards Free Library, Plaistow*

Mr W Carrington Smith JP, of the Philanthropic Society, instrumental in persuading Passmore Edwards to fund the cottage hospital, was successfully obtained an offer of £4,000 towards the cost of building a library in Acton. The District Council purchased a plot of land fronting the High Street and applied to the Local Government Board for approval to raise loans to meet the remaining costs. Lord George Hamilton, local MP and Minister for India, laid the foundation stone on 2 November 1898 and on 3 January 1900 Joseph Choate, the American Ambassador, opened the library.[21]

Designed by Maurice Adams, in the English Renaissance style, and constructed by local builder Sidney Powell the library has been described as 'one of the most picturesque library designs, with an unusually large amount of well-executed decorative arching'.[22] As usual *Building News* published drawings and a description of the new building. The library is in red brick under a green slate roof but its most important feature is the sculptural facade. Mostly in Bath Stone, a substantial chimney-topped gable surmounts two projecting 2-storey bays. There are ionic columns, arches, sculpted figures, scrolls and carved panels galore as well as a scroll flanked roundel window high up on the gable. The original single-storey wing to the left has since been extended to provide a second floor. Internally the library had been designed to maximise the amount of useable space. It was light and airy with tall gabled windows, glazed lantern roof lights and internal glazed screens. Electric lighting was installed and warm air heating was provided from a boiler room at the rear.[23]

On the left of the entrance was the newspaper room, 50 feet by 30 feet and it was here that the opening ceremony took place, although a crowd of more than a thousand local residents gathered outside. Right of the entrance was the lending library, with a 30 feet counter separating it from the book store behind, with its shelving for 20,000 books. As with most libraries at this time the reader chose their book from a catalogue; there were more than 8,000 books available at the time of opening, and a library assistant brought this to the counter. It was not until 1922 that readers could browse the shelves to choose their own books. All the public areas, including a reference library and magazine room were on the ground floor, the first and second floors being used for the librarian's accommodation and stock rooms, accessed by both a circular staircase and lift.[24]

*Acton Free Library, designed by Maurice Adams and opened in 1900*

Originally the library opened from 9am until 10pm on Monday to Saturday and, during the winter months, from 6.30pm to 9.30pm on Sunday evenings. Sunday opening was extended from 3pm until 9pm in 1904 and this continued until after the end of the Great War, raising a great deal of concern when young boys turned up at the library on Sundays instead of going to church. But the content of the shelves also caused concern; the librarian was asked to resign when Hardy's *Tess of the D'Urbervilles*, appeared in the catalogue, a novel described as 'giving an unwholesome travesty of domestic and matrimonial life'.

After a difficult start the library prospered. In 1931 a separate children's library opened and prior to the Second World War the librarian's flat was cleared and the space used for a new reference library and a meeting room where regular lectures could be held. Further reorganisation of the library took place during the 1950s and after 1965 when the library was transferred to the control of the newly formed London Borough of Ealing.

In 2010 the fate of the Passmore Edwards building is unclear as plans are in place to relocate the library to a modern building.

# Sixteen
# Hospitals & Convalescent Homes

'Hospitals are the perpetual preachers of the gospel of human brotherhood – a gospel never more wanted than now, when mammon worship claimed so many adherents'.[1]

Whereas a wealthy man might associate himself with, and be a patron of, the local hospital, Passmore Edwards, aware of the mammoth growth in population in London and the increasing need for better health care, was to be associated with no less than thirteen separate hospitals and to fund the construction of eight convalescent homes. He also contributed to appeals from several other hospitals in a minor way. 'Hospitals', he said, 'sprang from unselfish motives, and people who supported them did so from no hope of personal gain, whether it be the rich man who gives a guinea or a poor man, sixpence'.[2]

### Charing Cross Hospital

Dr Benjamin Golding first opened his home to treat the poor in 1815 and went on to found the Charing Cross Hospital in 1821. Initially called the Royal West London Infirmary and Lying-in Institution the title was changed to the Charing Cross Hospital in 1827 and the purpose-built hospital and medical school opened in 1834. The hospital had treated over 370,000 patients by the time of Golding's death in 1863 and continued to prosper and expand over the years to reflect both the growth of the area and scientific advances in medicine. As a charity the hospital depended on subscriptions and donations and the 'Roll of Great Benefactors' is lengthy. It is not known when Passmore Edwards first became involved with the hospital but by 1896 he had given £11,749 towards their work.[3] But Edwards did not only give his money. Both he and his wife, Eleanor, were to take an active part in the support of the hospital over a number of years. It was usual that local *ladies* were the backbone of many of the hospitals that existed at that time, working not only to provide the funds to construct or maintain the hospital but also to produce much needed linen for the hospital's use. Eleanor was a member of the Ladies Guild at Charing Cross, which apart from fundraising held *soirées*, where the ladies gathered together to sew garments and the other linen necessary for use in the hospital. In 1890 it was the task of making a hundred flannel garments for patients that occupied them.[4] Around the same time Passmore Edwards, who was on the Board of Governors, gave books to form a library for the nurses apartments.

In 1888 an appeal was launched to finance a convalescent home but Edwards was dismayed at the slow progress. At the Triennial Festival Dinner of 1891, the Lord Mayor, who was presiding, read a letter from Passmore Edwards asking for 'the privilege to be allowed to build and furnish at my own expense a convalescent home to accommodate fifty beds'. As evidence of his sincerity he enclosed a cheque for £5,000 and an undertaking to send the remainder of the estimated cost when the foundation stone was laid.[5] Initially it was proposed that the home would be built at Clacton but this was thought to be too bleak during the winter months and an alternative site was looked for within 30 miles of London. When the local gentry heard of their interest in a site at Reigate they put pressure on the landowner and effectually prevented the sale. The next site they looked at was at Sevenoaks but again the negotiations were defeated by collusion amongst the local landowners, as were negotiations for a site near Limpsfield. The well-to-do clearly felt that the poor and needy of London should 'know their place' and that was not as their country neighbours. It was at this stage that Edwards stepped in once more to take an active part in the negotiations. Learning of a similar site, a farm at Limpsfield, he attended the auction, arriving early and sitting at the front, daring not to look right or left in case he was recognised. The farm was the last lot to be auctioned so after sitting for two hours Edwards bid for and purchased it for £4,100. Even then, when it became known who had made the purchase, and for what purpose, the landowners gathered around to try to persuade him to surrender his bargain.[6]

The landowners' actions were, perhaps, understandable, as Limpsfield became a favourite place for the building of schools and institutions. As well as the Charing Cross Convalescent Home there was the Caxton Home, built by Passmore Edwards in 1894 for the members of the printing trade, a convalescent home for women and children, a home for boys on the edge of the village and a school and home for children of missionaries working abroad.

The Charing Cross Hospital Home was opened by the Prince of Wales, accompa-

*Charing Cross Convalescent Home, Limpsfield*

nied by the Princess of Wales and Princess Victoria, on 12 July 1896. The presence of the Prince was enough to ensure a large company of other worthies attended, with the potential for being signed up as contributors and supporters, and a special excursion train carried the guests from London. Designed by J J Thomson, the home stands on an escarpment with fine views for many miles around as the land drops quickly away just a few yards from the front elevation.

A copy of an Ordnance Survey map that appeared at auction in 2006 suggested that the convalescent home was earmarked to play a vital role during the Second World War, as a secret command centre for use by Churchill at a time of invasion, but there was little additional evidence to support this suggestion.

Although Edwards' one condition in providing the home was that the hospital should remain in perpetuity under the control of the governors and council of Charing Cross Hospital, this was not to prevent them selling the home to the National Sailors and Firemen's Union in the 1920s and eventually, in 1959, it to the Marie Curie Cancer Care Charity. The building has until recently been used as a research institute for the charity, with more than 70 world-class scientists involved and whilst operating from the former convalescent home, Marie Curie scientists have published groundbreaking work on bladder and skin cancer. However, a reorganisation at Marie Curie resulted in the closure of the centre putting the Passmore Edwards building at risk.

**West Ham Hospital**

Whenever Edwards attended any public ceremony he was sure to be approached by someone looking for his help – and his money. Opening the library in Canning Town – one that he hadn't funded, although he had provided 1,000 books – his help was solicited to assist with the building of a new wing for the West Ham Hospital, Stratford. A Mrs Mary Curtis first opened a dispensary in a small house in Romford Road in 1861, with one small room equipped to receive the most serious victims of accidents, too poorly to be taken even the three miles to the London Hospital. The rapid growth of the district called for more generous provision and by 1879 a purpose- built hospital was opened in West Ham Lane, on land given by Mrs Curtis.[7] However, even this could not match the demand for surgical and medical treatment in the district and in 1890 the

*Architect's drawing of the Passmore Edwards Wing of West Ham Hosptital*

Duke of Westminster opened the West Ham Hospital, built at a cost of £7,000. But the process of expansion to meet the growing needs of the area, a population approaching 300,000, was seemingly endless and it was to meet this need that Passmore Edwards' help was solicited. He offered £3,000 of the initial estimated cost of £3,700[8] of a new building and laid the foundation stone in April 1894. The new wing, designed by Lewis Angell, the hospital's architect, consisted of two 12-bed wards, bringing the total beds to 63, and was opened by Edwards the following September; declared open 'in the name of the Great Architect of the universe.'[9]

One of the wards, named the Eleanor Edwards Ward was for children and was fully furnished at Edwards' expense, whilst the other twelve-bed ward was named the J R Roberts Ward, who both furnished the ward and donated £1,000 towards the hospital funds.

West Ham Hospital developed into the West Ham and East London Hospital in the early years of the twentieth century, with a further extension opened in 1911 by the Duke of Malborough, who also funded the renovation of the original building. By then there were 110 beds but the hospital served a total population approaching one million of the poorest of London's poor.[10]

Relying on subscriptions and voluntary funding, through Hospital Sunday and Saturday Funds and through the King Edward's Hospital Fund, the hospital struggled to remain open, eventually transferring to the National Health Service with the birth of the welfare state at the end of the Second World War. The hospital finally closed in 1983 and the buildings having since been demolished and the area redeveloped.

**Willseden Cottage Hospital**

By 1890 Willesden had a population of around 60,000, which was increasing at the rate of about 7,000 every year. With no hospital within three miles of the parish the authorities appointed a committee, which quickly responded by securing a site on a lease from All Souls College, Oxford; appointed local architects, Newman & Newman; and began construction. But even with the proceeds of a grand fete and bazaar run over three days at the Hampstead Conservatoire, which raised over £800, and the sterling work of the Ladies' Committee, who raised £795,[11] as the hospital neared completion the attempts to raise the funds to pay for it had fallen sadly behind the builder's progress. With insufficient to pay the builder, and nothing at all for the necessary furnishings and equipment, a public appeal was launched but brought in only one response. It was at this point that Passmore Edwards stepped in, as he had done the previous year at the Whitechapel library, offering to fund the entire costs and suggesting that the money already raised should be invested as an endowment towards future operating costs.

*The Children's ward at the Passmore Edwards Cottage Hospital, Willesden*

The hospital was of sixteenth-century cottage style, of brick with tall chimneys and stucco facade and accommodated nine patients in two four-bed

wards, one for male and one female patients and a single bedded room for 'special' patients. Whether they were designated as special through their illness or through their ability to pay is unclear but it was more likely the latter. Offices and rooms for a matron and her assistants made up the rest of the buildings.

Almost as soon as the hospital had opened and received the first patient in 1893 it was appreciated that further accommodation would be needed to meet the needs of a still expanding population, and in 1897 a new appeal was launched to mark Queen Victoria's Diamond Jubilee. Once more it was Edwards who came forward with the £3,000 required to extend the hospital to accommodate twenty-four beds. It was only at this point that the hospital authorities voted to call the hospital the Passmore Edwards Hospital for Willesden[12] which, in those early days was run by a matron, one trained nurse and one assistant.[13]

The 'celebrity' Edwards suggested to open the hospital in 1893 was Lady Balfour, accompanied by her brother the Right Honourable A J Balfour, Leader of the Opposition in Parliament, and to open the extension, in 1899, he chose Lady Bannerman and her husband Sir Henry Campbell-Bannerman, the current Leader of the Opposition. He chose these, he said, to show that hospital provision was above party politics, 'having claims on all Parties and all sects as they conferred benefit on all alike'.

The original hospital committee had been forward thinking in securing a six-acre site for the hospital, with the majority being used as gardens to provide fresh fruit and vegetables for the patients and this allowed the hospital to expand without relocating, purchasing the freehold in 1921. As time went on then, the hospital undertook further expansion, changing to the Willesden General hospital, which included a training

*The former Cottage Hospital at Willesden Green is now a mental health resource centre for the Central & North West London NHS Trust*

school for nurses, and eventually, in 1991, the Willesden Community Hospital, preserving the original Passmore Edwards facade, and incorporating the principles upon which it was founded.

**Wood Green Cottage Hospital**

Though Wood Green had a population only half of that of Willesden in 1890, it was growing at an equally rapid rate. Clearance of thousands of houses during the redevelopment of London forced the working classes to live in even more overcrowded conditions or move out to the suburbs such as Wood Green. It was for these reasons that Edwards said that he 'cheerfully undertook to provide a hospital' there. The forced exodus from London was taking place with scant regard to the needs of the workmen and it was these workmen, he said, who constituted the broad basis of the strength and prosperity of the nation. But accidents and ailments occurred wherever people lived and it was essential that a hospital should be provided to meet their needs.

Whilst it was Passmore Edwards who laid the foundation stone, in August 1894, it was his wife Eleanor's turn to take the silver key and declare the hospital open the following June. At half past three, the time arranged for the ceremony, neither Passmore Edwards nor his wife had appeared. An hour later the crowd was becoming anxious as to the cause of the delay but just before five they arrived, their explanation for the delay causing much amusement. They had apparently got on the wrong train and were at Highgate before discovering their mistake and had to retrace their steps.

*The Wood Green Cottage Hospital*

In response to the vote of thanks, Edwards said that there was 'a trifling misunderstanding current. People thought that he had nothing but sovereigns to fling about the world'. He said that was a mistake. 'He put his pence together, and his shillings and when he had a thousand pounds to bestow he was glad to do it'.[14] This was in contrast, he noted, to those described in the *Spectator* in 1896, 'the millionaires who found nothing and build nothing except palaces for themselves'.

Edwards' main philanthropic work was completed over a period of only fourteen or fifteen years and the amount given was over £250,000. Whilst he realised significant sums on the sale of the *Southern Evening Echo* and the *Echo* he had accumulated his wealth, perhaps, over the preceding twenty to thirty years. Considering that he had 'owed several thousands' in 1854 and even in 1866, after paying off his debts, he was not then considered to be well off – and was cautioned against doing so, his rise in wealth and his later philanthropy is even more remarkable.

Designed by Charles Bell and built on land purchased from the Church Commissioners the hospital was a small brick and tile-hung building with accommodation for four men and four women patients and included an operating theatre, convalescent rooms and staff accommodation. As the population expanded so did the hospital, having 25 beds by 1904 and 52 from 1922. Plans to rebuild were put on hold by the Second World War although the hospital was renamed the Wood Green and Southgate Hospital. After the war, with the coming of the welfare state, the hospital was again extended to 73 beds by 1973.

Miss Elizabeth Martin was typical of the nursing profession of her day. Trained at Leeds Infirmary and first appointed sister at the Northern Counties Hospital, Bury, Miss Martin served her country during the Great War as sister and finally assistant matron, seeing service in Croatia and Italy, for which she was awarded the Royal Red Cross. In 1920 she was appointed matron to the Passmore Edwards Cottage Hospital in Wood Green, where she remained for the rest of her life. Matron Elizabeth Martin collapsed and died on duty at the hospital on 17 November 1948.[15]

The hospital closed in 1983 and was demolished and replaced, in 1990, by Passmore Edwards House, a three storey sheltered housing development, continuing, at least, the name of the original benefactor.

### Caxton Convalescent Home

By the early 1890s, members of the printing trades were already running a convalescent home at Swanage, Dorset, but with over 30,000 men following these trades in London there was a need for further provision. Initially it was decided to build the new home at Swanage and they began to prepare drawings – but Passmore Edwards had other ideas. The area purchased by Edwards for the Charing Cross Convalescence Home at Limpsfield was larger than the hospital needed and they wished to sell the surplus part, valued at £1,000, and use the money to help maintain the new home. Edwards let it be known that if the printers were to choose the Limpsfield site then he would fund the building of the home, at a cost of £3,000.

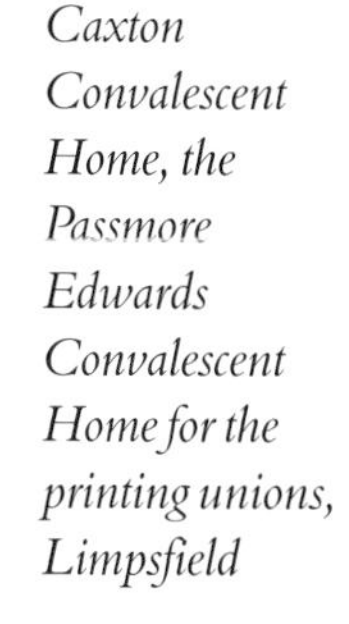

*Caxton Convalescent Home, the Passmore Edwards Convalescent Home for the printing unions, Limpsfield*

Although asked to lay the foundation stone of the Caxton Home, Passmore Edwards declined saying he thought that having funded the home, it might cause some resentment amongst other newspaper proprietors if he was to lay the foundation stone. He considered that this would not be good for the home's continued existence and upkeep. Instead he suggested that the Lord Mayor of London, who was also associated with the printing trade, might be a suitable alternative and this was acted upon,[16] although Edwards did attend the ceremony.

Having declined the invitation to lay the foundation stone, Edwards, by then installed as President of the Institution, agreed to open the home and this took place in September 1895. In the home's first annual report a section of Edwards' speech was printed in which he described the home in glowing terms. 'There was,' he said, 'something in the look of the place which was comforting and health restoring'. Set just below the ridge of the North Downs and within nine acres of grounds, the red brick home was situated on the edge of 1,500 acres of common and pine forest and looked out over miles of undulating countryside towards the South Downs. 'In all England there could not be found a more ideal place for a convalescent, jaded by the monotonous wear and tear of the printer's craft, to refit him for work and the duties of life'[17]

Alfred Saxon Snell, FRIBA, designed the home and the total cost was £6,000. Accommodation was provided for thirty patients on the first and second floors, with the matron's and servants' quarters at the rear, accessed by a separate staircase. A sitting room and games room were supplemented by a small library, stocked with 512 books from Passmore Edwards and added to by other donors. Outside there were games areas and formal gardens, as well as vegetable gardens and orchards, ensuring that the home was supplied with fruit and vegetables throughout the year, and an adequate supply of new laid eggs from the home's poultry.

Popularity of the home increased rapidly, to the extent that, in 1908, the building was extended with a new dining hall, which was also used for concerts and other entertainments, kitchens and an office, at a further cost of £2,600.

During the Great War a decision was taken to commemorate the response to the call to arms from those in the printing trades by creating a new wing in which a roll of honour would be placed. Built to accommodate eighteen patients the new wing cost £6,000, as much as the original building.

The Printers' Charitable Corporation, which traces its origins back to 1827, worked closely with the Caxton Home, eventually taking over control, and finally closing and selling the building for residential use.

In his autobiography Edwards said that he had also provided an endowment for a pension for the printing trades. No additional information is available about this but the Printers' Charitable Corporation amalgamated the individual funds providing such pensions in 1992 under the name of the Association of Printers' Trusts.[18]

**Tilbury Cottage Hospital**

For the majority of those working at the Tilbury docks there was only a week's work between them and poverty, and either accident or illness, with no local hospital to turn to, was feared. As far back as 1882 attempts were made by the friendly societies to found a cottage hospital in the area but response to the appeals was not forthcoming. Twelve years later, Passmore Edwards responded to a renewed appeal by offering to provide the money for the building. The Tilbury Docks Company, the major employer in the area, not only provided the site but also a subscription of £500 towards future maintenance.

Edwards opened the hospital in June 1896. In his response to the vote of thanks he said that as he passed through the somewhat dilapidated streets in Tilbury he could not help but thinking how it was that Englishmen, who are so capable of conducting great enterprises were apt to neglect ordinary homely duties. The reason was not, he said, because they lacked the ability, the means or the disposition. Whilst they were capable of solving significant industrial, social and political problems, and whilst there was no lack of fine homes and luxurious apartments for the wealthy and well-to-do, there was a half-hearted approach to the provision of sufficient suitable housing for ordinary working people or in supplying hospital facilities.[19]

The hospital, decorated with red brick with Bath stone dressings, designed by Rowland Plumbe FRIBA, initially provided accommodation for just eight beds.

On Thursday 27 October 1898, the destroyer HMS *Ariel* was steaming up the Thames when, near Gravesend, a serious accident occurred. Second Class Stoker North, who was working below with two others, began to draw the forward furnace but his rake caught and dislodged one of the boiler pipes. With 150lb of steam pressure suddenly released the three were enveloped in a stream of steam and boiling water. The injured men were rescued by the crew and put ashore at Gravesend by means of the customs launch, and immediately dispatched to the Tilbury Cottage Hospital. Fullager, the leading stoker was the most seriously injured, his head and upper body seriously scalded, both internal and externally and succumbed to his injuries shortly after arriving at Tilbury. North, and his colleague, Fellern, were both seriously scalded on the head and hands but due to the treatment they received at the hospital survived.[20]

Within two years the need for increased accommodation at the hospital saw the chairman, Sydney Holland, start an appeal fund and with £230 raised contacted Passmore Edwards for assistance again. Edwards wrote to offer £500, half of the sum needed to increase the accommodation by another eight beds.

In 1924 the running of the hospital was taken over by the Seaman's Hospital Society and with a planned expansion it was renamed the Tilbury Hospital, the name Passmore Edwards limited to the original building. Now being responsible for the treatment of sick and injured seamen in the whole of the Port of London, hospital accommodation was increased to fifty beds and outpatient, X-ray and operating theatre facilities extended and improved. Shortly afterwards an Indian businessman, Mr P J Singhanee of

*The Passmore Edwards Cottage Hospital, Tilbury*

Poona, gave nearly £6,000 to provide a ward for Indian seamen. The Duke of York, later King George, opened the Singhanee Ward and laid the foundation stones for the other new wards. These new buildings were constructed entirely of concrete block, on a concrete slab, leading to the hospital's local name of the *concrete hospital*, but the Society invested almost £30,000 in making it a first class hospital with all the modern equipment then available.[21] The hospital transferred to the newly formed NHS after the Second World War but was demolished in 1982.

## Convalescent Home for the Metropolitan Hospital

The Metropolitan Hospital was fortunate to have been left £10,000 'exclusively to maintain good Samaritan Societies or Convalescent Homes'. Unfortunately the terms of the legacy meant that this could not be used to construct a home, so it was decided that they should ask Passmore Edwards to provide one. Passmore Edwards readily agreed but delays in finding a suitable site led him to tell the hospital that if they could not agree on a site then he would have to withdraw his offer, he had others asking for help. Eventually a three acre site at Cranbrook, near Staplehurst, was offered, Charles Grieve was appointed architect and the foundation stone was laid on 14 October 1896.

*Convalescent Home for the Middlesex Hospital, Cranbrook, Kent*

The Metropolitan Hospital not only served an area occupied by the poorest of London's residents but sailors either injured in the docks or returning home from foreign shores, went there for medical help. Princess Louise travelled by royal train from London to Staplehurst station in July 1897, to open the home, and was welcomed by hundreds of supporters.

The home was built at a cost of £3,000, to accommodate eighteen patients, six male, six female and six children, together with a matron and two nurses.

The mistrust that existed over the presence of convalescent homes in the rural areas was transparent. While many local people were employed at the home there was concern that the patients from London would bring with them diseases that would affect the local population. By the turn of the century the London County Council converted the home for the use as a convalescent home for children recovering from tuberculosis the concerns were just as strong.

### Raymond's Story

Raymond Armfield was just one of the youngsters sent to the Cranbrook home suffering from tuberculosis. An insight into his life is to be found only from a couple of letters written by the matron and now in the Cranbrook museum. From these letters we learn that Raymond returned home to London late in 1937 after his treatment at Cranbrook. Matron tells him of the preparations being made to celebrate Christmas and of the folk who wished to be remembered to him, one being Leonard – now getting up a little, with crutches. In February of 1938 the matron responds to Mrs Armfield's letter giving news that Raymond was now working, which was fortunate, as Mr Armfield had lost his job. Matron reminds Raymond that he should keep in contact with the Metropolitan Hospital Tuberculosis clinic and says that the home can supply a replacement surgical boot for Raymond when it is required.

Following the Second World War the home was used as a remand home for errant boys and in the early 1980s the home was sold and converted into a residential home for the elderly.

Today the former home is divided into three private residences.

**Cottage Hospital and Nurses Home, Acton**

The Acton Cottage Hospital was one of the Passmore Edwards buildings commenced in 1897 during the Diamond Jubilee of Queen Victoria. At this time Acton was expanding rapidly. The District Council, formed in 1894, wanted to provide facilities for the inhabitants but the provision of a general hospital was not within their powers. Passmore Edwards responded to an approach by the President of the Acton Philanthropic Society with an offer of £2500 to build a cottage hospital, subject, of course, to the community providing a site and undertaking to maintain the hospital. The question of a site was answered by a gift of half an acre of land in Gunnersbury Lane, given by Lord and Mr Leopold Rothschild, who lived at Gunnersbury Park. A local appeal raised an astonishing £1,178 13s 7d.[22]

*The central section of the Acton Cottage Hospital, 2009*

Designed by Charles Bell FRIBA and built by an Acton builder, George Hooper, the Passmore Edwards Acton Jubilee Cottage Hospital, Nursing Institute and Invalid Kitchen was opened in May 1898 with provision for twelve beds. In the early years the management committee struggled to provide the funds needed to keep the hospital open but the need for the hospital grew and in 1904 Edwards provided a further £500 to fund an extension that doubled the number of beds available. Innovative methods of fundraising were devised; collection boxes in shops and offices, subscriptions from employers, sponsorship of wards, beds and cots, as well as the usual Hospital Saturday Funds, bazaars and events organized by the Ladies Linen League.

Accommodation was raised again, to thirty beds, in 1909, when a children's ward, operating theatre, and out-patients' department were also added. In 1920, there were 35 beds, in 1923 a further extension of seventeen beds, built as part of the town's war memorial, and in 1928 a nurses' hostel, and the total number of beds increased to 62. By the time the hospital transferred to the NHS there were 84 beds.

After closure the later extensions were demolished and the central former Passmore Edwards building was restored. Now part of the Acton Care Centre, a care home with nursing for 125 residents, it continues to serve the community.

**Workingmen's Club Union Convalescent Home**

The history of the Workingmen's Club and Institute Union parallels that of the trade union movement in Britain. Though employment legislation increased both wages and leisure time there was little opportunity to use the increased leisure time in a positive way. There was nowhere the working classes could meet other than the public house, and little opportunity to improve their lives through education. Lord Broughton had already given support to mechanics' institutes, founded by Dr Birkbeck, but men wanted somewhere to relax and develop new friendships, not just follow a hard day's work with an evening at school. Rev Henry Sully, a Unitarian, was the founder of the Club and Institute Union, although it was Hodgson Pratt, the peace activist and another Unitarian, who made it work. The Union, formed to support and consolidate the men's social clubs that were beginning to form throughout the country, was established

*The former Convalescent Home for the Workingmen's Clubs and Institutes Union at Pegwell Bay, now the Pegwell Bay Hotel*

in 1862 at an inaugural meeting funded by Lord Brougham and who became the first president. In 1865 Hodgson Pratt was elected to the council and in 1869 he became chairman of the executive committee. Sully, who was against permitting smoking and the sale alcohol in the clubs resigned in 1867.[23]

As far back as 1878 the Union's council attempted to provide a seaside home for members and families. A large house at Margate was leased and converted to accommodate members and their families, at 3s 6d a week for a bed or 6s 6d for a family room. But with the cost of maintaining the home throughout the year whilst the home was used only during the summer months, led to accumulating debts and the home closed after only two years.

In February 1892, the council tried again, resolving to 'take into consideration the advisability of a convalescent home, and that a committee be appointed for the purpose of drawing up a scheme'. The appointed committee produced a very modest scheme, estimating an annual cost of £600 a year and subscriptions from the clubs varying from one to four guineas, but there was little support from the individual clubs and the proposals fell flat.

Passmore Edwards was very supportive of the Workingmen's Clubs movement, attending the Union's AGM as early as 1881. When he funded the Perranporth Convalescent Home in 1892 Pratt, who by then had been elected President, made him aware of the Union's aims and by June 1893, reported back to B T Hall, Secretary of the Union, that Edwards would like to see a deputation on the matter. After hearing of the Union's plans and receiving assurances that that the Union would guarantee to keep a home going if he gave them one Edwards brought the meeting to a conclusion with 'very well, go and find your site, and I will buy it, and build you a home on it'.

However, the search for a suitable site proved a difficult a task and it was Passmore Edwards, who in May 1894 informed them that he had purchased a disused hotel and grounds at Pegwell Bay, Kent, which he thought would suit their purposes. An inspection by the secretary followed and found that the builders and decorators were already in attendance, the conversion almost complete. All that was left to do was to provide the furnishings and appoint staff.

An urgent appeal for funds to furnish the home raised £250 in two months, clubs or individuals being asked for £5 and for which the name of the donor would be fixed over the door of a room within the home.

On the August Bank holiday of 1894 Passmore Edwards opened the first convalescent home for the Union, in the presence of the Hodgson Pratt, the Mayor of Ramsgate, Alderman Blackburn, and 600 Club members who cheerily braved the stormy weather.

From that stormy start the home was an immediate success. As each resident returned to his club he spread the tale of its charms and its fame spread far and wide. Excursions organised by the Home Committee took tens of thousands of men from the London clubs to Pegwell for the day. The home opened to accommodate 32 members, but within a couple of years it was clear that an extension would be required, though there were no funds available at that time.

An appeal went out to the clubs and, on the advice of Passmore Edwards, who suggested adding a central tower and provided £500 towards it, Maurice Adams was engaged to prepare drawings. Bed-rooms with bathrooms were added, and communal wash rooms on each floor, where residents could wash without, as then, doing so in bedrooms, an arrangement said to be 'of great economy and infinitely more satisfactory to residents'.

Altogether the first extension cost £6,471, of which the tower accounted for £1,200, and a further £600 was required for furnishings. Eleanor Edwards laid the foundation stone on 10 July 1897 and just 12 months later, on 2 July 1898, her husband opened the new wing, raising the accommodation to 62. The response of the clubs to the debt created from the building works was enormous and it was cleared by 1905 when the committee again met to consider further expansion.

*A weekly intake at Pegwell Bay, July1926*

The next project was to demolish and replace the wing on the terrace and this was opened on Easter Monday 1906. Finally, building works were completed in 1914, when a wing was added to the bedroom block, bringing the accommodation to 72, and a cafe opposite the main entrance was purchased and pulled down to make room for a small bowling green and garden.

In January 1919, Herbert Samuel Boyland, who had worked as superintendent of the home since the opening in 1894, passed away suddenly at the age of 58. The service that he and his wife, the matron, had given to the home had won the affection of thousands and their testaments appeared on club notice boards across the country. Mr Boyland's work locally, especially for victims of the Great War, brought him great respect amongst his neighbours and a notable gathering at his funeral. Mrs Boyland continued in her post for a further eight years before retiring after 33 years service.

Ernest Jones was born around 1877 in Birmingham and after serving in both the RNAS and the RAF repairing the early aeroplanes he settled down in Willesdon with his wife Emily, working at the radiator factory. But by early 1925 he was taken ill and admitted to the Passmore Edwards hospital. Found to be suffering from cancer he was discharged but as a member of the Workingmen's Club was entitled to a stay at the Pegwell Home. Ernest was at Pegwell Bay in July and wrote home that he felt well enough to take the tram for a trip to Broadstairs. However his improvement was short lived and he died a few months later.

The Pegwell Bay Home continued under the WMCIU control until 1969, when, after suffering flood damage, it was decided that repairs would be too costly and the building was sold and converted back to a hotel, now operating as the Pegwell Bay Hotel offering 42 en-suite rooms.

**Falmouth Cottage Hospital**

In Cornwall Mrs Fitzgerald had been running a private hospital since 1853. When in 1893 she wrote to the authorities to say that she intended to close her hospital a committee was formed to raise the funds necessary to build a cottage hospital in the town. Mary Rogers, aunt of Reginald Rogers, the President of the Falmouth Dispensary, wrote to Passmore Edwards who immediately responded to say that 'Hospitals and Convalescent homes do blessed work' and 'It is essential for the community and the empire at large that the physical and moral health of every individual, if possible, be maintained.' He offered £1,000, enclosing a cheque for half of the money, saying that he did this 'for the sake of our dear old Cornwall, for which I entertain undying affection'. Lord Kimberley offered a site at the top of Killigrew Street for £70, the agricultural value. When it was realised that a larger building was needed Edwards offered a further £500, sending a cheque for the £500 with a promise of the remainder when the foundation stone was laid. Hearing that the committee had also raised £700 towards the running of the hospital Edwards said 'make that a thousand and I'll furnish the hospital when you have built it'. The town took him at his word and Edwards paid the £40 needed to furnish the hospital with his wife, Eleanor, becoming involved in the choice of the furnishings needed.

Designed by H C Rogers of Westminster the building is of Bridgewater brick up to the window sills above this the walls are rough-cast with brick dressings. The wards were on the ground floor with the upper floor of the central portion given over to accommodate the staff. Two terracotta panels sculpted by G Frampton RA were fixed above the bay windows, one including a sundial.

The day chosen to open the hospital was shared with the laying of the foundation stone of the library, Eleanor taking a gold key to declare the hospital open. As was usual practice at the time, it was Passmore Edwards that responded to the vote of thanks on his wife's behalf. He said that he had suggested that the hospital be dedicated to the memory of Robert Were Fox, the Cornish geologist and inventor and was disappointed that this suggestion was not taken up.[24] After the opening ceremony the party retired to a public tea served on the recreation ground opposite and this was followed by dancing on the green.

Under the matron, Miss Nicholl, the first two patients were admitted on 7 July 1894 and forty-two patients were treated in the first eight months, remaining in the hospital for an average of twenty-eight days. One of these was a Pickfords driver who fell off the shafts of his horse-drawn wagon driving along Greenbank; he broke both legs in several places, the wheels passing over him.

*Falmouth Cottage Hospital*

The need for additional space at the hospital was soon realised and funds were needed to provide equipment for an operating theatre, a dispensary, and a mortuary. Mr Allen, from Blackheath, was one of those to contribute. With his wife he had disembarked at Falmouth docks on an excursion to

Cornwall but Mrs Allen had been run over on the dockside and although taken directly to the hospital had failed to recover from her ordeal. Mr Allen was subsequently to receive £100 life insurance half of which he donated to the Falmouth hospital, in his wife's name and the other half to a London children's charity.

The site at the top of Kergilliak Street was not without its problems. The cottage hospital was on what was to become a busy road junction and drivers would sound their horn when passing, much to the disturbance of the patients. In addition the site did not allow for the expansion needed, which meant at times patients were refused admittance, and an appeal was launched in 1927 to fund a new hospital. So inconsiderable was the response that the proposal was abandoned until William Mountstephen and Albert Collins, formerly associated with Falmouth, but now living in Johannesburg, wrote to offer money for a new hospital. After initially looking at an existing house along the sea front, which would need conversion and extending, a site was found in Trescobeas Road and work started on the existing Falmouth General Hospital in November 1928.

In the final year of use the cottage hospital treated 217 inpatients, 312 outpatients, took 94 x-rays, carried out 325 operations, applied 2,526 dressings and gave 1,588 treatments of massage.

The old hospital continued in use for many years as a maternity unit and, following the introduction of the National Health Service, as a child welfare clinic. It continues to serve the community as a day centre run by Age Concern.

**The Friendly Societies Convalescent Home at Herne Bay**

In 1889 Mrs Charlotte Rusher handed over a convalescent home in Dover, which she had established some thirty years previously, to J E Nichols, George Vaughan and W H Chinn, members of both the South London district of the Manchester Unity, and the Ancient Order of Foresters. The gift consisted of two leasehold houses, fully furnished to accommodate 80 patients and a sum of £750 invested in consols, to be used for the purposes of a convalescent home for members of the Manchester Unity and other Registered Friendly Societies. The total value of the gift was estimated at £4,000.

It was not long before the accommodation proved insufficient to meet demand but although having over three million members and capital of over £23 million pounds, none was available to purchase a convalescent home. An Act of Parliament restricted the use of their funds to meet only sickness, funeral and other liabilities of the members. Provision could be made, for maintenance of a home but without additional outside help the capital needed could never be found.

After being approached by Mr Drummond, Passmore Edwards offered to build a home at Herne Bay to accommodate 50 patients, at a cost of not exceeding £6,000.

The chosen site, three hectares on the Beltange estate, on the cliffs east of the town of Herne Bay was just half a mile from the sea and had a road frontage of 100 metres.

Alfred Saxon Snell was appointed as architect and after his plans were agreed with Passmore Edwards, building commenced and the foundation stone laid on Saturday 6 November 1897.

It was soon clear that the total cost of the home was going to exceed the amount offered by Passmore Edwards and the trustees made an appeal to the Friendly Societies and branches operating in London to finance the undertaking and take on the liability for its future maintenance. This appeal was not entirely successful and the Trustees applied to the Charity Commissioners for registration as a charity.

Passmore Edwards eventually opened the home on 1 May 1899, when five special trains were chartered and thousands attended the ceremony.

The design proposed by Saxon Snell was to accommodate 50 residents on three floors. Built of Canterbury red brick with Monks Park Bath stone dressings under a Brosely red tile roof, the design was said to avoid the idea of an *institution* as opposed to a *home* and to permit additions without materially interfering with the original building.

On the ground floor the wide front entrance porch led to a small hall, with fireplace, and thence to the naturally lit main staircase. A corridor branched to the left and right of the entrance hall leading to the patients' day rooms and the administrative offices.

The day accommodation comprised a large general sitting and smoking room overlooking the gardens at the rear. In the front of the sitting room was the reading room and library, to which Edwards, of course, provided a number of books, with a large circular bay overlooking the front garden. A dormitory on the lower floor provided for those who would find ascending the main staircase difficult or impossible. A large lavatory, with washbasins and resident's lockers, and a bathroom was also provided on this floor.

The dining hall, a large room 38 feet by 21 feet with both end bays and side windows, included a raised platform at one end to enable concerts and other entertainment to take place. Also on the ground floor were rooms for the master and matron and a large kitchen. On the first floor were five dormitories for ten, eight and six beds and two for four beds each, plus rooms for staff and servants. On the second floor, and partly in the roof, there were three more three bed dormitories another with four beds and one single room.

When the Friendly Societies produced and published 'Spending and Saving', a 'primer of thrift and guide to the Friendly Societies' it was dedicated to Passmore Edwards, in recognition of his philanthropy, and particularly his establishment of the Conval-escent Home.[25]

During the Great War the home was requisitioned by the War Department, as was the adjacent Railwaymen's Convalescent Home, and temporary arrangements were made to accommodate patients at a hotel in Westgate.

*The former Falmouth Cottage Hospital, now an Age Concern Day Care Centre*

It was not until 1919 that the home was returned to the Societies and reopened. Together with the Railwaymen's Home, the two military hospitals had treated 10,000 patients. Immediately work began on the first extension to accommodate twenty

women in a ward dedicated to the memory of members who died in 'the war to end all wars'. Further extensions were provided over the years, including one for 10 women in 1930, and facilities at the Home brought up to date.

When war broke out in 1939 the buildings were once more requisitioned, initially for use as an emergency military hospital and later as accommodation for bombed out civilians.

Top: *From the air, the Friendly Societies' Convalescent Home (*right*) and the Railwayman's Home (*left*) at Herne Bay, Kent*

Below: *The Friendly Societies' Convalescent Home, Herne Bay*

As the war came to its conclusion the Kent County Council made proposals to use the home for the treatment of persons suffering from tuberculosis and then as a nursery for the many unwanted and orphan children resulting from the war years. But these proposals came to nothing and eventually the home was returned to the trustees and reopened.

The demand for more modern facilities and mounting maintenance costs led the trustees to decide, in the late 1980s to replace the Passmore Edwards home with a modern building.

In 2010 the new convalescent home, an attractive two-storey building built on the site of the original home, was finally closed and is the site taken over by Age Concern to replace the facilities they had until then run on two separate sites in the town. The link with the building's history remains only with the memorial stone from the original building incorporated into the new and a pair of elaborate iron gates.

**Tom's Story**

Tom was just nine or 10 years old when, in 1947/8 he went to stay at the Beltinge Convalescent Home. Asthmatic, and quite small and frail for his age he had recently undergone an operation on his appendix at St Thomas's Hospital, London, and was sent to the home to build up his strength. His father, having served in the merchant navy throughout the Second World War, had returned home to start an army surplus store in Kensal Road, W10. He was also a member of the Royal Antediluvian Order of Buffaloes, one of the organisations affiliated to the Convalescent Home at Herne Bay.

It was Tom's elder brother who drove Tom and his mother out of London and down to Herne Bay. After war-ravaged London the big iron gates of the Home, opening out on to large grassed areas stay locked in Tom's memory. As does the polished wooden floors, the tapioca pudding, which he had not seen before, the dormitory bedrooms and the queue for the weekly dose of 'Black Jack', syrup of Figs. For the next six or so weeks Tom remained at Herne Bay, playing games on the lawns, going for walks, all dressed in the regulation short grey trousers and shirt uniform and marching two by two. Tom said: 'It was a different world to me there, one of bewilderment to see things that I'd never seen before after going through the war, living in shelters, bombs dropping, being bombed out, hearing the doodle bugs drone stop and wait for the big bang, the sirens giving the all clear, then evacuation, being homeless, living in different places; so the convalescent home was like a little bit of heaven for me then and I felt better too, it was a bit strict and scary but ok, a place that is always in my memories of strange but happy days, then back home to London once more'.

**East Ham Hospital**

Silvanus Trevail was responsible for designing two of the Passmore Edwards buildings in London. The first was the free library at East Ham and the other a hospital in the same district, which at that time had a population of around 100,000 and was growing at the rate of 2,000 a year. The idea for the hospital came from the East Ham Council employees' Hospital Committee, established on similar lines to the Hospital Saturday Fund paying weekly penny subscriptions. Initially hoping to build a hospital in 1897 in

Top: *The Passmore Edwards Hospital, East Ham*

Below: *The entrance to the East Ham Hospital*

commemoration of Queen Victoria's Diamond Jubilee they launched an appeal, but this attracted only a few hundred pounds. As usual, when Passmore Edwards was approached he offered to pay £4,000 for the construction of the hospital if the committee would provide the site.[26]

The Council's former surveyor, W H Savage, advised Trevail to keep the design within Edwards's budget of £4,000.[27] Although Edwards clearly saw the need for a larger institution as he did not want the hospital to be a cottage hospital as was the case at other hospitals he had funded.

James Jerram, who built the East Ham library, was appointed as contractor and Savage acted as Clerk of Works, Lady Tweedmouth laying the foundation stone on 26 July 1900. The hospital was opened in 1901 with just 20 beds. Unlike Falmouth, the chosen site allowed for expansion and extensions were built in 1914 and in 1928, the hospital becoming part of the much larger East Ham Memorial hospital, designed by Mennie and Smith to provide 100 beds and completed in 1929.

Though the hospital was badly damaged by bombing in 1940 it became part of the NHS in 1948, and since then has been under the control of various hospital boards and trusts as the management of the health services developed. Today the hospital falls within the control of the Newham Community Health Care Trust. Set amid a modern, otherwise purpose-built, hospital the Passmore Edwards building is now home to both the Newham Community Mental Health Team on the ground floor and the Psychological Treatment Centre.

Originally a voluntary hospital, funded from subscriptions and donations, the need to maintain a healthy inflow of funds was essential. One of the ideas put forward was a charity football cup to be competed for by local teams, the trophy being presented by the leading doctor at the time, Dr McKettrick in 1904. This competition, one of the oldest in existence and now known as the East Ham Memorial Charity Football Cup Competition, has continued through the years providing much needed funds for the hospital and more recently the Sally Sherman Nursing Home, Alnwick Road, Newham.

**Sutton Cottage Hospital**

Sutton, just nine miles from central London, grew rapidly after the opening of the railway station in 1847. In 1899 a pair of semi-detached cottages provided by the Urban District Council at a peppercorn rent, were adapted to provide the first Sutton Cottage Hospital. It was soon seen that this would not meet the area's needs and after Mr R C Foster JP, later Sir Ralph Foster, offered a site in Hill Road, Passmore Edwards was approached. Edwards agreed to help and Cecil Sharp was commissioned to design the new hospital with a central block for a matron and the nurses and two four bed and two 2-bed wards, together with an operating theatre. Passmore Edwards laid the foundation stone on 1 May 1901 after travelling to Sutton by train with his wife, Eleanor. In his speech he said that he had been concerned that he would not be able to attend the ceremony as he had been involved in an accident just a couple of weeks previously. Crossing the road he had been knocked down by a cab. Whether or not he had received hospital attention himself he did not say. The hospital opened the following year; it cost £2,800. Even this accommodation was soon too small and an extension was added to bring the number of beds up to twenty. As the population grew the need for additional facilities increased and in 1927 a new site, on which the current hospital stands was purchased. Sir Alan Garrett Anderson, the son of the pioneering woman doctor, Elizabeth Garrett Anderson, opened the new hospital in September 1931.

*Sutton Cottage Hospital in 1912*

The Passmore Edwards building was demolished at some unknown date and premises known as The Alders erected on the site. This has since been acquired by J D Weatherspoons and is now known as the Moon on the Hill.

**Railwaymen's Convalescent Home**

Passmore Edwards had always taken an interest in the railway workers and often took up their causes over working conditions. When in 1881 the railway workers were calling for a reduction in hours, Edwards agreed to preside over a meeting held at Exeter Hall. The majority of the 135,000 railway workers at that time worked excessive hours, most working between eleven and fourteen hours a day, and some as many as twenty one. The call was for a nine-hour day and a fifty-hour week. Many accidents had occurred when signalmen fell asleep and it was proposed that the working hours for signalmen should not exceed eight a day. The lack of compensation available for railwaymen injured at work also concerned him. At a pre-election meeting in Salisbury during his campaign to become an MP in 1880, he said that it was only right that a man injured at work on the railway should be treated like any other and, if elected, he would do his best to see that this was the case.[28] While railway companies were liable for any injury to others caused by the negligence of signalmen, drivers or points men, the railway workers had no right of compensation for injuries caused by their colleagues. In 1883 Passmore Edwards added his name to an Amendment to the 1880 Employers Liability Act, which would prevent employers from contracting out of the terms of that Act and provide the railway workers with the protection they needed.

The Passmore Edwards Convalescent Home at Herne Bay was the first of ten homes opened by the railway industry for railway workers – the idea of John Edward Nichols, cashier of the London, Chatham & Dover Railway, who saw the need for a home where railway workers could go to rest and recover from sickness and ill-health. By then the number of those working on the railways exceeded 300,000.

Nichols, a member of the Manchester Unity of Oddfellows, having played a part in setting up the Friendly Societies' Home at Herne Bay was aware of the three acres of land adjacent to the Friendly Society home then under construction. When in 1898 he asked about Edwards' intentions for the land, Edwards initially said that he was considering building a nurses home on the site but seeing the disappointment this response produced he asked the reason for his interest. Although Nichols took this as an opportunity to inform him of the pressing need to provide convalescent care for men engaged in vital public services, such as railway workers, Edwards remained unmoved. Later that year Nichols again raised the issue of the railway workers, this time provoking him to repeat that he intended to build a nurses home, concluding that 'the case, Mr Nichols, is now closed'.

Nichols was, however, not so easily dissuaded and raised the matter a third time; this time Edwards agreeing not only to give the land but an additional £6,000 towards the cost of the building.

Central to Passmore Edwards offer was that 'nine men of good standing within their respective railway companies and of good repute among their fellow workers; length of service not less than twenty years, rank not to count, be assembled and informed of the scheme'. Edwards was to meet with this group as soon as possible so that a trust deed could be drawn up, but he stressed the need for speedy action. If such a home were to be built then he would lay the foundation stone on the same day as the one chosen to open the Friendly Society Home then under construction.

Nichols chose to enlist the help of the *Railway Herald*, his letter appearing in 7 January 1899. Within a week or so Nichols had sufficient replies to arrange a meeting on 19 January 1899 at which the selected representatives, including W J Day, an engine driver from the Great Northern Railway, and T Bartle, a checker in the goods department of the London and North Western Railway, were present.

With Mr W T Culver, the stationmaster at Canon Street, in the chair, the meeting unanimously accepted the motion that 'We the railwaymen, representing the men employed on the nine principal railways having termini in London, do hereby signify our willingness to become trustees of the Passmore Edwards proposed home, subject to his approval.'

The trustees, who included Nichols, were in a position to sign the trust deed by April 1899 and begin the process of setting up the organisation essential to attract the regular subscription income needed to support a home. There was also Edwards' expectation to meet, that the foundation stone would be laid on the same day as the Friendly Societies home, and this took place on 12 June 1899, the Earl of Amherst doing the honours, with full masonic ceremony.

On 31 August 1899 the trustees, now with Nichols in the chair, met to consider tenders for the new building and chose a tender from H Wall & Co of Kentish Town, of £8,367 for a come accommodating fifty beds. At the same meeting it was agreed to accept as an additional trustee a representative from the Great Central Railway, not in attendance at the original meeting.

By the end of that summer the project was in full swing. The full constitution of the

*The former Railwaymen's Convalescent Home at Herne Bay is now Elliot House, a residential care home for 71 people*

Board had been completed and the building, designed by Sexton Snell, was beginning to take shape. By the following year, however, although by March work on the building was so advanced that details of the opening ceremony were being discussed, growing financial concerns needed addressing.

Nichols, as both chairman of the Board and Passmore Edwards' accredited representative, had been given a free hand in the building scheme and proposed that the building should be enlarged to accommodate 100 patients rather than the original fifty. This would almost double the cost and the sum offered by Edwards. An appeal went out for further donations but the response was poor and Nichols' approach to Passmore Edwards received the short response. 'Provision for 100 beds was not thought of or mentioned that I know of when it was decided to provide the Home. Please not calculate on more than my promised £6,000 from me. Yours faithfully, J Passmore Edwards'.

An application for a loan from the Railway Guards Friendly Society for £2,000 was not successful and matters came to a head when the builders obtained a writ for possession of the unfinished building pending settlement of their account. The only response from Passmore Edwards, following an appeal from the chairman of the Great Eastern Company, was to offer to take the building over for a nurses' home as originally planned.

Finally the trustees were successful with a request to their bankers, Glyn, Mills, Currie & Co for an overdraft of up to £2,000, the deeds of the property being used as security and a formal guarantee on behalf or each of the trustees, but one. Passmore Edwards followed this with a further £1,000 principally for a building maintenance fund but agreeing that this could be used for the much-needed furnishings. Finally, the beginning of 1901 brought the completion of the building, installation of furnishings and equipment, appointment of Mrs Yates, the first matron, and the rest of the staff; all being ready for Sir Henry Campbell-Bannerman to open the Home on 8 June 1901, the railway companies providing free travel for those travelling to the ceremony.

During the first six months 131 workers took advantage of a fortnight's rest at the home, free of charge, and during 1902, the first full year, the number was 465 and in 1903, 725. Eager to see how the home was progressing Passmore Edwards made a surprise appearance at a meeting of the trustees in 1903, many of whom had not seen their benefactor. By 1904 subscriptions, at halfpenny or one penny a week, amounted to almost £3,000 and the number of 'patients' 1,030; all receiving at least two weeks free care. By the end of that year the final repayment to the bank was made the home being significantly in credit.

The home had only been open five years when it welcomed five unexpected guests, survivors from a railway company steamer that had foundered off the Dutch coast. The *Berlin*, operated by the Great Eastern Railway Company set sail from Harwich on the evening of 20 February 1907 bound for the Hook of Holland with 96 passengers on board. During the night weather conditions worsened and as dawn approached, and the ship approached Rotterdam, she was struck by a heavy sea swinging her broadside on to the entrance to the port. As the helmsman attempted to bring her round to regain her course the waves struck again driving her against the massive granite sea wall. The front of the ship broke away and passengers waiting to disembark, and members of the crew were thrown into the sea. It was two days before a lifeboat could land rescuers on board the ship, by which time only eleven passengers and five of the original 52-crew members were alive. After being landed back in England the five men were taken to Herne Bay to recuperate.[29]

The success of the home led to an additional wing to provide a further 50 beds being opened by Princess Louise in July 1906 but even this did not meet the growing requests for admission. This and the effect on patient's health from the lengthy journey to the Home from other parts of the country resulted in a search for further premises and the setting up of a 'New Home' fund.

In 1911 a home at Leasowe Castle on the Wirral opened followed by the Ilkely Home in 1915, and in 1919 Bridge House at Dawlish. Before the Great War, Mrs Calver, the wife of the Secretary of the Convalescent Homes had been given the Old Wool Hall at Lavenham by Princess Louise, and this had been converted and opened as the Railway Women's Convalescent Home. In 1921 Mrs Calvert offered this home to the Railwaymen's Convalescent Homes and as a result the organisation was renamed the Railway Convalescent Homes.

In 1922 the railway companies agreed to offer free travel to the homes, the cost of which had previously restricted poorer workers. With this concession and the introduction of direct deduction of contributions from wages the Convalescent Homes purchased a further home near Rothesay, one at Trenython, near Par, Cornwall, a Home solely for women at Margate, one at Buxton and finally a home at Llandudno.

At the outbreak of the Second World War Herne Bay again became a military hospital not reopening as a Convalescent Home until 1 January 1946.

The Golden Jubilee was celebrated at Herne Bay in 1951 signalling the peak of the home's success. 41,520 railwaymen had made use of its facilities and the home, further extended in 1914 and 1928 could accommodate 115 beds, admissions reaching 7,000 per year. However, the nationalisation of the railways reduced the number of employees and the birth of the NHS saw a reduction in need for Convalescent Homes. It was decided to reduce the number of homes but modernise those that remained and in the early 1970s the Herne Bay home closed for major refurbishment, including the provision of a lift for disabled patients. But faced with continual financial problems the home was not reopened, instead being leased to a company to be used as a residential care home, Heronswood, which opened in 1980. After 15 years the home went into receivership and again closed. Reopening as Elliott House, after a one million pound refurbishment, the building continues to provide care for the elderly. The Railway Convalescent Home Charity, now 'rch' today operates only the Dawlish Home in Devon but continues to provide convalescent care for those in need.

**Liskeard Cottage Hospital**

After his gift of the Falmouth Cottage Hospital Edwards was approached about providing a similar institution for Liskeard. Upon receiving assurance that the Borough Council would maintain the hospital, and a site being offered by Mr Carrington Marshall of St Neots, Edwards agreed. It was, said Edwards, the first hospital to be maintained by a local authority. William Stanton, the current Mayor took the matter in hand and appointed James Hicks to produce the plans and superintend the work. As a freemason, Stanton asked Lord Mount Edgcumbe, Lord Lieutenant and Deputy Grand Master of England, to lay the foundation stone with masonic rites. On 19 May 1895 more than 200 masons, in masonic clothing, headed by the Provincial Grand Master, processed from the Temperance hall to the site. Following an address by the Chaplain, Lord Mount Edgcumbe took a silver trowel to spread the mortar before lowering the stone. Testing for level with plumb, level and square, he declared the stone truly prepared and duly laid. In accordance with masonic custom he then sprinkled corn and poured wine and oil on the stone, as emblems of abundance, strength and gladness, and of healing and harmony.[30]

Hicks' design was to accommodate the patients in a number of small wards, it being the opinion of some eminent medical men of the time that they are preferable to large wards. Being maintained by the Borough Council strict rules and code of practice were introduced. Needy patients from within the borough, a radius of twenty four miles, were admitted free of charge whilst more prosperous folk and people from outlying districts, were required to pay, and thereby help to support the institution. Those suffering from contagious diseases, epilepsy or being 'of unsound mind' were not admitted. Patients could be charged up to two guineas, the amount decided by the management committee, and family members were required to sign an agreement to pay the charges, presumably in case the patient's treatment was not successful. All patients were required to have 'decent clothing and proper change of linen', but no doubt there were charity organisations that would assist with this. Anyone misbehaving was turned out of the hospital and not readmitted without the consent of the committee.

The medical staff, consisting of doctors from all medical firms in the borough, where responsible for the medical management of the hospital but reported to the committee and were expected to abide by the general code of conduct. At least one of these, the 'Surgeon of the Day', was on duty at the hospital at any one time to attend to all accidents and urgent cases brought to the hospital unaccompanied by a doctor.

The matron was responsible for attending to all patients and for the good conduct of nurses, servants and the patients, and was required to live at the hospital. The building also acted as the headquarters of parish nurses, who went out into the community to treat the sick.

The annual report for 1899 showed an income of £195 19s 3d from subscriptions, £9 14s 10d from donations and only £26 10s from inpatients. Outgoings amounted to £275 2s 11d. A total of 66 patients were admitted of which 45 were cured, six 'very much improved', three 'relieved' and six died. Another 12 died 'shortly after'.

During the Great War the hospital accepted a number of wounded Belgians and in 1918 a ward was given over to the Red Cross for the treatment of discharged servicemen.

In 1921 the hospital management committee were successful in obtaining funding from the King Edward's Hospital Fund. A sum of £250 was offered to provide a children's ward, if a similar amount could be raised locally. The money was raised within

three weeks and the scheme went ahead. Electricity did not arrive at the hospital until 1925 but with it came X-ray equipment and in 1927 a much-needed extension was begun. Funded by local donations the extension was opened in the following year, the streets of Liskeard once again being decorated with flags and bunting as the ceremonial party made their way from the Guildhall to the hospital, reminiscent of the day in 1896 when Eleanor Edwards performed the original opening ceremony.

The story of the Liskeard hospital is that of cottage hospitals across the country.

The hospital was much loved and well supported by the people of not only Liskeard, but the whole of south-east Cornwall. Although there were only a small number of beds it had a casualty department and treated patients with a wide range of physical complaints.

Under the NHS, consultants from Plymouth hospitals visited to provide weekly outpatient and operating lists for ENT, gynaecology and orthopaedics, ensuring that there were always doctors available on site. The hospital has been described as a place where the nursing staff knew many of the patients and could talk to them and deliver a personal service; where GPs and specialist consultants could meet informally and discuss patients and develop a team approach to their care; and, during a clinical session with a very junior trainee there was time to teach one to one without continual interruptions – sessions highly valued by all concerned.

Throughout the life of the hospital it received the support of the local community, with events like the carol concert at Christmas, mince pies and a glass of wine shared with doctors, nurses and patients; and the many fundraising events held to purchase additional equipment, such as an ECG machine or the defibrillator, used to save a life within a week of being purchased. Following the tragic death of Dr Taylor a local appeal was launched to purchase a CB radio system, which, in the days before mobile phones, allowed nurses to summon doctors in an emergency. One doctor, at least, entered into the CB world with enthusiasm, 'Breaker, breaker, Green Flash to Mother Hen' crackling over the airwaves.

Denis Wilkins worked at 'Passmores', as it was known, from the late 1970s until it closed in 2002 and has fond memories of the cottage hospital: the matron, who managed the hospital as well as the administration and knew everything about everybody. The band of nurses who would turn their hands to any number of different tasks and carry them out with aplomb. One minute bed-bathing an elderly and perhaps slightly demented patient on the ward, next scrubbed up for a tonsillectomy or hernia repair or dealing with a suspect heart attack in casualty; true multi-tasking. The intimacy of working in a small hospital, where the staff and patients were known to each other, though there was little privacy when treating half a dozen patients in a small ward

*Liskeard Cottage Hospital, Cornwall, from a postcard dated 1910*

'When did you have your heart attack, Mr J'. 'Think it was in 19xx, doctor', 'No, it was 19yy, Tom', would be shouted from the other side of the curtain by the next patient.

In 1996, to celebrate the hospital's centenary, doctors and nurses dressed in period costume for the day, but the inadequacy of the Victorian building to meet the demands of the Community Trust were clear. In 2002 the hospital closed, services transferred to a new hospital building, and 'Passmores' was destined to fade into the history books. However, plans by the Primary Care Trust to demolish the hospital and redevelop the site for housing were met with protests from townsfolk. Concerns were raised about the loss of the town's historic buildings and that this would be the first Passmore Edwards building in Cornwall to be demolished. However, although the Town Council voted to refuse permission for the demolition, the deputy Mayor, Councillor Ferguson, rightly said that the building could only be saved if a new use could be found for it. Being called Passmore Edwards was not sufficient.[31] A suitable use was found as part of a sheltered housing complex, Passmore Edwards Court being completed at the end of 2010.

# Seventeen
# A Caring Community

In the late nineteenth century, there were as many as 150,000 people in Britain suffering from epilepsy. While many were able to live and work normally, for those unable to find or continue in employment life was hard. There was no special provision for epileptics and those without the means of support would find themselves admitted to the workhouse, hospital or even the asylum. As many as 1 in 5 of those in the county asylums were suffering from epilepsy.[1]

In Europe, rural communities began to be set up where epileptics could live and work and in England, in 1892, as a result of an initiative by doctors at the National Hospital for the Paralysed and the Epileptic, the Ladies' Samaritan Society and the Charity Organisation Society, the National Society for the Employment of Epileptics was founded. Their aim was to provide a home, or homes, for those with epilepsy able to work but unable to find employment due to their illness.

The new society started work on two fronts. While one committee searched for a suitable site at which to base the proposed 'colony', another addressed the task of finding the necessary funds. 2,500 appeal leaflets were printed and the Lord Mayor agreed to host a Mansion House meeting in January 1893.

A week before the meeting, Passmore Edwards came forward to add his support to the venture, and money for a farm, but asked that his offer should not be made public until the day of the meeting. After announcing several sizeable subscriptions the Lord Mayor said that he had received a letter from Passmore Edwards in which he offered to purchase for the Society a 'suitable and conveniently situated farm or station of about 100 acres, with the necessary farm buildings and cottages'. Enclosed with the letter was a cheque for £1,000 and a promise to pay the remainder when the farm was selected. His only condition was that the farm should be placed in the hands of suitable trustees and that it should maintained for the permanent benefit of those with epilepsy.

After looking at several farms a decision was made to buy Skippings Farm, near Chalfont St Peter, Buckinghamshire, which was on the market at £3,900. On the edge of the Chiltern hills and only 21 miles from London, Skippings Farm consisted of a farmhouse, 135 acres of good farming land and a deep well promising inexhaustible water supplies. Passmore Edwards added £3,000 to the £1,000 already given and after being invited to join the executive committee gave a further £1,000 towards farm expenses. The trustees, in whom for the farm was vested, were Passmore Edwards,

Edward Montefiore Micholls and John Pearman. Completion of the purchase was accomplished by November 1893 and in recognition Passmore Edwards was asked to become a Vice President of the Society. Both he and Eleanor, who was a committee member and life governor, were to remain directly involved with the Society for the rest of their lives. Edwards fully supported the colony, financially at least, during the early days but his name also ensured that others were encouraged to come forward with both large and small offers of help. The committee suggested calling the colony after Edwards but he declined, perhaps because he knew that the success of the colony was going to need a much greater investment than he alone could provide.

To enable the colony to open as early as possible the building committee erected two temporary iron buildings with several smaller ancillary buildings providing initial accommodation for the staff and the 16 colonists, the first of whom arrived in July 1894.

Once work had started on the 'Iron Home' the building committee started planning the first permanent home. Passmore Edwards again offered to cover the cost, estimated at around £1,600 and designed by the architect Keith Young. Young proposed a two-storey cottage for 18 colonists in two dormitories, the matron and other staff, and Edwards laid the foundation stone in September 1894 marking the official opening of the colony at Chalfont St Peter.

Over the following five years Passmore Edwards was to fund the building of a further four homes and an administrative building.

Passmore Edwards House was built in local brick to the first floor level and roughcast above. Ready for occupation by August of 1895 half of the residents of the Iron Home moved into the new cottage. In 1899 the adult men were transferred to another home funded by Frederick Greene from Cranleigh, Surrey, Greene House, and Passmore Edwards House became a home for boys aged fifteen and over.

The founders had always accepted that women's homes would also be needed and it

*Passmore Edwards House, Chalfont St Peter, the Administritive Centre*

was Passmore Edwards who offered to provide one. The foundation stone of Eleanor House was laid with full Masonic ceremony by Lord Addington, Provisional Grand Master and Lord Lieutenant for Buckinghamshire, with corn, wine and oil being spread on the stone, for abundance, joy and peace. Ernest Shearman designed an attractive building in red brick with half-timbered oak gables and a red tile roof to accommodate twenty-four women and it was completed early in 1897.

To mark the coming Diamond Jubilee of Queen Victoria, in 1897, Edwards offered to fund another home for men, to be designed by Maurice Adams, with drawings appearing in Edwards' journal, *Building News*. The Duchess of Malborough opened Victoria House, while the Duke laid the foundation stones for two further homes, one for boys and the other for girls, later named Pearman and Milton House, both designed by Maurice Adams and funded by Passmore Edwards. They were just three of twenty-five Passmore Edwards's buildings started or completed during the Jubilee year. Each of red brick and stone, the homes were to accommodate twenty-four children in two dormitories, a sick room, kitchen, dining room and playroom. Accommodation was also to be provided for the 'mother' and nurse with an additional two servants accommodated in the girls home. However, by the time that the homes were completed, Parliament had passed the Elementary Education (Defective and Epileptic Children) Act, limiting the size of any home for children to fifteen and meaning that the Society could not use them as planned. The Society decided to open the homes for older children, Milton House being used to accommodate twenty women and girls and Pearman House for twenty-four young men.

Other benefactors provided additional homes and buildings and additional land and as the size of the colony grew so did the need for an administrative building. Several members of the committee wanted to mortgage the farm in order to raise the capital for this and future expansion. Edwards argued strongly against this, increasing his original offer of £2,500 towards such a building, made in 1899, to £3,000. As the opening of the Passmore Edwards Administrative House approached in 1904, Passmore Edwards requested that his first home be renamed the Susan Edwards House, after his mother. Unfortunately, this home was seriously damaged by fire in the 1980s and although reduced to a single storey building and used for a few years further as a sewing room, the building was finally demolished in the 1990s.

Left: *Milton House, a home for boys, named after Milton's association with the area*

Right: *Pearman House, a home for girls, Chalfont St Peter*

Within nine months of the arrival of the first residents at Chalfont an orchard had been planted and vegetable gardens laid out, poultry houses were in production and beehives were installed. Initially the surplus land was rented back to the farmer being taken when needed, but by 1896 the committee were planning to take over the farm themselves, providing work for the residents and supplies for the colony. Additional work opportunities existed in the laundry and dairy and for men in carpentry, basketry and boot making. As the colony expanded services and facilities improved, offering a school for the children, evening classes for the adults, entertainments and sports, as you would expect to find in any village.

**Rosa Honor Lewis's Story**

Rosa was born in June 1857, the tenth of her father's eleven children, the seventh by his third wife Sarah who passed away suddenly when she was three years old. Her father, being left with six children 'farmed out' some to their older siblings' own families but Rosa remained at home, at least until her father died when she was just nine years old. The 1871 census shows Rosa to be at the Orphan Asylum at Marylebone, and in 1881, at 23, an inmate at the Harrow Road Workhouse in Paddington. Although Rosa's family were aware of her position there was little they could do to assist. There is no record of when Rosa was diagnosed as suffering from epilepsy or when or how she was rescued from the workhouse but in 1901 she is listed as being a resident of the colony at Chalfont St Peters where she could find work as a seamstress. Rosa was to live at Chalfont for the next 20 years. Later descendants of a relative who had emigrated to America in 1872 heard of Rosa's condition and sent money to Rosa's niece to provide some comfort for her. Rosa, however, became ill and suffering from stomach cancer was transferred to Paddington General Hospital where she died in 1925.[2]

**The NSE**

The name of the society was changed to the National Society for Epilepsy (NSE) in 1907. The NSE has remained at Chalfont, providing residential care and public education from that time and, since its beginning over a century ago, has been the largest UK charity supporting research into epilepsy.

In 1972, following a report by the Department of Health on the care of patients with epilepsy, a new NHS treatment unit was established at the Chalfont Centre. Especially for patients with severe and complicated epilepsy this unit, the Special Assessment Unit, was run jointly by the National Hospital and the NSE and is the origin of the current NHS clinical inpatient and outpatient service for epilepsy at the Chalfont Centre.

Whilst the Society has to address the issue that the original homes, funded by Passmore Edwards and others, are becoming unsuitable for today's needs the Chalfont Centre will continue to provide care for those with epilepsy.

# Eighteen
# Libellous Claims

Apart from his appearance in court following the Salisbury election Edwards frequently found himself before the court as a result of his newspapers. This was most likely to be following the publication of allegations, about which the subject disagreed and sued for libel. Both the *Echo* and the *Weekly Times & Echo* reprinted stories contained in other newspapers and were occasionally sued when these stories could not be substantiated. He was also party to one court appearance that potentially could have reshaped British history.

## The Prince and the Publisher

On 17 March 1891, the *Echo*, along with the *Daily News*, published a story alleging that the Prince of Wales, later King Edward VII, was involved in a scandal revolving around Sir William Gordon-Cumming cheating during a game of baccarat at which the Prince had acted as banker. It was alleged that Gordon-Cumming, who was a Lieutenant Colonel in the Scots Guards had been forced to sign a statement that he would never play cards again as a condition that the matter was hushed up, and that the Prince was party to the arrangement. When the allegations were leaked Gordon-Cumming, who had denied cheating, sued the other signatories of the statement for libel. In breaking the story both the *Echo* and the *Daily News* scuppered any attempt to deal with the matter out of court when they printed a dispatch from the Press Association that 'There is every reason to believe that the trial of the action instituted by Sir William Gordon-Cumming in connection with the baccarat scandal will be a very short affair. The plaintiffs' determined to go into court, and will not hear of any retraction until his case is laid before a jury and he has, on oath, given an emphatic denial to the charges preferred against him. But, by acting in consonance with the Royal personage who has been mentioned in connection with the matter, it is stated in well-informed circles that there will be no cross examination and no attempt to prove the allegations; that an apology will be tendered, and the business of the jury will be to fix such damages as under the circumstances Sir William Gordon-Cumming may think fit to accept as compensation for the injury done to his character and reputation.'[1]

The defendants' solicitor immediately took action against the Press Association and the printer of the *Echo*, charging them with contempt of court and with damaging their clients' prospects of a fair trial. The printer responded to say that his role was merely to print the paper and that he had no editorial responsibilities. Passmore Edwards also came forward to swear an affidavit in which he accepted full responsibility for the *Echo*'s contents.

Edwards admitted that the *Echo*, like many other evening newspapers, had picked up on the story published in the *Daily News* and printed the Press Association paragraph in an article on betting. As soon as he had been informed of the inaccuracy he acted as quickly as he could to retract the item but the printing system did not permit the article to be withdrawn immediately. Instead the article had a statement added that the facts had been disputed and that the defendants intended to 'fight to the last', an action that the *Echo* supported. He added that the *Echo* used more than seventy articles a day from the Press Association and had hardly ever known of such a problem before. The action taken by Edwards was sufficient to persuade the justices that his actions were fair. The manager of the Press Association was either unable, or unwilling, to disclose just where the information had originated but its publication ensured that the baccarat scandal would be settled in court and that the Prince's part in the affair would be made clear. After seven days in court, of which the Prince attended six, the jury retired, but only for twenty minutes, before returning to state that they found for the defendants – Gordon-Cumming had cheated – a verdict that did not find favour with the general public. The Prince's popularity was already low and with the stories of his gambling and his womanising came rumours of great debt. The Queen attempted to force the Prince to give up gambling but to no avail and on attending the racing at Ascot on the last day of the trial he was met with boos and hissing. The potential effect on the monarchy was discussed across Europe and in the States with the prediction that the monarchy would not survive the death of Queen Victoria. While the *New York Times* reported[2] that 'royalty was a burden to the British taxpayer for which he fails to receive any equivalent'. W T Stead, the editor of the *Review of Reviews*, stated that many country gentlemen were of the opinion that the Prince would never become King, being a 'wastrel, a gambler, and a whoremonger'. It was to be another five years before his popularity returned.

### Colonel Hughes-Hallet

In 'Powder and Shot', an editorial column of the *Weekly Times & Echo*, on 29 May 1892, the following appeared.

> It is reported that Col Hughes-Hallet, formally MP for Rochester, is going to honour a new Parliament with his presence, if he can get returned. He should stand with Sir Charles Dilke for some double-barrelled constituency where the electors are not particular, and then we should have a suitable champion of purity on each side of the House in view of eventualities. Hallet and Dilke, Sodom and Gomorrah might have been proud of such a distinguished pair of representatives.

Hughes-Hallett had been the successful candidate for the Rochester seat at the 1885 election, defeating Passmore Edwards, after which there had been talk of foul play by Hallet but no legal action was taken at the time.

However, this publication in the *Weekly Times & Echo* resulted in Col Hughes-Hallet suing Edwards, the action being heard in the High Court before Mr Justice Hawkins. Edwards admitted the publication, but not the alleged meanings, and paid 40s into court. Though he did not plead justification Edwards gave notice of 'certain matters to be alleged against Col Hughes-Hallet, in mitigation of damages'. The case was widely reported, including in the *West Briton* in Cornwall. From the account that follows it is difficult to understand just what Hughes-Hallett hoped to gain by his action.

Mr Gill, in opening the case for Hughes-Hallett, said the *Weekly Times & Echo* described itself as a Liberal newspaper of political and social progress. The question raised by the case was how far the private life of a man who had at any period occupied a public position was the property of the sensational journalist anxious to make money out of scandalous disclosures. Malice, and only malice, said Mr Gill, inspired the libel. So long ago as 1885 Passmore Edwards contested the parliamentary borough of Rochester. At that election Col Hughes-Hallett had the misfortune to be Mr Edwards's opponent, and had the further misfortune to defeat Mr Edwards. It was impossible, said Mr Gill, for a man to compose a more infamous libel than this, which Mr Edwards published of the man who defeated him. Mr Gill said he did not propose to put his client in the box. In accordance with practice of the time, he simply proposed to prove formally the publication, and to leave it to the other side to introduce outside matter affecting Col Hughes-Hallett's reputation.

Mr Wills, in opening the case for Passmore Edwards, said that the reference to Sodom and Gomorrah as a suitable constituency for Col Hughes-Hallett merely referred to *uncleanliness of living*, and that in respect of this Col Hughes-Hallett's reputation so stank in the public nostrils that nothing that could be said could affect it. Col Hallett, said Mr Wills, had no reputation to protect or guard. For uncleanliness of life, for seduction, for procuring from the lady seduced, by improper representations, the sum of £5,000, for appropriating the property of others, for making false declarations as to money entrusted to him, for all these matters Col Hughes-Hallett's reputation was public property. For (said Mr Wills) in the *Pall Mall Gazette* in September 1887, the whole circumstances were published and no action for libel was taken by Col Hughes-Hallett to protect his reputation then.

The lady in question was a stepdaughter of Col Hughes-Hallett's first wife, the sister of another Member of Parliament and a daughter of a judge. Col Hughes-Hallett had admitted having 'immoral relations' with her when she was 22 and he was a married man. There was, alleged Wills, every reason to believe that the affair, which resulted in the young woman having a baby, had been going on for some years before it was discovered and read extracts of letters from Hughes-Hallett to the woman which showed this to be the case. Col Hughes-Hallett had also procured from the young woman the sum of £5,000, which he falsely claimed he had invested on her behalf. The affair came to light when the young woman was staying at the country house of her uncle. Col Hughes-Hallett arranged for an invitation for himself and in the middle of the night he was discovered in the woman's room by her uncle. Hughes-Hallett was kicked out of the house, then and there.

Mr Wills, said that this was the reputation which Col Hughes-Hallett sought to protect. The affair had been published in the *Pall Mall Gazette* and copied into other papers throughout the country and never challenged. All Col Hughes-Hallett had done was to offer the young woman's brother the 'satisfaction' of a duel.

According to Wills the affair did not end at that point as Hughes-Hallett had promised to marry the woman and, having his eye on the £40,000 which he knew the woman possessed, he tried to persuade her to continue the affair to give his wife an opportunity of obtaining a divorce. Wills went on to tell of Col Hughes-Hallett's dealings with two elderly relatives of his wife, a Mrs von Schomberg and Miss Page, who had entrusted him with money which, instead of investing he had used to secure his two elections for Rochester.

Kibblewhite, the editor and manager of the *Weekly Times & Echo*, and Passmore Edwards appeared in court. Kibblewhite said that it was he that had written the paragraph objected to and that though Edwards was the proprietor he took no part in preparing the paper for publication. Kibblewhite received information that Col Hughes-Hallett would stand for the new Parliament, and therefore he wrote the paragraph in question. He said that he did not intend to impute that Hughes-Hallett had been guilty of any criminal practices but that he was not fit to represent any constituency that cared for the moral character or honour of its representative. When he wrote the paragraph he had no malice or ill feeling of any kind towards Col Hughes-Hallet.

When Passmore Edwards was called as a witness he confirmed that he was the proprietor of the *Weekly Times & Echo*. He added that when he contested the Rochester election it had cost him £250. This brought the response 'Then I am not surprised that you did not succeed: it is not sufficiently liberal' and laughter from the court.

In summing up Mr Wills said Col Hughes-Hallett first obtained £5,000 by false pretences from a girl of honourable family. Then he debauched and degraded her, then he insulted her by denying that he was the father of her child, then he debauched the constituency of Rochester by spending £1,100 in secret service – which meant bribery – then to cover the money, he sold £2,000 worth of property, which two elderly ladies had placed in his charge; then when one of these elderly ladies died he insulted her memory by insinuating that there were confidential relationships between himself and her, and so on. Col Hughes-Hallett's reputation was so bad that nothing that could be said of him could injure it, and Col Hughes-Hallett had no right to ask for consideration from any man.

After Mr Justice Hawkins had told the jury that 'A man was entitled to damages to the extent to which his character was injured' the jury, after deliberating for only twenty five minutes, found for the defendant, adding that the reference to Sodom and Gomorrah was 'ill-advised'.

**Sir Richard Burton**

Whereas Edwards was taken to court on many occasions as a result of his publications one event was to lead to a demand for satisfaction in an entirely different way. When in 1862 he wrote an article condemning Burton, then Captain Burton, for his role in an alleged insult to a London Scientific Society, Burton's response was to send a brother officer to see Edwards, and hand him a challenge to a duel. He had to accept the challenge, offer an apology or do nothing. Burton, as a professional soldier, was presumably a good shot, Edwards' experience of guns merely an afternoon's hunting as a lad, which he later regretted. Edward's decision was to do nothing, and he, thankfully, heard nothing more from Burton.

# Nineteen
# Education, Education, Education

Passmore Edwards' name is usually followed by the words 'the Victorian Philanthropist' and his contribution to society thought to be merely through his libraries, often seen as places of recreation. Edwards' primary concern was, however, for moral welfare, the health and social development of the country and at the base of all this was education – essential to our wellbeing as a nation. Almost everything he did was to improve the education prospects of the working classes. He believed in a strong, self-sufficient England as head of the British Empire and he often contrasted the state of education and industrial advances in England with those in Germany and America. Edwards considered that education was essential to both the individual and the state and that there was, and always would be, an increasing demand for educated men and women to keep our industries going, and to maintain our institutions and our national way of life. Though he shared an interest in the issues that concerned his contemporary, Samuel Smiles[1] – Chartism, free trade, universal suffrage and parliamentary reform – Edwards' promotion was beyond the writing of books extolling the virtue of individual self-help. Edwards wished not only to educate but also to provide the means of education. The early publications, the *Public Good*, the *Biographical Magazine*, encyclopaedia and almanacs, were all aimed at the working classes and self-improvement; the low prices making them affordable, but leading to Edwards' bankruptcy. The *English Mechanic* and *Building News*, were hugely significant in the field of adult education; his newspapers, the *Weekly Times & Echo* and the *Echo*, priced so that all could afford them.

Escape from poverty lay in the freedom gained through education and 'if he could fund the ladder the poor would climb'.

Combining his hatred of war with his love for education he said 'I would like to see a Minister of Education as well equipped and paid as a Minister of War and he would expend as much money all round on education as we now spend on military or naval defence; as I believe that in diffusion of knowledge and in knowledge wisely applied, will be found, in the present race of nations, and in the near future, the chief source of national security. But Parliament, which hesitates to grant an additional shilling for educational purposes, will grant at the bidding of a Minister an additional pound for the Army or Navy or both'.[2]

The Elementary Education Act of 1870 had set the framework of schooling for children up to the age of twelve and so, with a couple of exceptions, it was the needs of adult education, or at least for those above the age of 12, that Edwards sought to fulfil; as he did when as a young man he started a school for the uneducated men and boys of his home village of Blackwater.

In Cornwall the institutes included facilities for technical education, the Hayle Institute included science laboratories, classrooms and a library, and the authorities at both Bodmin and Launceston took advantage of Passmore Edwards' offer of funding a free library by incorporating a technical and art school into the building. In Falmouth Edwards' funding of a library gave the Borough Council the opportunity to build both new municipal offices and an art and science school. Elsewhere his contribution was wide and varied, including schools, colleges, a settlement, lecture programs and scholarships. Asquith[3] said of Edwards, in 1902, that he had done more than any single Englishman to help the people to equip and educate themselves for civic and social duty.

**Helston Art & Science School**

The Helston Corporation responded to Passmore Edwards' offer of a free library by asking for an arts and science school instead. He readily agreed and a part of the garden of the former Helston grammar school was acquired freehold from Captain Rogers of Penrose, on the payment of one shilling a year. Edwards offered to pay the £1,600 construction costs but, as usual, expected the community to pay £300 for the furnishings and fittings. He even suggested where the corporation might go to secure donations, mentioning Lord Robartes and John Williams of Scorrier.

Although there are four foundation stones set into the front of the school, they are not engraved, as there was no ceremony to lay them. Although the date 1897 is displayed above the door, it was 12 May 1899, more than 12 months after the school was completed, that Edwards visited Helston to formally open it.[4] It was his first, and probably his only visit to the town, James Hicks, the architect, having made the necessary arrangements with the Town Council.

As was the Cornish fashion, the Mayor – Mr E A Pengilly, members of the Corporation, mayors from other Cornish towns, freemasons and members of Friendly Societies, ministers of religion, magistrates and many other worthies joined in the procession from the town hall to the new science and art schools.[5] Presented with an engraved silver key Edwards declared the school open, saying that if the key typified the school's beauty and utility then it would answer its purpose.

With the formal opening of the school completed the party withdrew for a luncheon, and the customary speeches and toasts. In response to a vote of thanks Passmore Edwards said that he had been pleased to erect a science and art school in Helston, because 'the building in the broadest sense was public property'. Liskeard was the only town in Cornwall, and as far as he knew in the country, to take under its control a hospital as municipal property, and now the Corporation of Helston followed with the science and art schools; accepting an obligation to maintain them out of public funds. This, he said, was a step in the right direction for true socialism. This he called Corporation Socialism and 'the more they had of it the better'.

Though he declared himself a loyal member of the Liberal party, he did not use the word 'radical'; in later life he moved towards the new socialist movement. He supported the trades unions, subscribed towards supporting industrial action, promoting the new socialists such as Keir Hardie, who he praised for his honesty and resolution, and funding Independent Labour Party candidates, though there is no evidence that he joined the ILP.

The festivities at Helston continued into the evening with seventy ladies and gentlemen sitting down to dinner at the Angel Hotel. During the dinner Edwin Durning Lawrence, Liberal Unionist MP for Truro, who presented the schools with a lecture table for the technical school and two scholarships for the art school, spoke about Parliament and the House of Lords. On hearing Lawrence say that the House of Lords had always been filled with great artists, like Lord Leighton, great poets, like Tennyson, and great men of science, like Lord Kelvin, Edwards replied that these were exceptions, showing his general dislike of those that populated what he called the 'House of Landlords'. When Lawrence continued in his praise of the present government, Edwards interrupted him to ask whether this was an electioneering speech. 'No Sir,' said Lawrence. 'Well I object to it,' replied Edwards. Lawrence, trying to recover his position, said that he had perhaps been led astray by talking as he did. He only desired to say that he would always do what he could for Cornwall. He supported the Government because he thought it was doing the best for the country. Edwards was not to be won over. Desiring not to throw a note of discord into such a gathering, he said that he was 'a Party man', a strong party man, but he had never, in any speech he had made on any similar occasion showed to which party he belonged. They should remember that they were all assembled as Cornishmen, as Englishmen and as citizens of the British Empire, rather than to show any proclivity to one side or the other. Although this was met with applause, the *West Briton* commented the following week that the harmony of the evening had been sadly disturbed by Edwards' rebuke and that 'opinions will differ as to whether he had been justified in his action'. Certainly Lawrence did not seem to be too upset by the occurrence as the following week, when speaking at the Royal Institute for Cornwall, meeting in Truro, he spoke of them being near a great educational building, the new technical school, founded by a man who was not yet a styled saint but had built these great establishments in many parts of the country. He referred, of course, to Passmore Edwards.

*The former Art & Science School, Penrose Road, Helston*

The Helston School was soon over taken by amendments to the education acts and, taken over by the County Council, it was enlarged in about 1904 and again 10 years later to form a County secondary school, remaining in use until the 1970s. Since then it has been used as a community centre. In 2008 the Helston Town Council gave the community centre management committee notice to quit, the reason given being that they believed the original deeds for the land were subject to a covenant restricting the use of the building to arts and science. The fact that the community centre was home to many local organisations including a drama group and a youth music group seemed to be of no consequence. The management committee did not accept the views of the Town Council, which offered no alternative accommodation, and took the case to the courts. This resulted in an offer to the community groups to purchase the building. But negaotiations broke down and the centre was due to close early in 2011.

**Cornwall Central Technical Schools, Truro**

The establishment of an institution to promote technical education in Cornwall had been proposed by Sir Charles Lemon in 1836, and he offered a substantial sum of money to support it. However the offer was not taken up and although another attempt was made in the Jubilee year of 1887 it was to be more than 60 years before the Institute was created.[6]

It was Silvanus Trevail, then Mayor of Truro, who saw an opportunity to realise Lemon's scheme. During the negotiations with Passmore Edwards over the building of Truro free library, which did not make any provision for technical education, Trevail put his ideas to Edwards and was successful in receiving a promise of £5,000 towards the cost. Trevail then set about gathering financial support wherever is was available; from the Department of Education, £500 from the Honourable Drapers Company, £600 from the County Council Technical Instruction Committee; ultimately tripling Edwards' offer. But Trevail had more than the costs to deal with. Apart from those that distrusted Trevail's methods, opposition came from other boroughs, where Councillors resented 'County' money being channelled into Truro, whilst Truronians feared the institute would become a white elephant, or more likely an albatross, a financial burden on the ratepayers.[7]

The foundation stone was laid with full masonic ceremony. As usual a half-day holiday was declared and the crowds turned out to see the event. More than 400 masons came together from all parts of Cornwall to process the short distance from the municipal buildings to the school site. The new Mayor, Alderman Dorrington, lead the procession and conducted the proceedings, welcoming Edwards as the only freeman of the city. On the invitation of the Acting Provincial Grand Master, Edwards took the engraved silver trowel and declared the corner stone 'plumb, level and square' and 'properly prepared and truly laid'. In accordance with masonic rights, corn was scattered and wine and oil poured on the stone before Edwards handed the plans to the architect and charged him to see that they were faithfully carried out.[8]

During the speeches Edwards reminded those present that some fifteen years previously the Prince of Wales had laid the corner stone of the cathedral with similar ritual. Whilst the cathedral was dedicated to religion, the building they had just commenced would be devoted to education 'of head and hand'. Whereas every small town and many villages enjoyed a chapel or church, and often both, there were very few institutions where the industrial arts were taught. The Central Technical Institution, which he suggested should be dedicated to Sir Charles Lemon, was necessary in the interest of both skilled craftsmen and the community at large. England, he said, with its mineral and geographic advantages, and its judicious mixture of races should be first and foremost in the broad and ever widening field of industrial action, a sentiment as much matched to today's challenges as of those of our late-Victorian forefathers.

Completion of the schools was delayed by administrative problems but eventually the building was ready and opened by Lord Mount Edgcumbe, Lord Lieutenant and chairman of the County Council, in October 1899. Adjacent to and in line with the library, and in the same Plymouth limestone with Bath stone dressings and of a similar English Renaissance style, the school included chemistry, physics and biology laboratories as well as metal workshop, art rooms and a museum. Trevail announced that 500 science students and a similar number of arts students had already enrolled at the Institute. In importance it was on a par with the formation of the Camborne School of Mines, established by Lemon, and Falmouth College of Art.

**John's Story**

John left the Truro Combined Technical School in 1956 aged of 15, and thought his association with Passmore Edwards had finished, other than occasionally to pass below the benefactor's name as he visited the adjacent public library. Little was he to realise that he would benefit from the Passmore Edwards legacy a few years later. In 1964 John was involved in a car accident, which resulted in serious injury requiring a three-month stay in the City Hospital, formally the Cornwall Infirmary to which Edwards had given the convalescent home at Perranporth. And it was at the Convalescent Home that John spent the final six weeks of his treatment and recuperation.

*The Cornwall Technical School, now part of the Truro Community Library*

When Truro's new comprehensive school at Penair opened in September 1979, and the Penwethers School became the Richard Lander school, the old 'tech' in Union Place was closed. Many of the rooms used by the school were adapted for use by the library service in 1982 and others provided accommodation for voluntary services organisations. Fortunately a proposal in the 1990s to sell off the two buildings for retail purposes was strongly resisted and a £1.4 million restoration of the now combined library and school has recently been completed to once again provide a building with which Passmore Edwards would be well pleased. Trevail's Tudor Renaissance design and the stained glass screen showing the emblems of the former Cornish boroughs, now combined in the new unitary authority that is Cornwall Council, mark the county's history, the IT hub, the hot-desk facilities offered to budding young entrepreneurs and the engagement with local community activists, are a sign of a progressive Cornwall. Passmore Edwards often considered the day when Cornwall could no longer rely on its mineral resources. He would surely approve of the part his buildings continue to play in the county's future; 'an architectural ornament to Truro and a source of commercial advantage to the district'.

**Art School and Technical Institute, Camberwell**

Sir John Millais, President of the Royal Academy, was prevented from laying the Foundation stone to the South London Technical Institution through illness, so in July 1896 it was Passmore Edwards who declared the memorial stone well and truly laid. The art school's history is closely linked to that of the adjacent South London Art Gallery, with which Edwards was also involved. Speaking at the laying of the foundation stone to the library and lecture hall he funded three years earlier, Edwards anticipated the time when the gallery would also be associated with a technical art school. Had he already decided that his money would bring this about?

*Camberwell College of Arts*

The art school was designed by Maurice Adams and opened in January 1898 by Edward Poynter, President of the Royal Academy, and dedicated to the memory of Lord Leighton, first President of the gallery. Edwards gave £5,000 towards the costs. Adams' design, in Portland stone and red brick, comprised four large studios and workshops for craftwork, which were located in the half basement. The style of the building is Renaissance, richly decorated with carvings by William, later Sir William, Goscombe John, who also executed the sculptured pediment that contains life-size figures representing architecture, sculpture and painting. Originally, the college offered classes that included architecture, cabinet design, woodcarving, wood block and stencil cutting, and after the Great War a fine art department was created.

After the Second World War the college saw an exciting period with several eminent artists teaching at Camberwell. The abstract painter Robert Medley was appointed Head of Painting in the 1960s and during this period the school had a thriving art history department. In 1973, the School expanded into a modern purpose-built block next to the original premises.

In 1986 Camberwell School of Arts and Crafts became part of the London Institute, an association of London's art, design, fashion and media schools, and in 1989 it was renamed the Camberwell College of Arts. Five years later the London Institute gained University status.

Long regarded as one of the country's leading art and design colleges with filmmaker Mike Leigh, musician Humphrey Lyttleton and artist Sir Terry Frost having studied there it is now known as the University of the Arts, London. After more than 100 years, this element of Passmore Edwards' legacy remains one of the world's foremost art and design institutions.

**London School of Economics**

On 30 May 1895 Beatrice Webb wrote in her diary 'Yesterday the formal opening of the new building of the School of Economics, a day of satisfaction for Sidney, Hewins and myself, Our child born nearly seven years ago in the back rooms in John Street with a few hundred a year from the Hutchinson Trust, despised by the learned folk as a young man's fad is now fully grown and ready to start in the world on its own account'.[9]

The will of Henry Hutchinson, a member of the Fabian Society, established a trust, with Beatrice's husband, Sidney Webb, as chairman – to dispose of the residue of his estate. When Hutchinson committed suicide in 1894 Webb decided to use the £10,000 available to establish a Central School of Economic and Political Science. Despite objections from leading Fabians, such as Bernard Shaw and Ramsay MacDonald,[10] who considered that the money should be used to promote Fabian socialism, Webb pressed on, formed a committee and appointed William Hewins as first director of the school.

Initially renting premises at 9 John Street, Adelphi, Hewins opened the School in October 1895, offering twelve courses of evening lectures and a three-year course in economics, economic history, and statistics. More than 200 students enrolled in the first term and this had risen to 281, including 87 women, by the end of the session. The following year, the school moved to more spacious premises at 10, Adelphi Terrace and with that move came the establishment of the British Library of Political Science. Seeking a permanent home for both the school and the library, the Webb's listed potential benefactors and launched their appeal; Beatrice wrote, 'In vain I flattered Passmore Edwards'.

Sidney, who had previously written for the *Echo*, was, at first, no more successful, as correspondence held at the London School of Economics' archives show. At the beginning of February 1899 Edwards wrote to Sidney to say that although he agreed with Webb's aims, he could not see how he could help. The Library Acts had been adopted in Bow, Bromley, Limehouse and Plumstead and they were all knocking on his door for substantial assistance, or in other words to provide the necessary building. Should he build four libraries at £5,000 each or spend £20,000 in the way Webb suggested. Besides, he also had pressing appeals before him to build polytechnics at Hackney, Camden and Brixton. However, the very next day Webb received a further letter from Edwards, asking how many rooms would be needed, and how large, so that he could judge the costs involved; and a few days later, after further representations from Webb, another letter arrived to say that he hadn't sufficient knowledge of the issues and asked Webb to visit. By the end of February Edwards wrote to say that he was prepared to provide a building and suggested that the trustees should include the Rev Mandell Creighton, Bishop of London. The conditions of his offer, drafted by Webb, included that there should be adequate provision for evening study; recognition by the University of London of the subjects taught; and that the London County Council should provide adequate support from its annual grant to the university. With these assurances Edwards confirmed his offer of £10,000 for the building in a trust deed between himself, the Bishop of London, R Haldane QC, and Sidney Webb.

Webb's work appeared to have been done, but with Edwards' close involvement in every one of his bequests, negotiations were to be both long and tasking. After telling Edwards of an offer of a site by the London County Council, he asked to see the site and questioned the length of lease the Council were offering. It was usual that Edwards required a freehold site to ensure the future of the building. At Blooms-bury he had reluctantly accepted a 999 lease for the site for the Settlement and now he was being asked to accept an eighty year lease, for a building that would be 'for national and perpetual use'. When the Council asked that he provide security on his offer he again objected, saying that this was the first time and last time, he would do this. 'My word is as good as my bond,' he said,'and I should not and would not make a promise without fulfilling it'.[11] But again Webb reas-

*Passmore Edwards Hall, London School of Economics*

sured Edwards, who agreed to transfer 135 National Bank shares, 120 Union Bank of London shares and 110 London Joint Stock Bank shares, a total of £11,500 as security. But even then, progress did not run smoothly. In order to ensure that the land would, indeed, be used for education purposes, the Council's legal advisors recommended that the site should be purchased specifically for purposes of technical education. The disadvantage would be that the Council was restricted in the period of lease it could then offer to the trustees. Edwards had long distrusted the legal profession, having the view that lawyers generally managed to get the best end of the stick, 'whoever may be hurt by its use'.[12] Whilst he had reluctantly accepted a lease of eighty years he was now being asked to consent to a lease of only twenty one years, after which the Council might take possession of a building that had cost £15,000. 'I am quite prepared to fulfil my contract to the letter. Am I not justified in expecting similar treatment from the Trustees?' Webb was again successful in placating Edwards who, within a few days, agreed to a tender being accepted for construction of the building, but confirming that his contribution would be limited to £10,000.[13]

The Bishop of London laid the foundation stone in July 1900 and Edwards paid the architects certificates as they were presented. By then the school had been admitted to the newly established faculty of Economics and Political Science within the University of London and in the year of opening, in 1902, the school was incorporated, with Sidney Webb as chairman of the governors.

Passmore Edwards Hall, in Clare Market, designed by Maurice Adams, had cost £18,000, Edwards being persuaded to add another £1,000 to his original offer; Lord Rothschild giving £5,000; and the remainder coming from a long list of other subscribers. In the early years the majority of the classes were held in the evening with regular daytime classes not established until 1906. Expansion was rapid over the next decade, there were 2,137 students by 1912, and the requirement for additional accommodation needed to be addressed. Though delayed by the First World War, construction started in 1920 and by the start of the Second World War accommodation had more than doubled. As part of this expansion the Passmore Edwards building was reconstructed and incorporated into the new buildings, now totally unrecognisable. The only links to the School's origins is in the Student Services Centre, created in 2002, the Passmore Edwards Room, and the foundation stone.

It cannot be argued that without Passmore Edwards' money the LSE would not have developed, Webb's determination would have overcome such a set-back, but it may have taken a number of years before the money was raised and this may have affected the way in which the school developed. Over the years the LSE has greatly influenced British society, developing relationships in politics, business and the law. Amongst those that have attended the LSE in recent years are Ed Miliband, Cherie Blair and Shami Chakrabarti, director of the civil rights organisation, Liberty.

**London Society for the Extension of University Training**

By 1900, 400 towns and districts had adopted the Free Library Acts. Though free libraries gave working-class people an access to literature they had little knowledge, or instruction on what they should be reading, and with the early indicator system, where the books were chosen and collected from a service counter, the potential reader had no introduction to the work they were choosing. Even where the books were available to browse there was little help in book selection. There was clearly a need to teach people not only what was available but also what to read. However, the wording of the Library Acts did not permit the authorities to spend library money on this aspect.

Passmore Edwards funded a series of lectures to be given by the London Society for the Extension of University Training at six of the free libraries in London; at Hoxton, Southwark, Brixton, Peckham, Fulham and Battersea.

The free course of lectures consisted of ten addresses by well-known University Extension lecturers on the great novelists of the nineteenth century and the success of the experiment was immediate and encouraging. The lectures were open to all and many were turned away at Brixton and Camberwell because of lack of room even though additional tables and chairs were provided wherever possible and many were allowed to stand.

Following each lecture a discussion class took place and weekly questions were set, the lecturers correcting and returning the papers sent to them. At the end of the course of lectures those who had submitted coursework were admitted to an exam with successful candidates awarded the certificate of the LSEUT. Between a third and a half of those who attended the lectures went on to attend the classes and examination.

At Fulham it was noted that the audience consisted largely of clerks and small trades people, with a fair sprinkling of manual workers and that the quality of the written work was higher than had been expected. At Southwark the audience was more from the lower and working classes, said to be 'intelligent but with little literary education'.[14]

One of the attendees at a course run by the Society, a course entitled 'The Chemistry of Everyday Life' was a fourteen-year-old office boy, Albert Mansbridge. After completing the course, and being awarded a certificate with distinction, Albert went on to make considerable further use of University Extension lectures and in 1903 created an 'Association to Promote the Higher Education of Working Men', later renamed the Workers' Educational Association, today the UK's largest voluntary sector provider of adult education.

Edwards similarly provided the Royal Historical Society with £100 a year for three years, for lectures on Historical Methods, again aimed at the working classes.

### Contributions of Books

It became an accepted fact that the gift of a Passmore Edwards library would be accompanied by a number of books, usually 500 or 1,000 volumes, and he offered 1,000 volumes to any library that was opened in London. Yet the gift of books had commenced before even the offer of 500 books that accompanied the Blackwater Institute and would continue for the rest of his life; going to those that occupied his buildings and many other institutions with which he had no direct connection. In total, he probably supplied as many as 80,000 books during his long life.

An opportunity to create a library at a convalescent home, working men's club, village institute, school, hospital, or nurse's homes was seldom ignored and contributions of between 50 and 2,000 volumes were distributed in Cornwall, London and across the country. At Christmas 1883 he presented 2,600 books to schoolchildren in his constituency at Salisbury and in his last years he worked with the Rev E W Matthews to construct the Ocean library for the British and Foreign Sailors Society and was to provide 5,000 books for its use.

The books donated were from a standard list, although this was enlarged and amended over time. The printed catalogue of the small library at Blackwater gave an insight into the subjects covered in the standard list, which we can assume reflected on Edwards' own interests.[15] Best[16] recorded that Shakespeare, of course, and the great authors of the time were included – Charles Dickens, George Eliot, Sir Walter Scott, Thackeray, Mrs Henry Wood, but not Jane Austen; and the poets – Keats, Byron, Pope, Dryden, Shelley and Milton, together with 'some anthologies and a few classic texts'. More than 30 volumes each were listed from Thomas Carlyle and Lord Lytton whilst the works of the historians: Gibbon, Macaulay and Hume, were included together with 'some deep theology, but not a great deal'. Only one book of particular Cornish interest was included, the life of the evangelist Billy Bray, who had lived nearby. Overall, Best described it as 'a popular library, half the books being of the useful, informative kind – biology, astronomy, games, pets, history, geography, 'the wonders of nature', famous voyages, famous men and women and some popular morality and religion'. This was a library designed more to educate than entertain.

The Passmore Edwards Collection at the Friendly Societies Convalescent Home, opened in 1899, included a wider range and more contemporary literature. Wilkie Collins was there, as was Mrs Gaskell, the Glasgow born novelist William Black and Mary Elizabeth Braddon. The biographical section now included the *Life of George Eliot* and, of course, the life of Ralph Waldo Emerson, the writer to which Edwards said he owed more than to any other, 'one of the luminaries of the human race'.

# Twenty
# Art Galleries & Museums

Just as his libraries often included art and science schools there was often space for a museum, providing accommodation for local collections. These museums have long gone, although the Camborne library retains a few exhibits in the upstairs reference section.

*The restored and reopened South London Gallery, 2010*

**South London Art Gallery**

William Rossiter, born at Holborn in 1831, was the son of a portmanteau maker and

educated himself by attending the Workingmen's College. In 1868 when the South London Workingmen's College opened, Rossiter was its first manager and after the college was extended to include a free library, Rossiter borrowed pictures to hang on the library walls to create a gallery during the summer months. When the gallery increased in popularity Rossiter moved, first to Battersea, then, in 1889, to live at Portland House in Peckham Road, Camberwell, where he constructed a new gallery in the garden with support from Gladstone and Lord Leighton, President of the Royal Academy and Trustee of the National Portrait Gallery. At that time the area was described as the very heart of the great intellectual desert of South London.[1]

The South London Fine Art Gallery was opened in 1891 with 4,000 visiting every weekday and as many as 2,000 on Sundays, all ordinary working people and children. At the first annual meeting Passmore Edwards offered £3,000 to build a lecture hall and library, declaring that he wished to support the gallery due to three factors. Firstly the gallery was open on Sundays – 'they must liberalise and emancipate their Sundays'. Secondly, entrance was free and finally young children were not only welcomed, but also provided with both instruction and recreation. He was more concerned with the gallery's contribution to the moral wellbeing of the inhabitants of South London than the quality of the collections. Designed by Sir Ernest George and dedicated to Lord Leighton, the Passmore Edwards Hall was opened in March 1893, by which time the gallery was receiving a grant from the parochial trustees so reducing the financial instability. By 1896 the gallery had been transferred to the St Giles Vestry, passing to the Borough of Camberwell and finally the Borough of Southwark. In 1898 Edwards funded an extension to the gallery, designed by Maurice Adams, giving an entrance onto the Peckham Road, office space and linking to the art school to which Edwards also contributed.

When war broke out in 1939 the gallery was handed over for use by the Ministry of Supply and in 1941 the Passmore Edwards lecture hall and library was severely damaged during an air raid and was demolished.

After the war the gallery reopened to house collections of Victorian works of art and a twentieth century collection of local artists but in June 2010 a £1.8 million development project was completed extending the gallery into the adjacent terraced house and constructing the Clore Education Centre on the site of the Passmore Edwards Lecture Hall.

**Whitechapel Art Gallery**

After Canon Barnett and his wife moved to St Jude's, Whitechapel, in 1872, they began to hold art exhibitions, aimed at the working-class residents of Whitechapel, borrowing exhibits from artists and friends. These free exhibitions ran for twenty years with growing popularity, to the point where Barnett wanted to build a permanent picture gallery. He chose a site adjacent to the Whitechapel library, which had been funded by Passmore Edwards, and Barnett naturally included Edwards in his appeal to finance his new social education project. Edwards offered £5,000, 'sufficient to build a suitable gallery' and another £1,000 towards the cost of the land and later offered a further £1,200 but then withdrew that offer. But more on that later.

When the Whitechapel Art Gallery opened in 1901 it was an immediate success. 206,000 visited the first exhibition and in 1906, 150,000 attended an exhibition of Jewish art and antiquities. With only a small endowment from the London Board of Charities, the gallery depended on donations from visitors, which sadly did not exceed £100 during that first exhibition, less than a quarter of that needed to keep the doors open.[2] The gallery continued to struggle for many years, the trustees at one time considering asking the London County Council to take over control and it was not until after the Second World War that the situation improved and by the mid 1970s the Whitechapel was considered as the major independent gallery in London.

Originally known as the workingman's art gallery the Whitechapel has since become internationally acclaimed for its exhibitions of modern and contemporary art exhibiting artists including Pablo Picasso, Jackson Pollock, Gilbert & George and Lucian Freud.

**My little weakness**

It has often been written that Passmore Edwards' withdrew his offer of a further £1,200 because Canon Barnett refused to name the Whitechapel Gallery after him. A study of the correspondence in the Whitechapel Gallery archives shows that the matter is not so straightforward.

Whereas the Whitechapel library was already under construction before Canon Barnett took Edwards to see it, he approached Edwards early on with his project to build a picture gallery. Edwards had previously told the wife of the artist Frederick Watts that he would like to 'do for Whitechapel what I had done for the South London Art Gallery' but 'the time and my ability to do so had not yet arrived'. Barnett's plans were not, however, to Edwards' liking; they were too big. Edwards proposed a gallery as an addition to Toynbee Hall, as the library and hall in South London had been an addition to the art gallery. 'I can't carry out your big scheme and must confine my attention to smaller ones,' he was to write – he was 'to do it in that way or not at all'.

Eventually Edwards agreed to give £5,000, the amount that Barnett said the gallery would cost and which Edwards considered sufficient to build a gallery in keeping with his own criteria. But the plans drawn up by Harrison Townsend were costed out at over £7,000 and an appeal was launched to raise the extra money. In addition the site, adjacent to the free library was valued at £6,000. Edwards thought that Townsend was an extravagant architect, insisting that his own architect, presumably Maurice Adams, could build a suitable building for

*The Whitechapel Art Gallery, opened in 1901*

£5,000, but went along with Canon Barnett's proposals, even to offering another £1,000 towards the land. Having the library and the gallery side by side, 'as brother and sister Institutions', appealed to Edwards. 'As I have been associated with the public library movement and as the Whitechapel library was the first I provided' and, as he had already pointed out he had paid the entire cost of the library, 'I shall indeed esteem it an honour to have my name associated with it'.

In order to secure an endowment on the gallery Barnett applied to the Central Governing Body of the London Board of Charities for assistance and in accordance with their wishes arranged for a board of trustees to be appointed. The Board also wanted confirmation that the capital costs of the construction had been guaranteed and Barnett wrote to ask Edwards whether he would be prepared to pay his contribution before building had started. Edwards was very unhappy about this suggestion, which he took personally. 'You may depend on my performing my promise but I do not see why I should be called upon to sell stock without commercial advantage. That is not the way in which I have made the money which I am trying to utilise for the public advantage'.

Eventually he was to provide a cheque for the full amount offered and within a few months, hearing that another £1,200 was needed to complete and furnish the building Edwards offers to provide it, 'on receipt of builders certificates'.

It was not until around the time chosen to lay the foundation stone that things began to go seriously wrong. Edwards had suggested that Lord Peel, the Speaker in the House of Commons, should be invited to do the honours but finding that Lord Peel's name would be inscribed on the stone, whereas Edwards' name was not to appear anywhere on the building, Edwards demanded an explanation and was absent from the ceremony.

Passmore Edwards had been disappointed that his help in funding the Whitechapel library was not recognised on the exterior of the building and Mr Plant, the Shoreditch librarian, had told Barnett of this disappointment. Barnett replied that if Edwards contributed to further developing the library or in providing another building in the area then he would reopen the matter. When Edwards was approached about the gallery, and gave £5,000, Barnett, surprisingly, did not connect this with his previous undertaking and it is clear that Edwards did not, at this stage, apply any such condition. When Edwards' concerns were raised, Barnett, having received donations from other parties, considered it too late to name the gallery after Edwards. And Townsend rejected Edwards' suggestion that his name should appear across the front of the two buildings 'The Passmore Edwards Free Library and Picture Gallery', as the style of the two buildings was so different.

As far as Edwards was concerned he had offered to pay for the whole building and had not been party to the decision to adopt a design that was to cost more than half as much again. Not only that but he had given, without being asked, the sum of £1,000 towards the land and offered the £1,200 needed to complete the scheme. 'I assure you I would not have done so had I thought that my name was to be omitted altogether, and of which I was not aware till two or three days before the foundation stone laying ceremony. I am prepared to do all I promised (and I have already advanced to Whitechapel nearly £13,000 in the shape of money and books) provided the understanding referred to be carried out. If not then the best thing to do is to say no more about it. You are the master of the situation.'

Amongst the almost daily correspondence taking place between Edwards and Barnett, Edwards makes his point by sending copies of pictures of the 'sixtieth building I have provided' and 'illustrations of nine other buildings that owe their existence to me and which will be opened or commissioned this year' and describing the good time he had at the opening of the convalescent home he provided for the Friendly Societies at Herne Bay.

Townsend, eager to have his plans published – Edwards' *Building News* was asking for copies – suggested an arrangement on the front of the gallery that 'would include his name yet not make it every eye and centre of the building as he wants'. Another suggestion is an inscribed stone, recognising that the gallery was erected 'chiefly through the munificence of J Passmore Edwards Esq' but instead Barnett arranged for the library committee to agree to naming the adjacent library the Passmore Edwards free library and to have this inscribed upon the front elevation, seven years after the library opened. He wrote asking to meet with Edwards, instead of the seemingly endless correspondence but Edwards refused – 'I am inclined to think that we have given the matter too much consideration already'. He referred to his desire to have his name appear on the buildings as 'my little weakness' but when rebuffed by Barnett over this, who regreted that Edwards 'cared to blot with a name charity so noble as yours', Edwards asked 'does a man who preaches a sermon, or a dozen sermons, for the benefit of others and afterwards publishes them in his name, "blot" that name? I think not. And if the same man or another erects an institution for a similar purpose with his name on it why should he be judged by a different standard? One man by performance in duty in Church or State gets recognition and promotion. Why should not another man who may promote the public good in some other form receive some other form of recognition? I may without egotism say that I do many things from which I neither desire nor hope to receive credit or reward in any form'.

In 1895, three years before the argument over the Whitechapel gallery developed, there had been considerable opposition in Falmouth to the building of the Passmore Edwards free library. Some of those against had suggested that Edwards had given the money only on the condition that it would be named after him. In a letter addressed to the *Falmouth Packet*[3] he denied that this was the case, saying that he had never even suggested that any of the buildings he had provided should bear his name. He pointed out that his name was not on the Falmouth Hospital or the Perranporth Convalescent Home, which he could have easily called the Passmore Edwards Convalescent Home if he had liked. Not one of the eight hospitals, libraries and homes that he had built in London up till that point bore his name, though every one of them might have done if he had wished it. The plans that had been submitted to him for the Falmouth library had his name on them and he approved of the design. However, 'if its permanent removal will provide public harmony the competent authority is at liberty, as far as I am concerned, to remove it'.

In the same year Mrs Ward was asking him to help fund her settlement in Bloomsbury. Initially offering £4,000 his contribution was to grow considerably. By the end of March he was to write – 'You are quite at liberty to pledge me to the extent of £7,000, and, if you will insist in calling it the Passmore Edwards Settlement, I must insist you increase my donation to £10,000. This you may rely on'.[4]

Although he did not insist on buildings named being after him it is clear that the fact that they were pleased him greatly and secured his greater support. There was also the publicity value, not just for him but also for the causes he was supporting. The proposal to build a Passmore Edwards library would generally, but not always, ensure both the support of the ratepayers, in adopting the Free Library Act and in encouraging others to donate, either land, money or books. The local authorities themselves would also be proud to have a Passmore Edwards library within their area.

By the spring of 1900 Edwards brought the debate over the name to a close. There was no point in going over the old story again and they should let the matter drop. The money had been spent at West Ham.

The loss of the additional £1,200 at Whitechapel led to the cancellation of the commission for a mosaic frieze by Walter Crane that was to be installed across the front of the building and the space remained plain and unadorned. The restoration of the former library and its reopening as part of an enlarged Whitechapel Gallery, in 2009, finally joined the two buildings together, as Edwards would have wished them to be.

**West Ham Museum**

In 1897 the Essex Field Club, a naturalist society founded in 1880, was looking for a new home and the West Ham Corporation agreed to include a museum within the library and technical schools they were building. When Passmore Edwards agreed to give £3,000 a separate museum building was proposed and after opening the library and technical school in October 1898 Edwards went on to lay the foundation stone for the museum on the adjoining site. The architects responsible for the library and technical school were chosen to design the museum. W S Gibson and S B Russell designed a symmetrical building with few external windows but capped with a spectacular leaded glass cupola topped with an art nouveau finial. Inside, the light flooding from the lantern above fully illuminated the open octagonal space with minstrel gallery and mosaic floor.

The Countess of Warwick opened the museum on 18 October 1900, at the same time unveiling a bronze bust of Edwards given by the sculptor Henry Fehr. Following the opening Passmore Edwards reopened the technical school, rebuilt after being destroyed in a fire the previous year, which he referred to as 'the people's university'.

Once one of East London's best known attractions the museum closed in 1995 and the collections dispersed. The Essex Field Club, however, remains a key player in nature conservation in Essex, promoting the publication of natural history guides and scientific surveys in the county.

The building then remained empty and run down, rainwater leaking through the roof causing damage to the intricate plasterwork. In 2003 the Duke of Gloucester, patron of the Victorian Society, reopened the Grade 2 listed building, after it had been rescued and restored by the University of East London. The exhibitions of historic London had been replaced by a café bar, offices and an entertainment area, for the

Stratford Campus Students' Union. The technical school and former library are also now part of the UEL, with more than 3,000 students including many local residents, students at the 'peoples university'.

**Tahemaa**

One of the strangest of the Passmore Edwards bequests was his gift to the Salisbury museum in 1880, during the period when he was an MP for the town. Centrepiece of the Bournemouth Natural Science Society Egyptian collection is a painted coffin containing the mummy of a young Theban woman. She is thought to have been called Tahemaa who lived over 2,500 years ago. Why, or under what circumstances Tahemaa came to be brought to England we do not know, but it is likely that she was unearthed by tomb robbers sometime in the 1800s and sold to a tourist to be brought to England as a souvenir and eventually purchased on behalf of the Salisbury museum by Passmore

*The former West Ham Museum*

Edwards. There is certainly no evidence to suggest that Edwards had visited Egypt and, although he is known to have been keenly interested in archaeology and ethnology, it is not clear how, or why, he came to purchase it.

In 1922 the Salisbury museum merged with the nearby Blackmore Vale museum and as a result a new home was found for Tahemaa at Bournemouth. In 1993 Tahemaa was subjected to X-ray and CT scan in an attempt to find out more about her origins and how she died. Although the investigations could not conclusively point to the cause of her death they did indicate that she was around 25 years old when she died and Dr Richard Neave, of Manchester University, produced a clay facial reconstruction of her from the CT scan, a photo of which is shown here.[5]

**Newlyn Art Gallery**

On the day that Passmore Edwards opened the Redruth library in 1895 he was approached by a deputation of artists from the Newlyn art colony, including Stanhope Forbes, asking for assistance in providing an art gallery in Newlyn, and after reassuring Edwards over his concerns about the upkeep of such a gallery he agreed to the proposal. The site, on the sea front at Tolcarne in Newlyn, was given by Charles LeGrice with James Hicks chosen as the architect and John Symons the builder.

It was through the building of the gallery that Edwards found himself, together with Symons, summoned to appear before the West Penwith magistrates for a breach of the bylaws. Due to a misunderstanding as to the local authority area in which the site fell, plans and specification were submitted to the Paul Urban Council rather than the Madron Urban District Council. By the time the mistake had been discovered construction of the foundations had been commenced, at that time an offence. Mr J B Cornish appearing for Passmore Edwards reminded the Bench of his client's generosity to others and told them of his regret over this innocent breach of the bylaws. After being told that as soon as Edwards heard of the problem he had discontinued building operations and it would be very unfortunate if this mistake deprived Newlyn of the gallery, the magistrates dismissed the case. Despite this set-back the building was completed within six months.

*The reconstructed face of Tahemaa, an Egyptian mummy presented to Salisbury Museum by Passmore Edwards in 1880*

On 22 May 1895 Passmore Edwards and his son Harry travelled from Liskeard to Penzance to lay the foundation stone of the new gallery. He used a trowel presented by Stanhope Forbes made from an alloy of tin and copper with an engraved pattern including fish and seaweed. Edwards said that it had been his good fortune to lay many foundation stones and on each occasion he had been presented with a silver trowel, each having the same appearance, but for the first time he was presented not with a silver trowel but with something he should appreciate more than any trowel he had ever had, and for these reasons: It was made out of Cornish material; it was the result of art workmanship from that place; and it represented fish, tin and copper, on which Cornwall's fortunes relied. He should appreciate it and treasure it amongst his brightest memorials.

On 22 October, the Cornish Liberal MP, Leonard Courtney, opened the gallery in the presence of Lord and Lady St Levan, Mr T B Bolitho MP, and Stanhope Forbes, ARA, and dedicated the building to John Opie, the Cornish artist.

The artists had formed themselves into the Newlyn Society of Artists and were closely involved in the design of 'their' Gallery, modifying Hicks' design in several significant ways. Internally the reading room vanished from the final plan, a move that did not find favour with many locals but the most significant change was to the front elevation.

Hicks' design included for the facade to be decorated by a carved frieze but the artists clearly wanted work relevant to Newlyn and the art colony. The result is the four decorative copper plaques representing 'Earth', 'Wind', 'Fire' and 'Water', fine examples of repoussé work popular in Newlyn at the time. Designed by two of the Newlyn colony of artists – J D Mackenzie, and T C Gotch, the panels were beaten by Philip Hodder who had learned the art of repoussé copper beating at the industrial class in Newlyn.

Whilst free libraries could rely upon the 'penny rate' to support them there was no such support for the Newlyn Gallery and its early history is one of continued financial insecurity. A full account of the gallery and its artists can be found in *100 Years in Newlyn, A Diary of a Gallery*, edited by Melissa Hardie and published in 1995 to mark its first centenary.

*Newlyn Art Gallery, Cornwall*

The opening exhibition at the gallery took place in November 1895 with more than 140 paintings exhibited by 47 artists, two-thirds of which were Newlyn artists and seven from St Ives. Records suggest that 27 of these were sold and commission to the gallery amounted to a little over £32.

Until the 1950s a committee appointed by both the artists and the trustees managed the gallery; and while the money to run the gallery was generated by the artists and supported by the members' subscriptions, the responsibility for the maintenance of the building fell to the trustees.

The importance of the role of Stanhope Forbes in not only the founding but the continued existence of the gallery was recognised by the sculptured panel by the Reverend Allan Wyon affixed to the front of the building and unveiled in 1948 by Sir Alfred Munnings RA.

Although Edwards said the artists approached him, Forbes later suggested otherwise. In an article entitled 'A Few Reminiscences of Newlyn' that appeared in the *Cornish Magazine* in 1898 Forbes wrote – 'As we leave one cannot repress a slight feeling of regret at the recollection of those pleasant days when the field was gay with crowds of visitors who had flocked thither for our yearly private view. It was, I think, Percy Craft who with me a good many years ago first introduced to Newlyn this fashion, and by degrees the custom grew until almost everyone adopted it, and the numbers of our visitors swelled from a handful of personal friends to that large crowd that each year filled the meadow, strolling from studio to studio, gazing at the pictures and getting a glimpse of our workshops and our ways.

But when fate in the person of Mr Passmore Edwards decreed that we should possess an art gallery, it became inevitable that the pictures could no longer be exhibited in this novel manner, and seeing the many advantages which the possession of a properly constructed exhibition room has conferred upon us, it were ungenerous to cavil at so small a matter.

It was a kind and generous thought of the giver to bestow this admirable little gallery upon us, and not the less gratifying for being so entirely spontaneous and unsought for. The success it has met with so far, not only from the support which the public of West Cornwall has given it, but also from the valuable assistance of many eminent artists who have lent us interesting works, augurs well for its future prosperity'.

But the building of the gallery marked a change in the dynamics of the Newlyn artistic community; several of the founding members, finding it difficult to find their own niche, moved away. To attract new artists, Forbes started the Newlyn School of Painting and several new studios were built.[6]

In the 1960s a number of alterations were made to the gallery to increase the exhibi-

*Beaten copper plaques which adorn the Newlyn Art Gallery*

tion space and later the gallery was amalgamated with the Orion Gallery, Penzance, to form the Newlyn Orion Galleries Ltd and in 1977 the Newlyn Orion became a registered educational charity.

Further development took place in the 1990s and in 2005 the gallery secured £2.7 million to implement further improvements, including an extension to the original Passmore Edwards building. In Hardie's words – 'The Newlyn Gallery continues, as it was originally established to do, to serve as a show place for the contemporary artists *for the public good*'.[7]

# Twenty-one
# Honoured by his fellow man

*Portrait of John Passmore Edwards by G F Watts at Truro City Hall. Copy of Watts' painting in the National Portrait Gallery collection*

Although Edwards declined offers of a knighthood from both Queen Victoria and later by King Edward VII, he was pleased to be honoured by the London and Cornish boroughs that bestowed on him the freedom of the borough. Truro was first, presenting the freedom of the borough to Passmore Edwards on 6 June 1893, an occasion that saw business premises closing for half a day's public holiday and over 2,500 schoolchildren and their teachers lining the main street to welcome him.[1] By then the Blackwater Institute and the Perranporth Convalescent Home had been completed, the St Day School Room was under construction and he was to lay the foundation stone for the St Agnes Institute the next day. His marathon of funding public buildings had only just begun but in presenting Edwards with the casket containing the seal of freedom, the Mayor, Mr Thomas Chirgwin, said that Edwards had 'not only preached but practised the gospel of brotherhood'. In response to the honour bestowed upon him, Edwards presented the Dean and Chapter of Truro with a sixteenth century ebony and ivory pastoral staff, or crozier, for use by the Bishop. This remains on display in the north choir aisle at the cathedral.

On 23 September, the Borough of Falmouth followed Truro's lead, bestowing on Edwards the freedom of the borough. Again, a half days holiday was declared and the town was decorated throughout with flags and bunting and triumphal arches erected in the principal thoroughfares. Mayors from Falmouth, St Ives, Truro, Penryn and

Helston headed a procession of JPs, aldermen, councillors, senior borough officials, officers of the Friendly Societies, the clergy and others, totalling more than 2,000, which marched and escorted Passmore Edwards from the Falmouth Hotel to the town hall.[2]

Edwards was the first person to receive the honour from either Falmouth or Truro and on 16 October 1895 he was to become the first person to be similarly honoured by the London Borough of West Ham. Whereas in Cornwall the ceremonies had been made a public holiday the ceremony in West Ham was on a smaller scale but the casket containing the *script of freedom*, of solid silver covered with gold, was the most elaborate. The Borough of East Ham followed suit following his bequests of both a hospital and a library.

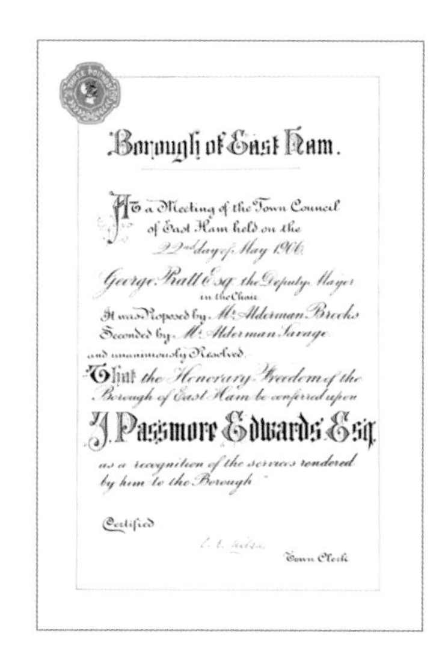

Borough of East Ham.

At a Meeting of the Town Council of East Ham held on the 22nd day of May 1906.

George Pratt Esq the Deputy Mayor in the Chair

It was Proposed by Mr Alderman Brooks
Seconded by Mr Alderman Savage
and unanimously Resolved

"That the Honorary Freedom of the Borough of East Ham be conferred upon

J. Passmore Edwards Esq.

as a recognition of the services rendered by him to the Borough"

Certified

Town Clerk

Freedom of the Borough of East Ham, granted to Passmore Edwards in 1906

A year later, on 26 October 1896, Edwards was the first person to be presented with the freedom of the borough of Liskeard, in Cornwall. As economical with his time as he was with his money the day chosen coincided with the opening of the Liskeard library, and he fitted in an inspection of the cottage hospital as well. The honour was declared to be in respect of the service he had rendered to the country, 'by erecting in great numbers, at his own cost, free libraries, technical schools, museums and other educational buildings in London and other parts of the country and in Cornwall'. Edwards had been responsible for providing both a free library and a cottage hospital for Liskeard.[3]

Whilst he was presented with the honorary freedom of the Stationers' Company, in 1899, Edwards did not receive the one honour that he would have desired above all. At the end of the century he had been considered for freedom of the City of London but the bad feeling about him at the time, due to his opposition to the Boer War meant that the honour eluded him. Though a different decision may have been forthcoming after the war, the matter was not raised again.

Another honour was a portrait painted by Frederick Watts and exhibited at the Royal Academy, and now in the National Portrait Gallery collection. A copy of this was presented to the City of Truro and is hung in the council chamber at City Hall. And as he had commissioned memorial busts of those he admired, busts were sculpted of him and displayed in several of his buildings.

In 1893 the satirical magazine *Punch* included Edwards amongst those it honoured in verse.

*A GENUINE PHILANTHROPIST*

*O PASSMORE EDWARDS, you, beyond contention,*
*Are worthy of Punch's 'Honourable Mention.'*

*Whenever there be any boons a-brewing*
*You're very sure, Sir, to be up and doing!*
*There's scarce a project schemed with kindly sense,*
*But profits by your large munificence.*
*Punch won't forget to pray when passing bedwards,*
*For you and for more bricks like PASSMORE EDWARDS!*

Thirty years previous Mr Punch had not been so generous. When Edwards, then editor of the *Mechanics Magazine* and candidate for the seat at Truro, had written to *Punch* to complain about an article on Cobden, *Punch* published a mocking response to what they called an amusing abusive letter under the title the 'Mechanical Donkey', alluding to Edwards' lack of education and in particular his spelling. 'Mr Passmore Edwards,' they said, 'complains of something which we have published, but as he describes it as a characture we hardly know what he means; and we also find it difficult to reconcile the facts that Passmore Edwards cannot spell, and that there are so many charity schools in London'. They suggested that they had enclosed a spelling book for Edwards, and 'when he shall be a little advanced in rudimentary knowledge, we will ask him to learn this couplet – all easy little words:–

In. This. World. There. Is. One. Ass. More.
Than. Punch. Had. Known. And That. Is. PAS. MORE.

Edwards, who had also previously attacked *Punch* for its treatment of Prince Albert, was quick to respond. *Punch*, he wrote, had so long pictured Cobden with long ears that he could not complain if they called him (Edwards) an ass. Had they praised him he would have thought that he had done something wrong and his reputation would have suffered amongst his friends. 'If my spelling is as bad as you represent then this is on par with your lot'. 'The older a man gets the better he is likely to spell whereas the older *Punch* gets the more flat, stale and unprofitable it becomes. At one time it respected fair play and broke many a lance for truth, now it sympathises with slaveholders abroad or rebel patriots at home'.

Although Edwards often played down the way in which he was portrayed in speeches at various opening ceremonies, saying that he was not worthy of the attention he was given, his refusal to accept a knighthood had nothing to do with modesty. He rarely had a good word to say about the landed classes – how many times do you see the name of Lord such and such, over a public building door? – it would be a betrayal of his class to accept a title. Whilst members of the Royal Family and others from amongst the aristocracy attended opening ceremonies, his choice was more often than not based on public office rather than inherited title. And, 'If the curtain could be lifted,' he wrote, 'so the light might be thrown on the motives and means used by many to get titles, both the wearers and the things worn would command only insignificant interest'.

# Twenty-two
# Save the Children

This is the title chosen by Passmore Edwards for a short, but important, chapter in his autobiography. He lived during a period when child mortality rates were high and the level of care exercised by the state was equally low. The economic and moral waste produced by the neglect, disease and death of children was, he said, incalculable and the nation should say less about its virtues whilst such waste existed. The best and cheapest way to improve the quality of citizens was to concentrate attention on moulding and guiding the young. 'Where would the British Nation be if it depended more on the number than on the ability of its people? And how can that ability be fully developed and utilised unless each British boy and girl has a fair opportunity for intellectual and moral growth?'[1]

In addition to his continued campaigning for free libraries and improved schooling, Edwards directed his giving towards the benefit of children, funding hospital wards, orphanages, schools, clubs and holiday homes for children.

**Home for Little Boys, Swanley**

This was the first of the Passmore Edwards bequests targeted directly at children.

The Homes for Little Boys date back to a former poor house in Tottenham, which, in 1864, was converted into a home for a few of the many homeless boys of that area. The success of the Tottenham home led to the founding of the Farringdon homes, a group of eleven cottages, each housing a number of boys, accompanied by workshops, classrooms and a farm, and which opened in 1867. This was followed by the homes at Swanley, Kent, with construction starting in 1883. Whether Passmore Edwards had a previous connection with the work of the Homes for Little Boys is not clear but early in 1895 he presided over the annual meeting of the organisation and as a consequence offered to add to the cluster of buildings already built at Swanley. His contribution was the Passmore Edwards or Assistant Masters House, opened in 1896 to accompany the Headmaster House and four Dames Houses, each of which was named after the separate benefactors. Each of the Dames houses was occupied by up to 30 younger boys whilst older boys occupied the Passmore Edwards House, and the most senior boys the head master's house.

Many of the young boys learned farming skills and perhaps found employment locally but a wide range of crafts were taught and boys left to become bakers, carpenters, printers, tailors, shoemakers and clerks. The arts and sciences were also taught, including chemistry, modelling and even photography. Christopher Casstine was an orphan who arrived at the Swanley Homes at the age of four and was later taught photography there. When he finally left in 1902 he set up a studio in Swanley and was a successful and well-known photographer in the area.[2] For those boys who set their sights on London the Home for Working Boys provided assistance and a temporary home until they could find their feet.

The Furness Home was funded by Sir Christopher Furness, a wealthy ship owner in 1909 and was used solely for boys who wished to follow a life at sea. Boys not only studied seamanship but also wore a midshipman's uniform, setting themselves apart from the other boys.

Renamed the Swanley Home School in 1938, the school has, over the years, seen many developments to meet changing needs; providing primary school education to local boys and girls, housing the Hextable Special School, and becoming more integrated into the local community.

In 1956 the Furness School was established as a boarding school for young children with learning difficulties. Reorganisation took place in the late 1980s to cater for secondary aged pupils with emotional and behavioural difficulties and in 2004 the school was re-designated as a school for pupils with behavioural, emotional and social development needs, accommodating twenty-four residential and 36 day boys from eleven to sixteen. In many ways the school continues to provide the same assistance to young people as that which impressed Passmore Edwards to contribute, more than 100 years ago.

*Passmore Edwards Home, Swanley School for Boys*

## The Victoria Home for Children

The Secretary of the Ragged School Union and Shaftesbury Society approached Passmore Edwards for help with funding a home for children with physical disabilities. He suggested it should be located at Bournemouth where a house had already been rented and opened as a temporary home. Passmore Edwards agreed and without a formal foundation stone ceremony, building commenced. The home, designed by Frederick Warman to accommodate twenty children was opened on 14 June 1898 by the Marquis of Northampton, President of the Ragged School Union, who said that in other homes children who were not able to walk on their arrival returned home able to walk. The Bournemouth Home, built close to Alum Chine and the sea, was intended to be not only a home but a *holiday home* where the children would have good air, shelter, care and protection, and healthy and agreeable recreation.

The majority of the children came from the East End of London but a few local children were also admitted since much of the money to maintain the home was raised locally. Initially with only a matron and two assistants, the staff undoubtedly worked very hard, some of the children being unable even to feed themselves. The children benefited both from convalescence after hospital operations and through physiotherapy, the average stay being around six months, although a few stayed much longer.

A reporter writing in the *Bournemouth Graphic* in February 1903 described the children she saw there. 'The youngest, a child of three, suffering from a bad form of rickets and with legs bandaged in splints, and utterly helpless, I found amusing itself with a huge rag doll, a recent gift to the Home. It was a delightfully warm morning and all those unable to walk were lying in invalid carriages out of door, breathing the pure, clean air which is such an essential part of their cure here; though it made one's heart ache to think that many of these little sufferers would never be able to walk, for the majority of the cases treated are either spinal curvature or hip disease.'

*The Victoria Home, Bournemouth*

Recognising the need to provide an education during lengthy stays, part time teachers were appointed and at the end of 1916 the home was registered as a 'residential school for crippled children' with the appointment of first full time teacher.

At that time the Shaftesbury Society had more

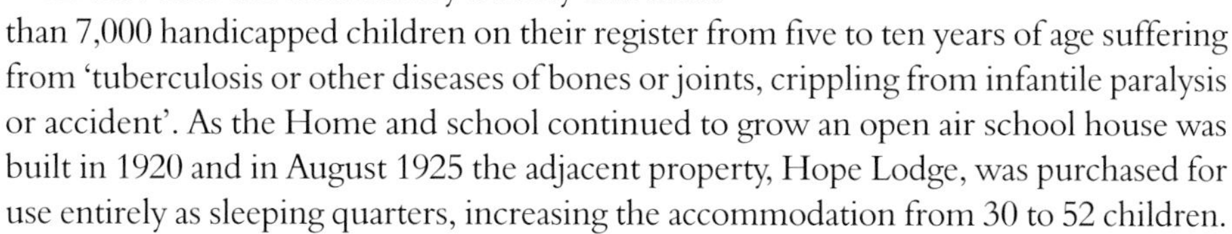

than 7,000 handicapped children on their register from five to ten years of age suffering from 'tuberculosis or other diseases of bones or joints, crippling from infantile paralysis or accident'. As the Home and school continued to grow an open air school house was built in 1920 and in August 1925 the adjacent property, Hope Lodge, was purchased for use entirely as sleeping quarters, increasing the accommodation from 30 to 52 children.

### Charles' Story

Charles was one of the many children who passed through the home. His account does not paint the rosy picture given in the official files, he had few very pleasant memories of the home, but he accepts that staff did what they thought was best for the children.

Surrey County Council did not have provision for the education of physically handicapped children just prior to the Second World War, so, at the age of five, Charles was sent to a local school until he could be 'suitably placed'. Placement was to be at the Victoria Home and being taken away from mum, dad, and gran for no apparent reason was very upsetting for the boy. The children of all ages had to make their own beds and the bedcovers all had to have boxed, hospital corners. Making a neat bed when merely five years old and only having one controllable hand, was not the easiest thing to manage. When the children went to bed at night, they were tucked in, with about a nine inch turndown of sheet and with their heads sticking out. The nurse smoothed this turndown and if they moved and crinkled it, they were in trouble in the morning and punished accordingly! Every Thursday there was a dose of Californian syrup of figs and every month a dose of castor oil in orange juice. If you'd been well behaved, you also got a quarter of a fresh orange. Charles' favourite time was being taken by school bus to the beach where there was a hut with buckets and spades, and barrows and rakes for the children to play with. Earlier generations of children were transported to the beach by handcart and later by a donkey and trap. Charles had been at the home for about 18 months when the war started and he was allowed to go home to his parents.

Life was no less rigorous for the staff as one young woman recounted from working there in the early 1930s.

> Our day started early – on duty by six o'clock to get the boys up, washed and dressed and taken over to the dining room for breakfast, after which they were taken outside to the toilets and then to the schoolroom. Having deposited them there we did housework. At ten o'clock we had a ten-minute break with cocoa and large slices of bread and dripping! After break it was back to more housework. After tea we took the boys to the 'playroom'. The poor mites didn't know how to play. There were no toys – just a big ugly bare room. We had two hours off duty each day if we were lucky enough to get off in time – it was a long day and by this time we were so tired that sometimes we were glad just to creep into bed. [Of the children, she said] – their physical needs were catered for adequately, but they were hardly treated as human beings. We were told not to get too close to them and, indeed, we never had the chance to do so. We were so harassed and rushed we never had time to talk to them individually or to show them any love or affection.

As the types of disability provided for became more severe the Almhurst Road premises were no longer adequate and in 1956 a new site in Bournemouth was purchased and specially designed premises constructed at a total cost of £70,000.

The Victoria Education Centre remains part of the Shaftesbury Society, a national Christian charity providing care, education and support for both children and adults with disabilities at over 50 sites.

The Victoria Centre, with its school, including for post 16 students, residential departments, the Victoria Horticulture Centre and an Assessment and Therapy Centre, is recognised as one of the finest specialist centres of its kind.

In the mid-1960s the original Passmore Edwards building in Almhurst Road was demolished and replaced with residential flats called Burnaby Court.

## The Sunday School Holiday Home at Clacton





The *Echo* had organised day trips to the countryside for thousands of children from the East End so Edwards was an obvious choice for the Secretary of the Sunday School Union to approach when looking for funding to build a Children's Holiday Home at Clacton on Sea, Essex. Edwards responded in his normal manner, by promising to supply the building, for the sum of £5,000.

The chosen site, of nearly two acres, fronted the Marine Parade and architect Charles Bell FRIBA designed a building to accommodate nearly one hundred children. Of course there were separate entrances and staircases to the dormitories provided for boys and girls but they shared the living rooms. The dining rooms, playrooms and all of dormitories, sleeping no more than eight or ten children in each, faced the sea. Some of the children would have come from homes where they shared with as many brothers and sisters and, perhaps, all in only a couple of beds. Bathrooms were provided on each floor but the WCs were outside.[3]

The home was open all the year round and amongst the thousands of children that stayed there was Sue Brewer's 'gran'. Born in 1896, May Emma Elsom was one of the five children of Francis and Catherine Elsom who lived at 7 Reedworth Street, Kennington, in Lambeth. To start with Francis, who was a carpenter, and Catherine rented just one room in Reedworth Road but as the children came along they rented additional rooms. By the time Walter, her youngest brother, was born Catherine's mother, Sophie, had joined the family, now in four rooms, but also including a lodger.

When old enough May joined her siblings at St Philips's (Archbishop Sumner Memorial) Church of England day schools, just along the street from where she lived. The schools – originally there were separate schools for boys, girls and infants – were in union with the Church of England National Society; religious and moral education being the responsibility of the parish minister; so the school was also used as a Sunday School and the young Elsoms would have attended regularly. May went to Clacton in 1903, but whether any of her brothers or sisters were with her is not known. Neither do we know just what impression the trip had on May, who was only seven years old at the time.

Lambeth was described as a very poor parish at this time and the area saw regular epidemics of scarlet fever, diphtheria, whooping cough, measles and chicken pox take their toll on the undernourished children.[4] May's youngest sister Katie died when only sixteen.

May survived her schooldays and became an embroiderer with the Queen Mary's Needlework Guild restoring tapestries at palaces and stately homes across the country, including a bedspread for Queen Mary's doll's house in Windsor Castle. May, who later married and had two children, died in 1982.

Passmore Edwards was in attendance on 19 May 1898, when Sir H H Fowler MP, laid the foundation stone, after which the party adjourned to the town hall for luncheon and the customary speeches and toasts. At the luncheon, the chairman reminded the diners that they met that day with a degree of sadness since Gladstone had died the day before, 'and all past differences of opinion, all the storms and tempests of years were hushed in the presence of that solemn event'. Gladstone had been a figure that

Edwards had admired and followed for many years, although his principles eventually led him to vote against his leader on the subject of Irish Home Rule, leading to Edwards' departure from Parliament. Although Edwards does not refer to Gladstone in his speech he would have doubtless been in his thoughts.

Edwards was back in Clacton in June the following year to take part in the opening ceremony. It was proposed that Lord Aberdeen, then Vice President of the Sunday School Union, would perform the opening but his cab was delayed by traffic congestion in London and he missed the train. Edwards stepped in to fill the breech and declared the home open, 'in the name of God and in humanity.'[5]

The contract price for the building was £6,596 and Edwards increased his subscription by offering another £1,000 just before the opening and an additional £1,000 was raised through contributions from the guests on the opening day.

The home continued to provide holidays for underprivileged children up until the end of the Great War when it was converted into a convalescent home, specialising in tuberculosis cases. At the outbreak of the Second World War it was taken over by the Government and became a headquarters for the Royal Artillery, with ack-ack gun sites located along the sea front. Edwards – 'I am a lover of peace and abhor war' – would have regretted this use of his building, even though it was being used for defensive purposes. Following the end of the war the Regional Holiday Board spent £11,000 on repairs before its reopening in 1950 for tuberculosis convalescent patients. As improvements in medical treatment almost eliminated the disease the need for such hospitals became less and the home fell quiet until it was extended and reopened as the Passmore Edwards Rehabilitation Centre in 1961. Here, up to 80 patients at a time, all of whom had lost the use of limbs through strokes or were amputees, could benefit from therapeutic treatment and at the same time learn to adapt to their new circumstances. Some of the rooms were converted into small flats where patients could learn techniques to help gain their independence. As well as physiotherapy and occupational therapy there was also an experimental workshop where advances in artificial limb design were undertaken.[6]

Alas, the need to make savings of £380,000 from within the Essex Health Authority budget led to the closure of the rehabilitation unit in 1985,[7] after 12,000 patients had passed through the hospital. The once beautiful building was demolished and replaced

Left: *The Sunday Schools Union Holiday Home, Marine Parade, Clacton, photographed prior to First World War*

Right: *East End children at Holiday Home, Clacton.*

with a block of uninspiring residential apartments to be known as Hestletine Court. Even then, for many years the older residents of Clacton still referred to that point on the sea front as 'Along by Passmore Edwards'.

Passmore Edwards was to later fund another holiday home for the Sunday School Union[8] but not on such a grand scale. The 'House Beautiful' was a children's convalescent home, opened in Bournemouth in January 1894. The home, 'for the many delicate children recovering from illness' was open throughout the year and boys aged seven to twelve and girls from twelve to fourteen who were members of the Sunday School movement were eligible to stay, at a cost of four shillings a week. The home was initially the property of a Mr G Lawson, a Bournemouth resident who loaned the use of the house to the Sunday School Union for seven years, rent free[9] and the manner in which Passmore Edwards later funded the home is as yet unknown.

**Teachers' Orphanage**

The opening ceremony for the Passmore Edwards House for the Orphans of Teachers began under leadened skies with the hymn 'Oh God our help in ages past'. The rain held off, at least for the first part of the ceremony, as Mrs Burgwin, the chairman of the National Union of Teachers Benevolent and Orphans Fund, gave a short history of the movement.

The Benevolent Fund had been founded in 1877 and as well as assisting teachers in need with loans and grants had already opened two orphanages, one in Sheffield, for girls and the other for boys at Peckham. These, however, were inadequate to meet the demands and when the need for an additional home was put to Passmore Edwards he offered to build a new orphanage at a cost of not less than £6,000, on condition that a suitable site could be found. Searching for a site the committee heard that Westwood House, in Sydenham was for sale and went to view it.

Westfield House had been built in 1766. Lady Charlotte Campbell, youngest daughter of the 5th Duke of Argyll and lady-in-waiting to Caroline, Princess of Wales, was the most notable resident before Henry Littleton, of Novello & Co, purchased the house in 1874 and had it remodelled as a renaissance fantasy palace with a magnificent music room complete with minstrel gallery.[10] Standing in five acres of landscaped gardens the house was richly fitted with mahogany doors and stairs, no expense having been spared on its decorations. Having stood empty for some years it was available at what was said to be a generous offer from the vendor, Mr J Whitlock Rabbitts JP, of £10,000.

*The Sunday Schools Holiday Home, Bournemouth*

Considerable work was required to make the house suitable for its new use and how this was accomplished without disturbing the house's finery is not clear but we are

assured that this was so. The coach houses were converted into workshops and a gymnasium but the music room, in which both Dvorak and Liszt had played, Liszt giving one of his last piano recitals there, was retained, and graced with the gift of a new grand piano from the Educational Musical Instrument Company.

On Saturday 23 September 1899, Passmore Edwards officially opened the orphanage before a crowd that included 1,200 teachers. In an account of the opening ceremony, subsequently published in the *Schoolmaster*, it was recorded that Passmore Edwards opened the building with a key on which was engraved 'Charity – old and young in the years to come will rise up and call you blessed'. In response to the vote of thanks Edwards read to the assembly a letter he had received from a resident in the neighbourhood who objected to the orphans being housed in the district. He then read aloud the reply he had sent

> My Dear Sir, You should address yourself to the Teachers' Benevolent Society, and not to me, in reference to the Teachers' Orphanage; but I believe it is too late to alter the decision come to, and particularly for the miserable reasons mentioned in your letter. Westwood House has not been inhabited for years, and you would prefer its remaining so rather than it should be inhabited and enjoyed by poor orphans who probably are as much deserving the favours of Providence as you are. You evidently object to their near neighbourhood because they are poor and if so it reflects no credit to your head or your heart. You will probably now have an opportunity to learn that teacher's orphans though poor, are clean, well behaved, and respectable – Yours faithfully, J. Passmore Edwards.

*The Orphanage, Sydenham, funded by Passmore Edwards for the National Union of Teachers*

Though Edwards gave £6,000 towards the founding of the orphanage the total cost was, as usual, considerably more and there was a deficit when the home opened. The teaching community in London took it upon themselves to raise an additional £10,000 to complete and run the home and both Passmore Edwards' wife and daughter attended a garden party there in 1903 to celebrate the completion of their mammoth task.

The home closed after the Second World War and was demolished in 1952, to be replaced by one of Sydenham's housing estates.

**Canning Town Boys' Club**

In 1889, students at Mansfield College, Oxford, founded the Mansfield House University Settlement in Canning Town. Like the Bloomsbury Settlement, Mansfield House provided educational and many welfare services, such as a sick benefit society and the 'poor man's lawyer' – free legal aid. As part of the development a Boy's Club was started in a row of tumbledown cottages and in 1890 it was decided to build a new club on the site. An approach to Passmore Edwards resulted in an offer of £5,000 towards the final cost of £7,800.

Designed by H C Lander, ARIBA, the club was opened by Mr Choate, the America Ambassador in July 1900. It was constructed in red brick with terracotta dressings and the three-storey building provided a wide range of facilities. On the ground floor was a clubroom with refreshments area, and a large hall, known as the Passmore Edwards Hall, which doubled as a gymnasium. In the half basement were slipper baths and showers. On the first floor were classrooms and a games room and on the top floor a

*Canning Town Boys' Club. Built for the Mansfield Settlement*

billiard room and workshops.

The club gained an excellent reputation for sporting achievement, with some members going on to become international sportsmen and representing England at the Olympic games.

Though the Boy's Club escaped serious damage during the Second World War, by the 1980s the Settlement entered a period of decline and with the buildings in need of expensive repair a decision was taken to sell them. The work of the Mansfield Settlement, however, combined with the Aston Charities Trust, continues. The former Passmore Edwards building, now restored and converted for housing, remains a local landmark and a reminder of a former age.

**Redruth Children's Hospital**

The Redruth Miners' Hospital was established in 1863 with money given by Sir Edward Nicholl and opened the following year. The Rt Hon T C Agar Robartes of Lanhydrock, whose family had interests in the mines around Redruth, gave the site and financially supported the hospital for many years.

In 1887 it was decided to build a women's hospital adjacent to the miners' hospital and Mrs Basset of Tehidy, President of the Hospital, opened this in 1890. At first priority was given to women who worked in the local mines and tin streams although treatment was available to all who needed it.

Mrs Basset, who also contributed £100 per year towards the running costs, gave half of the total cost of the new hospital and the total cost of furnishings. The land had been bought for a nominal £150 from General Sir Redvers Buller, who also gave £100 towards the building costs. In digging the foundations of the Women's Hospital, two roughly circular stones, about two feet in diameter, were uncovered together with wood ash and other stonework walling. This was believed to be the original tin smelting works, or blowing house, from which the area derived its name.

*Now restored, the former Children's ward of the Redruth hospital is now part of the Gweal Pawl residential development*

In 1898 Mrs Basset approached Passmore Edwards about the addition of a children's wing to be attached to the Women's Hospital. He agreed to meet the construction costs of £400, Mr

Trounson, a Redruth gentleman paying to furnish the ward at a cost of £200. Designed by Sampson Hill the Children's Jubilee Memorial Wing, following Queen Victoria's Diamond Jubilee in 1897, provided a single ward, with six cots, and a nurse's room on the first floor and a playroom and special care ward, with two beds, on the ground floor. There was also a small playground outside. When the ward was completed the costs had amounted to an additional £78, which Edwards agreed to pay.[11]

The two hospitals were amalgamated in 1901; a maternity unit was added in 1926 and further additions made in 1928 and 1935. In 1938, to celebrate the Coronation of King George IV, a Redruth Hospital Coronation Extension Appeal was launched and the resulting extension was opened in 1939 bringing the accommodation up to 79 beds, while a further 43 beds were made available during the war years.

By the time of the 1953 Coronation the hospital had 151 beds and was treating over 3,000 in-patients and 31,000 out-patients each year. These, however, were the peak years and a gradual run-down commenced in the 1960s with a transfer of services, and patients, to Truro, the hospital eventually closing in the 1990s.

After many years of standing empty the hospital site was handed over to developers who have created an imaginative residential development. Now set amongst a village-like collection of residential units known as Gweal Pawl the former Children's Ward and the other redundant hospital buildings have been carefully restored and converted into 'live and work' accommodation.

# Twenty-three
# Mary Ward

### Passmore Edwards Settlement, Bloomsbury

In the latter decades of the nineteenth century the cause of the social crisis affecting London and other large cities was perceived to be the geographical separation of classes. In the East End, in particular, those that could afford it left to live in the developing suburbs leaving the lower classes alone to populate large areas. Without the middle classes, thought to provide a moderating if not improving influence, the conditions in the impoverished areas worsened, whilst the middle classes lost touch with the realities of working-class life.

To counteract these conditions the settlement movement was created to restore contact between the classes. Built in working-class neighbourhoods a settlement was a building, part of which was home to a number of young middle class professionals who would invite the local working-class inhabitants to use the facilities provided by the settlement and as a social club.

*Relief of Mary Ward, from Mary Ward House, Bloomsbury*

The novelist Mary Ward, granddaughter of Dr Thomas Arnold of Rugby and niece of the poet Matthew Arnold, had written a three-part novel, *Robert Elsmere*, in 1888. In her novel, Elsemere, an Anglican priest, questions his faith but through the founding of the New Brotherhood, a settlement in the East End on the lines of Toynbee Hall, regains it. The novel was a great success, being read by many thousands. To begin with Mrs Ward worked with the University Hall in Gordon Square, renting rooms in Marchmont Hall to run classes, concerts and various clubs, and launching an appeal for £5,000 to establish a settlement. At first the results to her appeal were disappointing and her approaches to Passmore Edwards, then living at 51 Bedford Square, nearby, brought the response that he had his hands full and was unable to help. Then in May 1894, Mrs Ward received a simple letter in a buff coloured envelope, which was at first thought to be a bill but turned out to be a note from Edwards and an offer of £4,000. This was followed, within the month, by a further letter to say that she could rely on his contribution 'to the extent mentioned at *least*, and as soon as you like'. It was the start of a relationship that would continue for the rest of his life, a relationship that would see Edwards freely giving both his money and his advice.

Edwards took a close interest in all details of the proposals, commenting on the constitution and questioning conditions of the offer of a site from the Duke of Bedford in Tavistock Place. The price of £10,000 he thought was unreasonable, adding that he had strong objections to paying rich landlords big prices for the privilege of building institutions for the public good. Particularly, he noted, landlords such as the Duke of Bedford whose family had done so little for the district from which they gathered such high rents.[1] When Mary Ward reported back to Edwards on more promising negotiations with the Duke, Edwards warned against the kindness shown by the Duke as 'for every shilling he may give he will have two shillings in return'. His own experience was that he 'had never known a Lordly Landlord to do an uninterested act'. Did the 'experience' he referred to include the fact that in 1884 he was forced to move *Building News* and *English Mechanic* from of his premises in Tavistock Street, Covent Garden, when the Duke wanted to enlarge the Covent Garden market.

Peter Baynes closely studied the correspondence between Edwards and Mrs Ward for his work on Passmore Edwards and detailed their exchanges. Mary Ward had Edwards on her hook and she was not going to lose such a big fish. After a conversation

*The Passmore Edwards Settlement, later Mary Ward House, Bloomsbury*

between W Odgers QC, a member of the Settlement's Council and Edwards, Odgers wrote to Mrs Ward to say that Edwards would be pleased to see a Passmore Edwards Settlement and thought that Edwards intended to give £7,000. But to Ward there was a different slant. Whilst warning her of the Duke's largesse he hints at a desire to have a settlement, a mission or a polytechnic all of his own provision. At this stage there had been a hint that the Settlement's concert hall might carry Edwards name but the Settlement itself would carry another title. He also raised concerns over the proposed articles of association that placed the total control of the Settlement in the hands of the members, who would be free to dispose of it. Edwards also wrote that he had no memory of offering or hinting that he would give £7,000, thinking he had left a very different impression in her mind and it took another personal visit from Odgers to bring him round.

Top: *Portrait of Passmore Edwards by English painter Felix Moscheles, hanging at the Mary Ward Centre, Bloomsbury. Moscheles was President of the International Arbitration and Peace Association*

In March 1895 he wrote 'You are quite at liberty to pledge me to the extent of £7,000 and if you insist in calling it the Passmore Edwards Settlement then I must insist on increasing my donation to £10,000'. Before the Settlement opened, two years later he had increased his contribution to more than £14,000 and he continued to give his support to her work, meeting deficits and contributing towards future projects.

Two young architects who had appropriately been residents at the University Hall Settlement, Dunbar Smith and Cecil Brewer won a competition for the design of the Settlement. Both in their mid 20s this was their first major development and yet, according to Adrian Forty, it is a major architectural achievement that marks a change in architecture that both reflects the time and the social ideals of the settlement movement.[2]

Bottom: *Bust of Charles Dickens, Mary Ward House, presented by Passmore Edwards*

The Settlement was an immediate success, attracting ordinary local people who paid the few pence annual membership fee and took advantage of the settlement's facilities. They could learn practical skills, attend concerts, or use the gymnasium, and join the many groups, such as the coal club or boot club, as well as take advantage of the *Poor man's lawyer* – free legal assistance given by the lawyers amongst the Settlement's residents. Music was an important part of the Settlement, Gustav Holst was musical director for a while, and Edwards contributed, as reports of the Passmore Edwards Prize Choir, a ladies' choir performing at Claremont Hall, Pentonville shows.[3] The Settlement was also a centre for debate with George Bernard Shaw and Keir Hardie amongst the lecturers and the Jowett Lectures became a regular feature. The Settlement was also a firm favourite with Edwards, who was often to be found amongst both the contributors and the audience and he chose the Settlement to receive six of the memorial busts he commissioned.

**Ralph Waldo Emerson**

Edwards confessed that he owed more to the American Ralph Waldo Emerson than to any other writer. He was, he said, worthy of admiration as one of the luminaries of the human race and he presented a marble bust of Emerson to the Settlement in 1903 asking Joseph Choate, the American Ambassador, to unveil it. Following this Mary Ward unveiled a bust of Dr James Martineau. Edwards recalled that he had first heard Martineau preach at the Octagon chapel in Liverpool, nearly sixty years before and that one sentence used by Martineau had lived in his memory since; that whatever we do solely for ourselves perishes with us, but what we do disinterestedly for others lives forever.[4]

*Bust of Ralph Waldo Emerson, Mary Ward House*

Four other busts were placed in the Settlement; Charles Dickens, Sir William Herschel, Matthew Arnold and the classicist and theologian, Benjamin Jowett. All were sculpted by George Frampton RA, best known for his statue of Peter Pan in Kensington gardens

**Invalid Children's School and Summer Vacation Schools**

The Settlement's 'mother and toddlers club' was the start of the play centre movement and in 1899 the first school for physically handicapped children opened at the Settlement and again with the help of Passmore Edwards. This was the first such school to be formed in Britain and possibly in the world. His initial response was to offer only £10 a year towards the required £100 a year, adding that the state or local communities should undertake the responsibility. He remarked that Parliament would shortly be asked for, and given, another eight or 10 millions sterling for additional battleships but if £50,000 were asked for educating and strengthening invalid children 'it is not likely that it would be obtained'.

In spite of Edwards' reluctance to contribute, the Invalid Children's School opened the following year and was an instant success. So much so that plans were made to build an annex adjacent to the Settlement, at 9 Tavistock Place, with Edwards providing £1,000 towards the cost. In its new home the school was endowed by the London

School Board, who supplied trained teachers for the classes, whilst the Settlement provided classrooms, nurses to look after the children and mid-day meals. The school was so successful that the School Board resolved to start four other schools in different parts of London and by 1903 schools for the 'Physically Defective' had been adopted into the national school system.

In 1902, the first Vacation School in England was held at the Settlement, for London children otherwise left to roam the streets during the school holidays. Passmore Edwards would regularly include a cheque of £20 or £25 towards the Vacation Schools or '£5 for the Girls Seaside Holiday Fund'.

After the death of Mary Ward, in 1921, and with the agreement of the Passmore Edwards family, the centre was renamed the Mary Ward Settlement and in 1970 the Mary Ward Centre. Though the success of the Settlement rests firmly with the inspiration and hard work of Mary Ward, Passmore Edwards' contribution was no less significant.

The Mary Ward Centre continues to thrive, but, alas, not in Tavistock Place. Edwards had perhaps underestimated Mrs Ward's power of persuasion, or the Duke of Bedford's benevolence, as the terms of their agreement was a donation of £900 and a 999-year lease at a nominal rent of £10 a year, together with first refusal on two adjacent houses, the land on which the School was later built. This lease was later amended, increasing the rent to £45 a year but with an additional donation of £1,500.

During the 1930s the management council considered moving the Settlement to Islington, where some considered there was more work to be done than in Bloomsbury, and the lease was sold back to the Bedford Estate to kick-start an appeal and plans drawn up for a new building. Resistance from a few members of the council, and the fear of the impending war, meant that the move did not take place but the Estate allowed the Settlement to remain on a 6-month lease. This situation continued until 1959 when, to offset death duties, the Estate sold the property for redevelopment.

Though immediate action to get the building listed put paid to the redevelopment plans it did not stop the estate from wanting to sell the buildings. An appeal by the Settlement council brought only a substantial positive response from the Nuffield Foundation and Joseph Rowntree Trust, who were looking for a headquarters for the newly formed National Institute for Social Work Training. By now the LCC had closed the Physically Handicapped School and the Settlement's council was offered the annex in which to continue their work, on a 5-year renewable lease.

*The extension to the Passmore Edwards Settlement for the 'School for invalids', Bloomsbury*

In 1982, no longer able to afford the rent the Settlement finally moved to Queens Square where it remains today providing a wide range of courses; its aims, as they were in 1897 – 'To promote public education and social service for the benefit of the community'.

The National Institute for Social Work Training has also vacated Tavistock Place and it is now a privately owned conference centre, known as Mary Ward House. Whether Passmore Edwards' view that the building should have been held in trust, rather than the arrangements eventually made, would have enabled the Settlement to remain is a matter of speculation.

# Twenty-four
# Some Other Contributions

The final edition of the *Salisbury Times* of 1882 contained the following comment.

> Ah said a would be knowing one to me the other day. I know the motive why Mr Ededwards subscribes to our schools and societies – he does so partly for political reasons and would noty do so unless he expected to be returned again. Whatever may be Mr Es motive in connection with Salisbury I cannot say, but he cannot expect to be returned for Cairo and Yorkshire for Finsbury and Westminster, at all events. A short time since I saw that Mr E had subscribed £50 towards the Arabi Pasha Defence fund, last week I saw that he had sent £50 towards the Lord Frederick Cavendish memorial in Yorkshire, and £10 towards the Alhambra Fire Fund for the benefit of the suffers from the fire; and this week I see that Mr Edwards has sent £50 towards the Orphans Working Asylum Haverstockhill, where between 600 and 700 orphans are provided for.

In *Footprints* Edwards lists his 'beliefs' amongst that of Spinoza – 'that the good human life lies not in their possession of things which for one man to possess is for the rest to lose, but rather in things which all can possess alike, and where one man's wealth promotes that of his neighbour'.[1]

### A Few Sovereigns

> *There was a man whom some thought mad,*
> *The more he gave the more he had.*

Mr A Chapman, parliamentary agent for the Ancient Order of Foresters, quoted these lines at the opening of the convalescent home for the Friendly Societies at Herne Bay, in Kent. 'Not,' he was quick to add, 'because there was any suspicion of madness in Mr Passmore Edwards' case, but because of the long list of public buildings and institutions Edwards had made possible through his generosity'. In responding to the vote of thanks, Edwards' referred to his money by saying, 'It is mine; it is yours; it is ours'. I am only a steward having the command of a few sovereigns, and in going through the world I endeavour to utilise those sovereigns to the best of my ability, so as to get the maximum value out of them'. It is a principle he demonstrated throughout his life.

## The Cripplegate Institute

As at St Bride's, the Cripplegate Foundation was established in 1891 by amalgamating the non-ecclesiastical charitable donations previously administered as separate trusts. In 1896 the governors of the foundation built the Institute on Golden Lane, containing reading and reference libraries, news and magazine rooms, classrooms, a theatre and even a rifle range. Edwards' contribution was to equip a boys reading room and it was at the Institute that several of the memorial busts he commissioned found a home.

In November 1904 Augustine Birrell KC, Liberal MP and later Minister of Education, unveiled busts of Cromwell and Bunyan. Cromwell had been a subject included in one of the lectures Edwards delivered to mechanics' and literary institutes in his early days in London and in his autobiography he refers to this lecture, 'The Romance of Trifles', in which he showed that big things were composed of small things – the mole hill, the mountain, the globe and the solar system, composed of infinite number of atoms, the character and quality of the greatest things depended on the character and quality of the smallest component parts, and that humanity was made up of many individuals and the life of each individual was built of little incidents. For example, when Oliver Cromwell was making plans to emigrate to America a dream diverted his thoughts inducing him to stay in England. Edwards celebrated Cromwell's life, not for the execution of the King but for his acts of unity, incorporating the Isle of Man and the Channel Isles with the mainland and bringing Irish and Scottish members into his Parliament.

John Bunyan served in Cromwell's army but after the restoration of Charles II he was arrested for unlicensed preaching and spent more than 12 years in prison for his beliefs. It was during this time that he wrote *Pilgrim's Progress*.

Daniel Defoe, another writer, and pamphleteer, imprisoned for his beliefs was a subject of Passmore Edwards' desire to record, *fac simile*, in marble or bronze the heads of famous men and women. The fourth bust presented to the Cripplegate Institute was that of John Milton, the poet who had also served under Cromwell and though not imprisoned spent the last years of his life in hiding after the restoration of the monarchy brought about a warrant for his arrest.

The Cripplegate Institute survived until 1973, latterly as a secretarial college, when it was closed, the foundation becoming a grant giving trust. All of the busts presented by

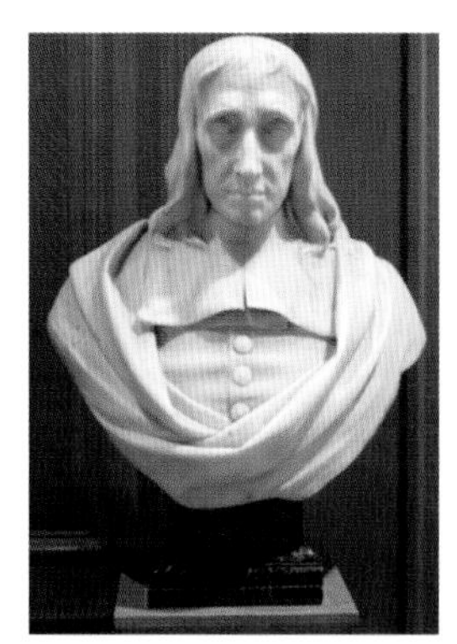

Left to right: *Busts of Cromwell, Bunyan, Defoe, Milton. Cripplegate Institute*

Edwards were removed to nearby St Giles church where they remain today.

**Mithian Institute**

By far the smallest building that Passmore Edwards contributed to is the Mithian Institute. Was it that it was so small, or that he thought that his contribution was insufficient to claim it as one of his, for when opening the technical school at Truro he referred to his nineteen buildings, each representing one letter of his name. Including Mithian there are twenty.

The villagers of Mithian, which was in the same parish as Blackwater, had planned to build a village institute for some years. Land had been purchased in the centre of the village and building work started, but insufficient money was available to continue. When Passmore Edwards was approached for help in meeting the deficit his response was to send Frank Symons around to complete the job.[2] He said that he was surprised how little this was to cost and he regretted that the foundations were too small to allow a larger building. 'If they had approached him earlier,' he said 'he would have been pleased to fund a more "imposing" institute'.

It was on the bright spring morning of Thursday 12 April 1894, that Passmore Edwards, along with his wife, Eleanor, and his children Harry and Ada, visited Mithian to perform the opening ceremony. Whilst the event was, like the Institute itself, not to be of the most imposing character, it suited the occasion perfectly. The visitors were welcomed by a shower of bunches of wild flowers tossed by the cheering children of the Board school who lined the lane and then went on to sing a well-rehearsed hymn.

Following welcome speeches by the Institute's Secretary, Mr J Tredinnick and the Treasurer, Mr S Martin, Frank Symons handed Edwards the key, and he unlocked the door and declared the Institute open, 'for the benefit of the public'.

Edwards' visit to Mithian was only short as he was to open the Chacewater Institute that afternoon, but he said that he delighted in meeting his 'fellow parishioners' and regretted that he could not stay longer. He hoped, when visiting Perranporth on some future occasion he would be able to spend more time in the village.

Edwards' departure did not mean the end of the celebrations as these continued, with a football match in the afternoon followed by a tea for all of the inhabitants.

*Mithian Institute, completed by Passmore Edwards when the villagers' funds ran out*

The Institute remains today at the centre of the village, with a front porch added prior to the Great War,[3] and is as much loved by villagers as when first opened. As at Blackwater the Mithian Institute became a male domain with a snooker table to supplement the library of books supplied by Passmore Edwards. There was a wooden partition that could be used to separate the building into two smaller rooms but one cannot imagine that this was often the case once the snooker table was installed. When the men's interest dwindled the Women's Institute moved in, their own building having fallen into disrepair and eventually, in the late 1980s a group of villagers formed the Mithian Village Association and the little building once more provides a welcome for 'one and all'.

**Bust of William Ewart**

Amongst the thirty busts that Edwards commissioned was a bust of William Ewart, who had introduced the first Free Library Act in 1850, presented to Westminster public library on 16 December 1904. Unfortunately, the library closed in the 1990s and the local authority has no record of the fate of the statue.

In 1905 Edwards asked for a copy of the bust to be made and presented it to the Manchester Central library, to commemorate the fiftieth anniversary of the founding of the first free library in Manchester, and Edwards was invited to Manchester to attend the anniversary celebrations. The library services in Manchester have no record of the present location of the bust.

**Joseph Lancaster and Michael Faraday**

Marble busts of Joseph Lancaster and Michael Faraday, executed by Henry C Fehr, were presented to the Borough Road Polytechnic, Southwark in 1904 and placed on marble brackets in the entrance hall. In 1930 the Polytechnic building was extensively altered and the busts were moved. For some time the bust of Lancaster was housed in the Polytechnic's Students' Union building but today it is on display in the University's National Bakery School restaurant, located in the University's tower block building on Borough Road.

*Bust of John Lancaster, given to the Borough Road Polytechnic. Now in the National Bakery School building at the South Bank University*

The bust of Faraday has, unfortunately, not fared as well as his companion. A Students' Union magazine from 1972, contained an article about the Lancaster bust, but asks the question 'where is Michael Faraday?' It would therefore seem that the bust has been missing for several decades and none of the university's current staff have any knowledge of what happened to it. The South Bank University does, however, continue their connection, through Passmore Edwards, to these two great men, commemorated as they are in the Lancaster Building and the Faraday Building.

**George Whitefield**

Whitefield was a nonconformist preacher, a contemporary of John Welsely and the Tabernacle in Tottenham Court Road was one of several founded by Whitefield. The foundation stone was laid on 10 May 1756 and Whitefield preached at the opening service, held in November of the following year.

Around 1904 Edwards presented a bust of Whitefield to the Tabernacle and there it was to remain until Palm Sunday 1945, when the Tabernacle was destroyed by a direct hit from a German V2 rocket, reputedly the last V2 to strike London.

Its site is now occupied by the George Whitefield Memorial Church, the American Church in London, a smaller replacement chapel opened in 1957, 201 years after the foundation of the original building. Whitefield's bust was lost.

In 1904 Passmore Edwards also presented a bust of the satirist and painter William Hogarth to the Chiswick town hall. Hogarth lived and is buried in Chiswick and the bust remains on display at the town hall.

Though Edwards wrote in his autobiography that he intended to celebrate the lives of other great men and women in this manner I have found no evidence of any being commissioned in addition to those he listed.

**An Oxford Scholarship**

In agreeing to fund the building for what is now the London School of Economics, Edwards endeavoured to provide education in those subjects needed by 'the business clerk, the journalist and the civil servant'.[4] But what was his motive for funding a scholarship at Oxford? His son, Harry, had attended Christ Church but had studied history, not the subject Edwards was to favour with a scholarship.

On 28 December 1900, John Churton Collins, Professor of English Literature at Birmingham, knocked on the door at 51 Bedford Square, and was met in the hall by Passmore Edwards.[5] Edwards, who said that he was due to lunch with his grandchildren, asked Collins to briefly explain the purpose of his visit, no doubt realising that this was no social call but a request for money. After Collins laid out his plan for an Oxford scholarship for the Comparative Study of Classical and English Literature. Edwards summed up by saying 'So, you want me to find the money for the Scholarship?' He then began to tell Collins of all the other requests he had received, what he had done and what he was expected to do, but, at least in Collins' mind, seemed willing to consider the matter.

On arriving home Collins immediately set about to develop his plan, writing to a number of leading members of the University, but not identifying the prospective donor by name, and then submitting these testimonials to Edwards. By now Edwards' enthusiasm had cooled and it took another direct approach before he was firmly on the hook.

An announcement in the *Times* in May 1901 declared that 'A decree was passed by Convocation accepting the offer by Mr John Passmore Edwards of the sum of £1,675 for the endowment of a scholarship for the encouragement of the study of English literature in its connection with the classical literatures of Greece and Rome, approving the regulations made for the scholarship, and recording the gratitude of the University for Mr. Passmore Edwards's munificence. The first examination for this scholarship will be held in the academic year, beginning at Michaelmas 1902'.

Originally the scholarship would provide a sum of £45 a year for three years. Today there are two prizes, each valued at £200. According to the *Oxford University Gazette*, one is awarded, 'if there is a candidate of sufficient merit, by the Moderators in Honour

Moderations in Classics and English, to the candidate whose performance in that examination they judge the best. The other prize will be awarded by the Examiners for the Final Honour School of Classics and English, to the candidate whose performance in that examination they judge the best. No special application is required for either prize'. Amongst recent winners is the opera singer, Laura Pooley.

In recent years the fund has also been used by the university to fund the Passmore Edwards symposia, on the interactions between English and classical literature and culture.

**'Jack's Palace'**

The British and Foreign Sailors Society was formed to administer to the needs of merchant sailors whilst in London. The Society had started by opening a hostel in an old war sloop on the Thames in 1818 and opened a sailors' institute in Shadwell in 1856. By the turn of the century the Society was working in more than a hundred ports, at home and across the world and with the lease of the headquarters at Shadwell about to expire and the expansion of the London docks meaning that the institute was no longer conveniently placed, the Society was looking for a new home.

The Lord Mayor launched the scheme to build a new centre at the Mansion House in 1900. Edwards was attracted by the Society's temperance principles but mainly because he saw the proposals, to build 'a home from home' where sailors of all nationalities would find shelter, as creating an international peace centre. Through the Archdeacon of London Edwards offered to present the Society with a building for their new headquarters, estimated at £5,000. As the proposals developed the costs, and

*'Jack's Palace', East India Road, Limehouse*

Edwards' contribution, increased. He eventually gave £14,000, the greatest amount ever received by the Society from one person. Edwards said that although he had cooperated with many others, and in many ways, to improve the conditions of life, nothing had given him more satisfaction than his active connection with the Society.

The architects Niven and Wigglesworth were chosen to design the building, to be constructed on a wedge shaped site fronting on to the East India Dock Road, Limehouse, close to the docks and similar homes for foreign sailors, and the foundation stone was laid in 1901. By the time the 'Sailor's Palace' was opened by the Prince of Wales, in May 1903, the cost of the building had risen to £18,000 but the total costs were more than £30,000, contributions arriving from heads of state, associations, and individuals, across the world.

On the ground floor were the Albert Victor Sailors' Rest, accommodation for the ordinary sailors, the American Room, a temperance restaurant and the smoking room whilst the first floor accommodated the Society's offices and boardroom, and the Passmore Edwards Ocean library started with his donation of 5,000 books. Through the Ocean library the Sailors Society was able to place collections of books on merchant ships throughout the world and exchange them when the ships visited a suitable port. The Princess of Wales 'launched' the library on the occasion of the opening of 'Jack's Palace' by placing a few books into a box that was to be sent to the crew of the steamship *Ophir*. On the second floor was the officers' and apprentices' flat and on the top floor, an observatory, navigation room and staff accommodation.

The addition of the Alexandra Wing, named after the Queen, almost doubled the size of the original proposal and contained a hall, Captain's and officer's dining room, a tearoom and the King Edward VII Nautical School.

The nautical school was for training officers for the merchant navy. In 1926 the school was recognised by the London County Council as a technical school and in 1949 it implemented a scheme by which senior courses were established at Sir John Cass College, while junior courses remained at the King Edward VII School. During the 1960s the department of navigation at Sir John Cass College merged with the King Edward VII Nautical College and moved from East Indian Dock Road to a new building at Tower Hill. At the same time Jack's Palace was closed and the building sold to the Toynbee Housing Association, today providing much needed social housing.

Since 1995 the Society has been known as the British and International Sailors' Society, and still works for the 'material, moral and spiritual welfare of seafarers in ports throughout the world'.

Edwards was amused that the hostel became to be known as Jack's Palace. He had been known as Jack when a lad and had now provided a home for sailors away from home. He often visited the site of the Palace during its construction, travelling with the Society's Secretary, the Reverend E Williams in his carriage – an East London omnibus – to watch progress. Just before Christmas of 1902 as they were alighting from the tram Williams said 'A thousand thanks, dear Mr Edwards'. 'What did you say,' he asked, a wonderful light playing in lustrous eyes – 'another £2,000?' On Christmas morning the Rev Williams received one of 'Edwards' delightful letters' and a cheque for £2,000. Williams said that he never knew a man do business of this kind so joyfully.

Left: *Drinking fountain at Christchurch Gardens, London*

Right: *Hoxton Square drinking fountain*

**Gardens and fountains**

In May 1890, Sir Edmund Currie unveiled a fountain in Victoria Park, funded by Passmore Edwards at a cost of £260, and erected by the Metropolitan Drinking Fountain and Cattle Trough Association. The fountain was a memorial to the political reformer John Bright. Edwards announced his intention to establish twelve further fountains in London and in different parts of the country.

In 1892 he offered £1,000 to erect a fountain to the memory of James Beal and J F B Firth, pioneers of London municipal reform and the LCC agreed to place this on either Blackfriars Bridge or on the Thames embankment[6] but no trace can be found today.

Some of the offers do not seem to have been taken up. In October of that year the *Pall Mall Gazette* contained a report that Passmore Edwards 'had shown a willingness to found a permanent scholarship at King's College School for a Chorister or to erect a fountain on the embankment' in the memory of the Rev Henry White of the Chapel Royal, Savoy; and as early as 1890 Edwards offered to erect a drinking fountain at Redruth, Cornwall, in memory of his mother, but the Council couldn't decide on a suitable location and Edwards withdrew the offer.

The Metropolitan Public Gardens Association was established in 1882 to preserve gardens, disused churchyards and open spaces within the area of the Metropolitan Police District. It actively campaigned to preserve open spaces with highest priority given to the most deprived inner city areas where overcrowding was at its worse. Passmore Edwards recognised the need for public open spaces to relieve the drudgery of life in the working-class areas and readily responded to a request for assistance from the association's founder, Lord Brabazon.

> My Lord
>
> In answer to your letter asking me to subscribe towards expenses in utilising for

public purposes the large parish churchyard of Woolwich, I cheerfully comply with your request. The very last thing I would sanction would be the desecration of 'God's Acre'. A graveyard, to my mind, is holy ground, and I never knowingly pass one without raising my hat. But for the sake of the living, and particularly in this overcrowded metropolis, where millions of our fellow citizens pass mostly, comfortless lives, I would make churchyards sweet resting places for the weary, and picturesque recreation grounds for the young.

You say that Woolwich churchyard is about four acres in extent and that it is near the centre of the town and situated on high ground, that it overlooks a fine view of the river Thames, that it would make a delightful garden, and that it the estimated cost of preparing it for public use would be about £1,200. The object aimed at is so good, and the derivable benefit so certain, that I most willingly respond to your appeal and undertake to meet the whole of the estimated charge. Please accept this as my New Year's gift to Woolwich, and believe me, –

Yours faithfully
J Passmore Edwards.

By the time that the Duchess of Fife opened the garden in May 1895, St Mary's graveyard, which had long been a wilderness, put on a new garb and bloomed with flowers.

Five years later Passmore Edwards added a drinking fountain and provided funds to keep the garden in good order. Although laid out by the MPGA the garden remained under the control of the local authority, as it is today. Southwark Council now maintains the garden but the fountain was removed in the late 1960s and its fate is not recorded. The garden surrounds St Mary's church, which dates back to 1732 and a stained glass window installed near the main door remembers the 590 people who lost their lives in the *Princess Alice* disaster of 1878. The *Princess Alice* was a paddle steamer in collision with a collier, the *Bywell Castle*, a short distance down river from the Woolwich ferry while returning from a day trip to Southend on Sea. The collier sliced the steamer in two, and it sank in a few minutes leaving the 700 passengers and crew to struggle for life in the polluted waters of the Thames. It was said that as many died from the pollution as from drowning and the disaster contributed to moves to start to clean up London's main artery. When a Mansion House fund was set up for the survivors and families of those who died Passmore Edwards was, as usual, near the top of the list of subscribers, giving fifty guineas.

Other fountains were provided at Stalbridge Common, Hackney; The Broadway, Hammersmith; Edgware Road, Kilburn; Duncan Terrace, Islington; Christchurch, Blackfriars; Hoxton Square; Leyton Square, Camberwell; Rotherhithe Street, Bermondsey; and Hackney Road, Shoreditch. These fountains were not just decorative memorials but provided a clean and free supply of drinking water within the reach of the poorest. The Association received support from temperance organisations concerned that beer was more easily obtained than safe drinking water. Many of the fountains also had troughs attached to them for dogs and Edwards commented on the debt owed to man's companion.

Like so much Victorian statuary and ornamental street furniture many of these fountains have since been removed and destroyed, but renewed interest in London's public open spaces has seen a few restored, although unfortunately no longer in use.

Although privately owned, the central garden at Hoxton Square was laid out by the MPGA and leased to the borough council. In 1901 Edwards added a drinking fountain. Now a public garden, protected under the Preservation of London Squares Act, 1906, it was restored in the mid-1990s.

The churchyard at Christchurch closed to burials in 1856. In 1900 the MPGA undertook to lay out the churchyard as a public garden and to install a Passmore Edwards drinking fountain. The Bankside Open Spaces Trust and Groundwork Southwark renovated the garden in 2000.

Albion Square, Hackney, was built in 1844 but by 1898 the central garden was derelict. Through grants from the MPGA the garden was restored and handed over to the Hackney Vestry, being reopened in July 1899 by Lord Meath. The *Hackney and Kingsland Gazette* said the new garden would 'vie in beauty with some of the prettiest gardens in the West End' and in 1910 the MPGA erected a drinking fountain in the centre of the garden, probably Passmore Edwards' last bequest. In 1999 the Albion Square garden celebrated its centenary by winning first prize in the Small Publicly Maintained Garden section of the London Garden Squares Competition.

*Albion Square Gardens. Set out by the Metropolitan Public Gardens Association with funding from Passmore Edwards*

# Twenty-five
# Ones That Got Away

The frequency with which Passmore Edwards presented his gifts to a wide range of communities led to numerous claims of gifts that either did not exist or fell by the way-side.

One such report was that Edwards had expressed a willingness to provide a free library at Margate.[1] The Margate Free Library Association did campaign for a public library in the town at the end of the nineteenth century but wrote not to Edwards but to Carnegie for support. Although the Carnegie Trust made an offer of £10,000 this lacked support from Councillors and the people of Margate had to wait until 1923 before their library was built. Edwards opened several other libraries, although he did not fund them. It is often thought that he funded the Walthamstow library, but Carnegie funded this, Edwards later presenting a bust of William Morris. Edwards also chose not to fund a library at Stoke Newington, the birthplace of his wife, but was still asked to open the library in 1892, presenting a thousand volumes of popular literature, 'selected by himself with great care and ability'.[2]

### The Albert Palace

In 1885 the Albert Exhibition Palace, a glass and iron structure originally built as part of the Dublin Exhibition of 1872, was re-erected in Battersea Park. The building in total covered an area over 6,500 square metres comprising of exhibition halls, conservatory, concert hall, aviary, and restaurants. Central to the concert hall was the grand organ, six distinct but connected organs with sixty seven stops and 4,200 pipes and at the opposite end of the concert hall an 'echo' organ, worked by an ingenious electrical arrangement from the solo keyboard. Not surprisingly, the venture was not a financial success and it closed in 1888. When in 1892 moves were made to demolish the buildings Passmore Edwards came forward to offer £13,000 to help purchase the building and hand it over to the London County Council, providing that they would maintain it in perpetuity. The Battersea Vestry offered £5,000 leaving only £2,000 to be found to meet the asking price of £20,000. Confident of raising the full amount the London County Council began the Parliamentary process then needed to give them the authority to acquire the building for use as a winter garden, where the local population could gather for recre-ation. Delays in securing the building led to the contents of the Palace being put up for sale to meet the ongoing costs. The organ, which had cost £5,000 to install was sold for just £600 but Hood Barnes, a member of the Council's Acquisition Team managed to persuade the purchaser to sell it to the Council for the same price he had paid. Although the enabling legislation passed through Parliament no progress had been made on completing the deal. By the beginning of 1894 it became known that Edwards had withdrawn his offer, causing Edwards to write to the *Times*, to explain.[3] He argued that he had not withdrawn his offer; rather it had never been accepted. Though his offer was clearly on the basis that it would be 'for the free use of the public', the Council had included in their application to Parliament provision 'to make from time to time such reasonable charges for admission to the building on such occasions as the Council may think fit; and also to let all or part of the building at a rental from time to time'. As far as Edwards was concerned he had offered one thing, they wanted another and his offer was never accepted. Hood Barnes retaliated, again in the *Times*, stating that his original conversations with Edwards had been clear that the Palace would be used for 'penny concerts' and the Parliamentary bill anticipated no more than this. He added that Edwards would have been fully aware of the wording of thebill and its passage through Parliament yet on not one single occasion had Edwards chosen to discuss his concerns with the Council. There is no further public statement from either party but the campaign was over. In May 1894 the structure of the Albert Palace was sold off in lots, to be demolished by the purchasers, and the land disposed of as building land. The Palace had originally cost £100,000 to build but was almost given away. The glazed roof, 1,900 square feet of glass, was sold for a mere £1 5s, the 800 tons of steelwork realised only £800.

### Actors' Orphanage Fund

Edwards remained alert to the areas where his money could be put to best use and although he used the expression 'the best for the most', some sectors of society that he assisted were very specific. Through meeting Sir Henry Irving, the Victorian actor, Edwards became aware of the Actors' Orphanage Fund. This Fund was used to place orphans of deceased actors in orphanages and schools or to help older children become independent through employment. The numbers of children supported by the Fund was small, only 21 in 1899, but Edwards clearly considered that more could be done. As with the orphans of teachers he offered to provide an orphanage for the children of actors if the fund would undertake to maintain and run it from their own resources.

Although the proposal brought about a lot of debate within the acting community the overall feeling was that their resources were too small to take on such a commitment. Reluctantly they told Edwards of their decision. His response was a gift of £1,000 to help the fund carry out its work.

### Cornwall Lighthouse

When Harry Passmore Edwards opened the St Agnes Institute he said that it had always been in his father's mind to erect a lighthouse on St Agnes Beacon. Like the later offer of a lighthouse at Falmouth, this was to be dedicated to John Couch Adams, but Trinity House thought that a lighthouse was not needed and the site was not suitable. If erected on the Beacon it would be so high it would be lost in the mists.

Falmouth's dismissal of Edwards offer of building a lighthouse on the Manacles did not deter him. He later declared that he intended to find a site on the Devon coast, again with the object of matching it with a similar light on the French coast, but nothing more came of it. Whether he considered it advisable to contact Trinity House to ask where a lighthouse would be most needed is not known.

When the *Monhegan* foundered on the Manacles, in 1895, with considerable loss of life, newspapers reported on Edwards previous offer to build a lighthouse and questioned the decision by Trinity House not to accept. It was, indeed, Trinity House's decision to reject the idea of placing a lighthouse on the Manacles, not the Borough Council's. The Falmouth Harbour Board had written to Trinity House with such a request in 1890, well before Edwards had made the offer to the Borough Councillors. Trinity House rejected the request on the basis that there was already a light at St Anthony and in poor visibility a ship's captain might mistake the Manacles light for the St Anthony light and turn on to the rocks in the belief that they were entering Falmouth.[4]

# Twenty-six
# Marriage, Children and Family Life

At the dinner organised by Edwards' former creditors in 1866 one of the speakers suggested that it was time Edwards found himself a wife, advice he seems to have taken, for at the age of forty-seven, he married Eleanor Elizabeth Humphreys, daughter of a porteait painter, Henry Vickers Humphreys. Eleanor was born in 1841 at Kennington, Middlesex and in 1861 is shown living at 23 Upper Street, Islington, the home of Emma Powell, both working as dyers' assistants. How she met Passmore Edwards is unknown, although he lived in Islington for some time, but they married at St Mary's Church, Lambeth, on 6 February 1870, by special licence, with Emma Powell as witness.

*Eleanor Humphreys, possibly in her wedding dress*

## Family Life

In 1871 the family are living at 31 Tavistock St, just round the corner from Edwards' offices at the Strand; no more than a mile, but a long way from Holborn where Edwards had lived when arriving in London 26 years earlier. The census shows Ann Wyatt, employed as general servant whilst her husband, Joseph, is described as Passmore Edwards' messenger.

Edwards does not refer to his wife and children in his autobiography. His publishing and political careers would have left little time for family life and in any case he would have considered that this side of his life was of no business to anyone else.

However, Churton, discussing his first visit to Edwards, at 12:15pm on 28 December 1900 to ask him to fund a perpetual scholarship at Oxford university, describes how Edwards received him in the hall at 51 Bedford Place. Edwards told him to be quick as he about to go to lunch with his grandchildren. When Passmore Edwards and his wife were seen at the wedding of Emma Broughton, sister of actress Phyllis Broughton, the reporter commented that he had never seen Edwards at such a festivity before but Eleanor appeared more frequently in the society press. A quiet, gentle but charming woman she helped to organise bazaars and charity functions as well as share in many of her husband's interests. She also helped organise the excursions into the countryside for thousands of poor London children, paid for by the *Echo*; was a member of the National Society for Women's Suffrage; the Women's Movement to Stop the War – the Boer War; and many other associations. In June 1888 Eleanor sent out invitations to a meeting in support of the National Society for Women's Suffrage at their home at Queen Anne's Gate. But it was Passmore Edwards who took the chair and the group called on the Government to grant the vote to women on an equal footing as for men.

But there are few other pointers to Passmore Edwards' family life to be gleaned from amongst press reports and other accounts other than in a letter written by Mary Ward, following Edwards' death, which said that 'his family were his friends and helpers throughout'.

Harry, when speaking at the retirement presentation of Mr W D Nott, former advertising manager of the *Echo*, said that he had been a friend of Mr Nott since he was seven when his father brought him into the *Echo* office. Was Edwards preparing his son for a future career in publishing or was this a father sharing his interests with his son, as his own father had done, taking him to hear lectures back in Cornwall?

*Eleanor Edwards, probably taken in 1893 by F Argall, Truro*

Often spoken of as a dour man, Edwards spoke with humour, often making himself the butt of his own jokes. At Blackwater, after opening the extension to the Institute in 1893, he quoted Shakespeare: 'there is a divinity that shapes our ends, rough hew them as we may' but there appeared to be two divinities attempting to shape his course in

Cornwall. Wherever he went there were both a photographer and a reporter. If he looked away, the photographer caught it, and if he talked nonsense, down it went.

His grandson, Robert Ingham Clark, who was only 15 years old when his grandfather died, wrote that Edwards was a hard man who drove himself hard, but others remarked upon his charm and the sparkle in his eye. Holyoake found him the most elegant adversary he had ever come across – 'A mass of wavy black hair and pleasant expression made him picturesque. He was slim, alert, and fervid'. Ingham Clark described him as 'looking Celtic rather than Saxon, an almost Semitic nose, very dark complexion, and long black curly hair and beard till age changed its colour. He had dark, large, flashing eyes which made him stand out vividly even in a room full of people.' He was certainly not a character easily forgotten. One man attending the opening of the St George in the East library remarked upon hearing Edwards lecture at the local Institute 50 years earlier.

During his early adult life, both in Manchester and for several years in London, he lived a very simple life with little money. It was during this time, from 1847 to 1859, that he was not only teetotal but also a vegetarian. What money he had he ploughed into his publications and later into paying off his creditors. He was also a member of a number of political and social reform groups, each of which would have required a subscription of varying amounts and though he received fees or expenses for attending some meetings, these were often no more than his costs. Later, when his fortunes had changed, he still found a need to be economic in his daily life, including lunching at the Democratic Club in Essex Street where lunch cost a shilling.[1] At the ceremony to lay the foundation stone at the Falmouth hospital in 1893 he said that his wants were no more than they were when he left Cornwall fifty years earlier. His dinner cost him scarcely more than it did then and he 'gloried in living laborious days and scorning delights'. In 1898 he put his longevity down to constant hard work sandwiched with occasional short holidays and accompanied by reasonable precautions, and recommending that one should always sleep with the bedroom window open all night winter and summer alike.[2]

But perhaps family life was not as 'austere' and 'frugal', 'making Eleanor's life grim in the extreme', as stated by Ingham Clark. In some respects he was not the miser that he is often made out to be. One only has to look at the property in which he lived from the time he entered Parliament, when he was living at Queen Anne's Gate, Kensington, to realise this. He was later to move to 51 Bedford Square, Bloomsbury, and finally Netherhall Gardens, Hampstead, where he died in 1911. When a painting of Milton as a young boy was wanted for an exhibition it was found to be hanging in Edwards' home, and was willingly loaned for the event. He had bought the painting, by Cornelius Janssen, from Christies in 1884 for 330 guineas. As well as his love of art, Aaron Watson said that he 'dealt privately in art, with as secure an instinct as if he had been one of the children of Israel'.[3] Edwards was such a well-known collector that the satirical magazines of the day often commented on the fact and his appearance at auctions and galleries. He admired marquetry and inlaid furniture, some of which remains within the family today.

Later in life he was to foster the hermit myth, otherwise being plagued by visitors asking for money. 'Why,' he wrote, 'should anyone who supplies a public library or a convalescent home be pelted with begging letters to build churches?' Even strangers wrote or turned up on the doorstep to ask for financial assistance for themselves, causing him 'contrary to my disposition and desire' to cultivate the life of the recluse.

To his children, Harry and Ada, he may have been seen, when he was seen, as a hard-working man who was rarely at home. He was 48 when Harry was born, with a working day that would have taken him away from home during most of Harry's waking hours.

The family did, however, accompany Edwards on his trips to open or lay foundation stones at the many buildings he funded, and many more that he did not contribute to. Eleanor, as well as taking a personal role in organising and choosing furnishings for the hospital wards that he funded, took part in many ceremonies and opening several buildings, although she is not recorded as having made a speech, Edwards doing this on her behalf. Harry too, having reached the age of majority in 1892, took his part in the ceremonies. It was Harry who laid the foundation stone for the Perranporth Convalescent Home in 1892, erected in memory of Edwards' mother; his father didn't attend; and it was Eleanor who opened the home some months later. Though Ada is often present at the ceremonies, there is no record of her taking an active part.

**Ada Edwards**

There is a mystery surrounding the birth of Ada, their first child. The census of 1871, twelve months after the marriage of Passmore Edwards and Eleanor, gives Ada as being five years old. She was baptised on 12 February 1867, the church register describing her as being the daughter of Eleanor, and John Edwards, publisher, living at 4 Russell Street, Brixton, and being just twelve months old. Passmore Edwards was a man of honour with a respect for the truth. He would not have declared that he was the father if that was not the case; he had recovered his wealth sufficiently to pay off his former creditors by the time that Ada was born, so why wait another five years before marrying Eleanor? And where, and

*Ada Edwards*

under what circumstances, did Eleanor and her child live during this time?

Ada was taught at home by a governess for a while, presented to court at eighteen, attended the social events expected of a young woman in her social position and could list amongst her friends Emma and Phyllis Broughton. Unfortunately there is no evidence of Ada's later education so we do not know how it compared to Harry's. In October 1889 Ada married Frederick Walter Fell Clark, manager and director of the family paint-manufacturing firm, Robert Ingham Clark & Co and they had three children.

**Harry Passmore Edwards**

Harry was given the education that Passmore Edwards had not received. After attending Westminster School from the age of twelve he went to Christ Church, Oxford, where he studied history, obtaining a third class degree. After graduating he spent a short time in Heidelberg before returning to London to become a director of the newly formed Strand Newspaper Company and, with apparently no experience of journalism, general manager of three successful publications; a position that had taken his father more than thirty years to achieve.

Robert Ingham Clark, wrote that his grandfather didn't see eye to eye with his uncle Harry. While Passmore Edwards lived for 'Peace at any price', Harry was a keen soldier,[4] joining at the age of seventeen the Middlesex Volunteers, the Artists Rifles.

After 1815, following the Battle of Waterloo and the Peninsular War, the local militia and volunteer forces were mostly disbanded. However, by 1847, when relationships with France were again strained, the Duke of Wellington led moves to alert the public to the state of Britain's defences. Seven years later the country was again at war, in the Crimea, followed almost immediately by the Indian Mutiny and the first Opium War with China. Initially the government rejected a call from Sir Charles Napier for the enlistment of volunteers to defend the country in case of invasion, but after 1858, with public concern outpouring in an almost uncontrollable wave of patriotic emotion, the War Office authorised the formation of Volunteer Corps.

This was the period through which Passmore Edwards had been most directly involved in the Peace movement. His addresses to the Chartist rallies in Nottingham and Loughborough, in 1847, had led to attendance at the 1848, 1849 and 1850 Peace Conferences. His pamphlets, *The War a Blunder and a Crime*, published in 1855, denounced the British involvement in the dispute in the Crimea and in 1858, *The Triple Curse*, the first Opium War with China and the actions of the East India Company. He toured the country speaking in favour of arbitration and campaigning against

*Harry Passmore Edwards in the uniform of the Artists' Rifles*

the Militia Bill[5] and everything that concerned war. His membership of the Peace Society, and the publication of the Peace Advocate at his expense, demonstrated the strength of his pacificist principles.

The 38th Middlesex (Artists) Rifle Volunteers was one of the earliest volunteer corps to be formed. Initially the Corps was composed of painters, sculptors, musicians, writers and poets, actors, and architects; amongst them the young painter and sculptor, Lieutenant Frederick Leighton, later to become Colonel and, in 1878, Sir Frederick Leighton and President of the Royal Academy.

Membership of the corps was on two levels; those enrolled for service in Great Britain had to provide their own uniform and equipment, pay an entrance fee of 10s 6d and an annual subscription of £1 1s; honorary members were under no liability for military service but had to pay an annual subscription of £2 2s or a one-off payment of £10 10s. Enlistment was by direct introduction by a serving or former member and with expansion of the corps non-artists were permitted to enlist, opening the door to Harry Passmore Edwards.

Officers were selected only from amongst the ranks and Harry slowly climbed the ladder, promoted to second lieutenant in 1900, lieutenant in 1904 and captain in 1909. At the outbreak of the Great War the corps became an officer training unit both in England and in France, often sending young men to the front with only the most basic of training as an officer. Harry was eventually sent to France in June 1916 and sent up the line the following year, but remained there only two months before returning to base for treatment for a suspected heart condition. His commanding officer, however, later reported that he 'lacked the physical and temperament needed to work in the trenches' and he did not return to the front line. Following demobilisation, in 1918, he returned to England and his position at Strand Newspapers.

Whereas his father had lived a simple life, Harry enjoyed the advantages of his position in society. He became Secretary of the Playgoer's Club, attained Grand Lodge rank within freemasonry in 1907 and was described as a moderate, but dedicated golfer who knew all of the major courses. In 1895 Harry married Grace Alice Hill and they had four children. Grace remarked upon having looked out of the window one morning to see her husband 'playing with his toys' – polishing his golf clubs ready for a day on the golf course rather than his office.

Silvanus Trevail saw the marriage as an admirable opportunity for the Cornish people to mark their appreciation of Passmore Edwards' generosity. Together with Falmouth Councillor Webber and other well-known gentlemen he lost no time in getting a county subscription scheme afloat to provide a wedding present for Edwards' only son. But directly Edwards heard of the project he promptly put his foot down and said he would have none of it.[6] Harry's view of this is not recorded. At Newlyn Art Gallery Stanhope Forbes called for '3 cheers for Mr Passmore Edwards junior' remarking that he hoped for all their sakes that he would follow in his father's footsteps. Harry had responded to say it was an unexpected pleasure to be the recipient of such kindness and he agreed with Mr Forbes in that he hoped it would always be in his power to follow in his father's footsteps for so long as it be his benefit to live on this earth. The day after, at Camborne, after Harry had opened the free library, Edwards remarked that he hoped his son would be a chip off the old block and a much greater man than his father.[7] It was a hard act to follow and although Harry did continue in some of his father's charitable works, being a trustee of the Railwaymen's Convalescent Home at Herne Bay and the Swanley School for Boys, he chose a different way of life.

# Twenty-seven
# His Last Days

Passmore Edwards became ill early in 1911. By March, he was so ill he needed constant attention and two nurses were living at his Hampstead home.[1] The *Times* court circular reported on 1 April that 'the condition of Mr Passmore Edwards showed no improvement' and daily recorded his steady deterioration.

It is the Rev Matthews,[2] with whom Edwards worked to establish the Sailor's Palace, who tells of Edwards' final struggle. He was with Edwards just a few hours before he died. 'On the little table,' he said, 'was the gold watch bearing the inscription: Presented to Passmore Edwards, Esq., October 29th, 1866, by friends who have special and unusual occasion to testify their appreciation of his integrity and uprightness.' In the sickroom there was a bookmark on which was sewn – 'Susan Edwards, your affectionate mother, born March 14, 1786. May you be happy, blest, and free from every ill. Good-bye'. This simple marker was kept in his books as he read them through all the years. Perhaps since that time, sixty-seven years earlier, when he had first left Blackwater to find his fame and fortune.

As he drifted in and out of a coma, he said 'Where is my mother?' 'In Heaven dear,' said his wife; 'would you like to go to her?' 'Yes I would,' he replied.

And so he passed away. The *Times*,[3] which Edwards had so vigorously opposed during his early life, wrote 'He did more good in his time than almost any other of his contemporaries'.

A decade earlier Passmore Edwards had said 'The man who imports the most wisdom into his daily doings will live the longest and the happiest and will serve his generation the best.'

He was laid to rest at Kensal Green cemetery, after a small private funeral, to be joined five years later by his wife, Eleanor, and many more years later by his son, Harry. As long ago as 1834 the *Penny Magazine* carried an engraving of the cemetery and included an article which Passmore Edwards may have read as a boy.

*Passmore Edwards is buried with his wife and son at Kensal Green Cemetery*

Only weeks before his death the Rev Matthews noted that Edwards longed to get better, sometimes half consciously saying 'My work is not yet done'. In reality, his work was not done. One can only guess at the numbers that have benefited from the Passmore Edwards legacy. Those previously denied hospital treatment and subsequently treated at one of the hospitals that he helped to fund; those who learnt to read and write through attendance at his libraries, or who learnt a craft at one of the arts, science and technical schools and, in the case of the Camberwell School of Art, still do. And the thousands upon thousands that made up the weekly turnover at the eight convalescent and children's holiday homes. Men like those at the Herne Bay Railwaymen's Home, who wanted their families to know how they were being looked after by sending them a postcard showing the facilities they were enjoying. The children from the East End pictured at the Sunday School Society Holiday Home at Clacton in 1903, are just a few of the many hundreds that stayed there over the years, and there are many more who lived and worked at Chalfont St Peter.

Edwards was, said Rev Matthews, a man of deeds, rather than words. The results of his deeds are amongst us still, perhaps to inspire us, in our own way, to do as he did and *live laborious days*.

# Notes

## Preface

1 *English Radicalism: 1853-1886*, Vol 4 -1886; S Maccoby, 2001, p 106
2 *John Passmore Edwards, 1823-1911, An account of his life and works*; P Baynes, 1994
3 *A Few Footprints*; J Passmore Edwards. 1904
4 *English Philanthropy 1660-1960*.

## One: A Blackwater Boy; making of the man

1 *The History of Blackwater*; Clive Benny & Tony Mansell
2 Memoir of Robert Ingham Clark; unpublished family papers.
3 *The Life and Good Works of John Passmore Edwards*; R S Best, Dyllansow Turan, 1981, p 8.
4 Until 1851 there was a tax on any property with more than six windows.
5 *Methodism in Blackwater, 1767-1973*; Thomas Shaw, 1973, p 24.
6 *Royal Cornwall Gazette*; 14 August 1890.
7 *Blackwater School Centenary Souvenir 1877-1977*; Blackwater CP School, 1977.
8 *A Few Footprints*; John Passmore Edwards, 1906
9 Outlined in the Appendix: Beliefs.
10 *Memoir of Robert Fell Clark*; family papers
11 *Cholera 1832*; Robert John Morris, Croom Helm, 1976, p 13.
12 Bible Christian Chapel.
13 *Methodism in Blackwater, 1767-1973*; Thomas Shaw, 1973, p 16.
14 *Salisbury Times & South Wilts Gazette*; Saturday 29 May 1880
15 *Robert Lowery, Radical and Chartist*; Brian Harrison & Patricia Hollis, Europa Publications, London, 1979, p 233.
16 The difficulty in travel prompted Edwards to sign a petition in 1845, calling on the High Sheriff of Cornwall to arrange a meeting to ensure the provision of a railway to connect Exeter with Penzance and Falmouth.

## Two: The Manchester School

1 *The Sentinel*; London, 14 September 1844.
2 *Manchester Times & Gazette*; Manchester, 12 October 1844.
3 *Manchester Guardian*; 23 November 1844.
4 *The Sentinel*; London, 16 November 1844.
5 Ibid; 28 December 1844.
6 *Manchester Guardian*; 4 December 1844.
7 Ibid; 7 December 1844.
8 *Oxford Dictionary of National Biography*; Dr Ralph Waller,

## Three: Victorian London

1 *Victorian London, The Life of a City 1840-1870*; Liza Picard, Weidenfield & Nicholson, 2005, p 2.
2 *A Social History of England, 1851-1990*; François Bédarida, Routledge, London, 1991, p 24.
3 *A Few Footprints*; Passmore Edwards, 1906, p 20.
4 *Victorian London, The Life of a City 1840-1870*; Liza Picard, Weidenfield & Nicholson, 2005, p 93.
5 *Radical Fights of Forty Years*; Howard Evans, *Daily News*, pp 5-7.

## Four: In Pursuit of Reform

1 *A Few Footprints*; Passmore Edwards, 1906, p 24.
2 An Irish radical politician, one time MP for County Cork and founder of the *Northern Star* newspaper in Leeds.
3 A London based radical newspaper, which supported the Anti-Corn Law League.
4 *The Times*; 11 April 1848.
5 *A Few Footprints*; Passmore Edwards, 1906, p 25.
6 *Nottingham Journal*; 14 April 1848
7 G J Holyoake (1817-1906), Secularist and freethought campaigner throughout the 19C. Holyoake was the last person in England to be sent to prison for atheism.
8 *A History of the Chartist Movement*; Julius West, Houghton Mifflin, 1920, p 259
9 *Manchester Times*, 20 Nov 1858.
10 *Berrow's Worcester Journal*; 22 May 1858.
11 *Peoples Journal*; London, Vol 7, 1849.
12 *Riotous Victorians*, Donald C Ritcher, p 52, Ohio University Press.
13 *Lloyds Weekly Newspaper* (London), 5 August 1866.
14 *Grand Tours and Cook's Tours: A history of leisure travel. 1750-1915*; L Withey, William Morrow & Co Ld, 1997, p 146.
15 *The Morning Chronicle* (London), 7 May 1861

## Five: Early Steps in Publishing

1 *Manchester Guardian*; 6 February 1847.
2 *A Few Footprints*; Passmore Edwards, 1906, p 20.
3 *The Public Good*; J Passmore Edwards, 1850.
4 *Lloyds Weekly Newspaper*; London, 23 November 1851.
5 *A Few Footprints*; Passmore Edwards, 1906, p 11.
6 *The Examiner*; London, 10 January 1852.
7 *Trewman's Exeter Flying Post or Plymouth and Cornish Advertiser*; Exeter, England 6 March 1861
8 *John Passmore Edwards, 1823-1911, An Account of his Life and Works*; Peter Baynes, privately published 1994, p 36.
9 Ibid.
10 *Derby Mercury*; Derby, England, 23 June 1852.

## Six: The Darkest of Days

1 Unpublished family papers.
2 *Bradford Observer*; 14 December 1854.
3 http://www25.uua.org/uuhs/duub/articles/jamesmartineau.html; accessed 9 July 2009.
4 *A Tribute to John Passmore Edwards*; An address given by Knighton Berry at St Ives Library, 31 May 2007.
5 *Bibliotheca Cornubiensis*, G C Boase & W P Courtney, Longmans, London, 1874.
6 *Manchester Times*; 27 May 1865
7 *City Press*; 4 November 1866.
8 *The Life & Good Works of John Passmore Edwards*; R S Best, Truran, Redruth, 1981, p 14.

## Seven: A Foot Soldier for Peace

1 *John Passmore Edwards, An Account of his Life and Works*; Peter Baynes, privately published 1994, p 34.
2 *The War, A Blunder and a Crime*; J Passmore Edwards, Houlston & Stoneman, 1855, p 4.
3 *Bibliotheca Corubiensis*; A-Q; G C Boase & W P Courtney, 1874, p 136.
4 *West Briton*; Truro, 16 March 1849.
5 *The British Peace Movement, 1870-1914;* Paul Laity, Oxford Historical Monographs, 2002, p 18
6 *Daily News* (London), 16 Sep 1862
7 *The Leeds Mercury* (Leeds), 12 April 1864.
8 *A Few Footprints*; J Passmore Edwards, p 29, 1905
9 *The British Peace Movement, 1870-1914*; Paul Laity, Oxford Historical Monographs, 2002, p 98.
10 *Hansard*; 20 July 1882.
11 *Manchester Guardian*; 15 July 1882.
12 *The Pro-Boers, An Anatomy of an Anti-war movement*; Stephen Koss, ed, 1977.
13 *The Times*; London, 12 January 1900.
14 *Lloyds Weekly Newspaper*; London, 4 February 1900.

## Eight: Crime and Punishment

1 *Daily News*; (London) 26 Aug 1859.
2 *The Science of Sherlock Holmes*; E J Wagner p 52-54, John Wiley, 2007.
3 *The Preston Guardian*; (Preston), 14 June 1856.
4 *The Abolition of Capital Punishment in Britain* (The End of the Rope, Part 1); Tom Phillips, *Contemporary Review*.
5 *Liverpool Mercury* 30 September 1859.
6 *Daily News*; (London), 27 December 1856.
7 *Supervising Offenders in the Community; A History of Probation Theory and Practice*; Maurice Vanstone, p 23-24, Ashgate, 2007.
8 *Daily News*; (London), 24 January 1857.
9 *Lloyd's Weekly Newspaper*; (London), 18 January 1857.

## Nine: Newspapers and Publishing

1 *A Few Footprints*; J Passmore Edwards, 1906, p 33.
2 *The Peoples Journal* had funded two lifeboats
3 *John Passmore Edwards, An Account of his Life and Works*; P Baynes, Privately published, 1994. p 47.
4 *Radical fights of Forty Years*; Howard Evans, *Daily News & Leader*, 1913, p 83.
5 *Bygones worth remembering*; G Holyoake, nd.
6 *Great London Dailies, Leisure Hour*; H W Massingham, September 1892.
7 *The English Mechanic*; 10 January, 1890.
8 *Radical Fights of Forty Years*; Howard Evans, *Daily News & Leader*, 1913, p 87.
9 'Famous Batchelor Women' by Sarah H Tooley, *The Women at Home*, date unknown
10 *Pearson's Magazine* July 1896.
11 *The Examiner*; (London), 5 August 1876.
12 *Radical fights of Forty Years*; Howard Evans, *Daily News & Leader*, 1913, p 85.
13 *Hansard*; (London), House of Commons debate, 26 February 1883, vol 276 cc 843-4.
14 *Irish Independent*; 9 June 1910.
15 *Radical fights of Forty Years*; Howard Evans, Daily News & Leader, 1913, p 87
16 Quoted in *Encyclopaedia of the British Press 1422-1992*; ed Dennis Griffiths, 1992, p 219.
17 A 'wayzgoose' was an annual entertainment given by master printers to their employees.
18 *Royal Cornwall Gazette*; Truro, 29 June 1893.
19 *A Newspaper Man's Memories*; Aaron Watson, Hutchinson & Co, London, 1925, p 127.
20 *The Derby Mercury*; (Derby), 8 August 1883.
21 *John Passmore Edwards, 1823-1911, An account of his life and works*; Peter Baynes, 1994, p 64.
22 *Belfast News-Letter*; Belfast, 29 July 1885.
23 *Glasgow Herald*; 28 August 1892.
24 *Freeman's Journal and Daily Commercial Advertiser*; London, 1 December 1897.
25 *Weekly Times & Echo*; 19 August 1894.
26 *Hearth & Home* (London) 5 Dec 1895.
27 *Newspaper Press Directory*, C Mitchell & Co, London, 1890.
28 *Allinson Essays, Extracts from the essays of T R Allinson*; Compiled and edited by Bob Metcalfe & Kat MacDonald-Taylor, Richmond Tower Communications Ltd, 2007.
29 *Weekly Times & Echo*; London,26 Aug 1894.
30 *The Liberty Review*; 27 Jan 1894 p 136.
31 *Odds, Intelligence and prophecies: Racing News in the Penny Press, 1855-1914*; Matthew McIntire, *Victorian Periodicals Review* 41:4, Winter 2008.
32 *Sporting Life*; London, 20 October 1877.
33 *Echoes of a Century*; Gordon Sewell, Southern Newspapers Ltd, 1964, p 28-30.
34 Ibid; p 32.
35 Ibid; p 36-43.
36 Speech during annual outing and dinner of the staff of Strand Newspapers and reported in the *Weekly Times & Echo*, London, July, 1894

## Ten: Slavery

1 *The Times*; London, 19 May 1853.
2 *Preston Guardian*; Preston England, 16 December 1852.
3 The word 'boycott' entered into the English language after Captain Charles Boycott, an agent for an absentee Irish landowner in County Mayo, Ireland, was ostracised by the local population when he evicted tenants from their land

after they had demanded a rent reduction. His workers and servants laid down their tools and the local businessmen stopped trading with him.

4 *The Anti-Slavery Reporter*; 1 November 1948, p 176.
5 *The Caledonian Mercury*, 7 Feb 1863.

## Eleven: Parliamentary Business

1 *The Examiner*; 1 July 1865.
2 *West Briton*; (Truro), 21 September 1868.
3 Ibid; (Truro),
4 *English Radicalism: 1853-1886*, Vol 4,-1886; S Maccoby, 2001, p 106.
5 *West Briton*; (Truro), 1 October 1868.
6 *Reynolds Newspaper*; (London) 15 November 1868.
7 *West Briton*; (Truro), 1 December 1868.
8 *Bristol Mercury*; (Bristol) 21 November 1868.
9 *Chatham & Rochester Observer*; 14 November 1885.
10 *Pall Mall Gazette*; (London), 11 May 1869.
11 *The Times*; 29 Jan 1879.
12 *Pall Mall Gazette*; London, 20 March 1879.
13 *Trewman's Exeter Flying Post or Plymouth and Cornish Advertiser*; Exeter, 6 March 1861
14 *Salisbury Times*; Sat Mar 20 1880.
15 *The Taint in Politics, a study in the Evolution of Parliamentary Corruption*; Joseph McCabe, Grant Richards Ltd, London, 1920, p 211.
16 *Salisbury Times*; 24 April 1880.
17 *Salisbury Times Supplement*; 20 March 1880.
18 *Chatham & Rochester Observer*; 14 November 1885.

## Twelve: Creating a Legacy

1 John D Rockefeller was reported to be the richest man in the world at that time.
1 *A Few Footprints*; p 43.
2 *West Briton*; 1 October, 1868.
3 *The Autobiography of Andrew Carnegie*.
4 *North American Review*; June 1899. p 653-665.
5 *West Briton*; Nov 1890.
6 *Passmore Edwards Institutions, Founding and Opening Ceremonies*; J.J.MacDonald, Strand Newspaper Co, 1900, p 68.
7 *Royal Cornwall Gazette*: 14 August 1890.
8 *A Few Footprints*, Passmore Edwards, p 50, 1905.
9 *Morning Chronicle*, (London), 19 September 1849.
10 *Liverpool Mercury*, (Liverpool), 30 April 1850

## Thirteen: Family Memorials

1 *The First Cornish hospital*; 1975, C T Andrews.
2 *Passmore Edwards Institutions*; JJ McDonald, Strand Newspaper Co, 1900.
3 *The First Cornish hospital*; 1975, C T Andrews.
4 Report of the St Austell Medical Officer. *Cornish Gazette*; 10 May 1890.
5 *Chart & Compass*; May 1911, p 105.
6 *A Few Footprints*; John Passmore Edwards, 1906. P 9.
7 *Newton Abbot Western Guardian*; January 1903.
8 *East & South Devon Advertiser*; Newton Abbot, October 1904.
9 *Lloyd's Weekly London Newspaper*; London, 10 May 1846.
10 *The Cornishman*; 28 September 1893.
11 *The Hayle Institute*; Patricia Adams, 1996.
12 *St Agnes & Mechanics' Institute 1893-1993 Centenary Booklet*; St Agnes Museum Trust, Clements Press, 1993, p 6-7.
13 *A Few Footprints*; J Passmore Edwards, 1906, p 6
14 *The book of St Day - The Town of Trynyte*; J Mills & P Annear, Halsgrove, 2003.
15 *West Briton*; (Truro), 11 May 1893.
16 Ibid; 19 April, 1894.
17 *Redruth Times*; 12 April, 1895.

## Fourteen: Cornwall Libraries

1 *Falmouth Packet*; Falmouth; 24 May 1894.
2 The Falmouth Misericordia Society was founded in 1807 'for the relief of poor strangers and distressed persons of the Town'.
3 *West Briton*; Truro, 10 May 1894.
4 *The St Ives Times & Echo & Hayle Times- Supplement*; 25 April, 1997, p 2
5 *The Library World; the Journal of the Library Association*, Vol 3; 1900, p 58.
6 *Falmouth Packet*; Falmouth, 2 February 1895.
7 *A Mural Miscellany*; Annie Dingle, Privately published, p 4.
8 *Silvanus Trevail, Cornish Architect and Entrepreneur*; R Perry and H Harradence, Francis Boutle, 2008, p 128.
9 Bodmin Library ; W H Gladwell, An essay, submitted in candidacy for the PG Diploma in Building Conservation at the School of Architecture at the University of Plymouth, 2000.
10 *Silvanus Trevail, Cornish Architect and Entrepreneur*; R Perry and H Harradence, Francis Boutle, 2008, p 35.
11 Bodmin Library; W H Gladwell, An essay, submitted in candidacy for the PG Diploma in Building Conservation at the School of Architecture at the University of Plymouth, 2000.
12 *Silvanus Trevail, Cornish Architect and Entrepreneur*; R Perry and H Harradence, Francis Boutle, 2008, p 129.
13 *Cornish and Devon Post*; 28 April 1900.
14 *Silvanus Trevail, Cornish Architect and Entrepreneur*; R Perry and H Harradence, Francis Boutle, 2008, p 116.
15 *Passmore Edwards Institutions, Founding & Opening Ceremonies*; J J Macdonald, Strand Newspaper Company, 1900, p 90.

## Fifteen: London Public Libraries

1 *The Oxford Art Journal*; Juliet Steyn, 13 February 1990, p 44.
2 *The History of Rate-Supported Public Libraries in London: 1850-1900*: Derek Jones 1973 & 2002, p 100.
3 *Library Architecture in Tower Hamlets*; Denise Bang & Jennifer Brown, 2006.
4 *John Passmore Edwards, Philanthropist, A History Essay Presented at the Architectural Association School of Architecture*; Nicholas Rose, June 1971, p 14.
5 *Passmore Edwards Institutions*; J J Macdonald, Strand Newspaper Co, 1900.p 1.
6 *Daily Telegraph*; Sukhdev Sandhu, July 2005.
7 Ibid; Mark Sanderson, 7 August 2007.
8 *The History of Rate-Supported Public Libraries in London: 1850-1900*; D Jones 1973 & 2002, p 62-63.
9 Ibid; p 32-33.
10 Ibid; p 87.
11 *Minutes of the St Bride Foundation*; April 1894.
12 *The History of the Rate-Supported Public Libraries in London: 1850-1900*; D Jones, 1973 & 2002, p 37-38
13 *South London Press*; London, 23 May 1903.
14 *The Liberty Review*; London, 15 December 1897.
15 *Daily News*; 11 June 1891.
16 *The Times;* London, 30 October 1899.
17 *The History of Rate-Supported Public Libraries in London 1850-1900*; D Jones, 1973-2002, p 96.
18 Ibid; p 76-77.
19 http://www.actonhistory.co.uk/acton; accessed 12 June 2009.
20 *The First Hundred Years of Acton Library*; A & T Harper Smith, Acton History Group, 2000.
21 *Passmore Edwards Institutes, Founding & Opening Ceremonies*; J J Macdonald, Strand Newspaper Company, 1900, p 49.
22 *Acton Town Hall – A Vision for the Future: Progress Report*; London Borough of Ealing, 25 March 2004. p 7
23 *The Building News*; 28 Oct 1898 & 5 Jan 1900, Strand Newspaper Co.
24 Ibid; 5 Jan 1900, Strand Newspaper Co.

## Sixteen: Hospitals and Convalescent Homes

1 *Passmore Edwards Institutions, Founding & Opening Ceremonies*; J J Macdonald, Strand Newspaper Co, 1900, p5
2 Ibid, p5.
3 *Historical Account of Charing Cross Hospital and Medical School*; W Hunter MD FRCP, John Murray, 1913
4 *West Briton*; (Truro); 8 May 1890
5 *Nursing Record*; 26 November 1891.
6 *Passmore Edwards Institutions, Founding & Opening Ceremonies*; J J Macdonald, Strand Newspaper Co, 1900, pp 20-21.
7 *The Times*; 24 November, 1911.
8 *Falmouth Packet*, (Falmouth); 4 May 1895.
9 *Nursing Review*; 27 April 1895.
10 *The Times*; 24 November, 1911.
11 *Well Done, the History of Willesden Hospital*; Len Snow, Brent PCT, 2006.

12 Ibid; 12 February 1898.
13 *The Nursing Record Hospital World Supplement*; 17 August 1893.
14 *Weekly Times & Echo*; 26 August 1894.
15 *The British Journal of Nursing*; March 1948, p 7.
16 *Passmore Edwards Institutions, Founding & Opening Ceremonies*; J J Macdonald, Strand Newspaper Co, 1900, p 10
17 Ibid, p 11
18 *Printers' Charitable Trust: Recruitment briefing*, 2008.
19 *Passmore Edwards Institutions, Founding & Opening Ceremonies*; J J Macdonald, Strand Newspaper Co, 1900, p 19-20
20 *The Standard*; London, 28 October, 1898.
21 *The Grays & Tilbury Gazette and South Essex Pictorial Telegraph*; 23 July 1923.
22 *Acton Hospital 1897-1997*; Acton History Group, 1997.
23 *The First Century*; George Tremlett, The Workingmen's Club and Institute Union Ltd, 1962,
24 *West Briton*; Truro, 19 April 1894.
25 *The Builder*; London, 26 July 1901, p 125.
26 *The Times*; London, 27 July 1900.
27 *Silvanus Trevail, Cornish Architect and Entrepreneur*; R Perry & H Harradence, Francis Boutle, London, 2008, p 135.
28 *Salisbury Times & Echo*; 27 March 1880.
29 *The Herne Bay Times*; 23 August 2001.
30 *Passmore Edwards Institutions, Founding & Opening Ceremonies*; J J Macdonald, Strand Newspaper Co, 1900, p 74.
31 *Cornish Times*; 13 January 2006.

## Seventeen: A Caring Community

1 *A Caring Community*; Jean Barclay, National Society for Epilepsy, 1992, p 2. Written during the centenary year, 1992.
2 Unpublished family papers.

## Eighteen: Libellous Claims

1 *The Times*; (London); 25 March, 1891.
2 *The King, the Press and the People*; Kinley Roby, Barrie & Jenkins, London, 1975. P 256.

## Nineteen: Education, Education, Education

1 *Author of Self Help*; appropriately self-published in 1859. It sold 20,000 copies in its first year.
2 *Passmore Edwards Institutions, Founding and Opening Ceremonies*; J J MacDonald, Strand Newspaper Company, London, 1900, p 11.
3 *West Briton*; Truro, 25 May 1899.
4 Herbert H Asquith, 1st Lord of Oxford and Asquith, Liberal Prime Minister of the United Kingdom from 1908 to 1916.
5 *Passmore Edwards Institutions, Founding and opening Ceremonies*; J J MacDonald, Strand Newspaper Company, London 1900, p 85.
6 Ibid, p 86.
7 *Silvanus Trevail, Cornish Architect and Entrepreneur*; R Perry and H Harradence, Francis Boutle, London, 2008, p 130-133.
8 *Passmore Edwards Institutions, Founding and opening Ceremonies*; J J MacDonald, Strand Newspaper Company, London 1900, p 86.
9 *The Diary of Beatrice Webb Vol 2 1892-1905;* Ed N & J Mackenzie, p 92.
10 *John Passmore Edwards, 1823-1911, An Account of his life and Works*; Peter Baynes, privately published, 1994, p 127.
11 Ibid, p 130-131.
12 *A Few Footprints*; J Passmore Edwards, 1906, p 42.
13 *John Passmore Edwards, 1823-1911, An Account of his life and Works*; Peter Baynes, privately published, 1994, p 132.
14 *Daily News*; Saturday 15 December 1900.
15 *The Life and Good Works of John Passmore Edwards*; R S Best, Truran Publications, 1981, p 18.
16 Ibid, p 18.

## Twenty: Art Galleries and Museums

1 *Art for the People*; G Waterford, Dulwich Picture Gallery, 1994.

2 *The Whitechapel Art Gallery Centenary Review*; Janeen Haythornthwaite, Whitechapel Art gallery, 2001.
3 *Falmouth Packet*; Falmouth, 26 March 1895.
4 *John Passmore Edwards, 1823-1911, An Account of his Life and Works*; P Bayne, 1994, p 117.
5 Unpublished papers; Stephanie Roberts, Bournemouth Natural Science Society.
6 *Cornwall and the Coast, Mousehole and Newlyn*; Joanna Mattingly, Victoria County History, 2009, p 142.
7 *100 Years in Newlyn - A Diary of a Gallery*; ed Melanie Hardie, Patten Press, 1995

## Twenty-one: Honoured by his Fellow Man

1 *Passmore Edwards Institutions, Founding & Opening Ceremonies*; J J Macdonald, Strand Newspaper Company, 1900, p 88.
2 Ibid; p 89.
3 Ibid; p 91.

## Twenty-two: Save the Children

1 *A Few Footprints*; J Passmore Edwards, 1906, p 48.
2 *A Century of Caring – Furness School 1883-1983*; R Chapman, 1983, p 5
3 *The Building News*; 20 May 1898, p 707.
4 History of Archbishop Sumners CoE School; School Website, Stuart Kerner.
5 *Passmore Edwards Institutions, Founding and Opening Ceremonies*; J J Macdonald, Strand Newspaper Co Ltd, 1900, p 56
6 *Clacton's Rehabilitation Centre*; Enid A Walsh, Essex Countryside,
7 *The Times*; 27 July 1982.
8 *A Few Footprints*; J Passmore Edwards, 1906, p 48.
9 *The Guardian*; Bournemouth, 9 June 1894.
10 *Sydenham and Forest Hill Past*; John Coulter, Historical Publications Ltd, 1999.
11 *West Briton*; Truro, 18 May 1899.

## Twenty-three: Mary Ward

1 *John Passmore Edwards, 1823-1911, An Account of His Life and Works*; P Baynes, 1994, p 114.
2 *Architectural Journal*; Professor Adrian Forty, 2 August 1989.
3 *The Musical Herald*; 1 March 1911.
4 *New York Times*; 9 August 1903.

## Twenty-four: Some Other Contributions

1 *A Few Footprints*; J P Edwards, 1906, p 68.
2 *West Briton*, (Truro); 19 April 1894.
3 *Mithian*; Tony Mansell, Trelease Publications, Mithian, Cornwall, 2003, p 18.
4 *John Passmore Edwards, 1823-1911, An Account of his life and Works*; Peter Baynes, privately published, 1994, p 133.
5 *Life and Memoirs of John Churton Collins*; L C Collins, 1912, p 164-172.
6 *Birmingham Daily News*; 15 November 1892.

## Twenty-five: Ones That Got Away

1 *Lloyds Weekly News*; London, 9 February 1896.
2 *The History of Rate-Supported Public Libraries in London 1850 to 1900*: D Jones, 1973, p 103.
3 *The Times*; 6 January 1894.
4 *West Briton*; Truro, 29 May 1890.

## Twenty-six: Marriage, Children and Family Life

1 *A Newspaper man's Memories*; Aaron Watson, Hutchingson & Co, London, 1925, p 234.
2 *The Windsor Magazine*; London, 1898.
3 *A Newspaper man's Memories*; Aaron Watson, Hutchingson & Co, London, 1925, p 128.
4 Unpublished family papers.
5 *The Ipswich Journal*; 10 April 1852.
6 *Falmouth Packet*; 29 June 1895.
7 *Cornishman*; 30 May 1895.

## Twenty-seven: His Last Days

1 Census return 1911.
2 *Chart & Compass. Journal of the British & Foreign Sailors' Society*, 1911.
3 *The Times*; 24 April, 1911.

# Appendix one
# Beliefs

*Passmore Edwards set out the basis of his beliefs in a chapter in his slim autobiography and this is replicated here.*

I believe, with Shakespeare, that a divinity is shaping our ends, rough hew them as we will, and that 'Heaven hath a hand in all';

With Schiller, that 'Justice is the keystone of the world's wide arch, sustaining and sustained by all';

With Elizabeth Barrett Browning, that 'no lily-muffled hum of summer bee but finds some coupling with the spinning stars';

With Herbert Spencer, that 'amid the mysteries which become the more mysterious the more they are considered, there will remain the one absolute certainty, that man is ever in presence of an Infinite and Eternal Energy from which all things proceed';

With Mazzini, that 'the word Progress, unknown to antiquity, is destined henceforth to be a sacred word to Humanity, as in it is indicated an entire social, political, and religious transformation';

With Thomas Carlyle, 'that modern majesty consists in work. What a man can do is his greatest ornament, and he best consults his dignity by doing it', with Victor Hugo, that 'between the government that does evil and the people who accept it there is a certain solidarity';

With Frederic Harrison, that 'man's morality towards the lower animals is a vital and, indeed, a fundamental part of his morality towards his fellow-men';

With J. S. Mill, that 'we are entering upon an order of things in which justice will be the primary virtue, grounded on equal and sympathetic association, having its root no longer in the interest for self-protection, but in a cultivated sympathy, no one being left out, but an equal measure being extended to all';

With Emerson, that 'there will be a new Church founded that will have heaven and earth for its beams and rafters, and service for symbol and illustration';

With Humboldt, that 'centuries are but seconds in the process of developing humanity';

With Longfellow, that 'affection never is wasted: if it enrich not the heart of another, its waters, returning back to the springs, shall fill them full of refreshment'; with Spinoza, 'that the good human life lies not in the possession of things which for one man to possess is for the rest to lose, but rather in things which all can possess alike, and where one man's wealth promotes that of his neighbour';

With Ruskin, that 'that country is the richest which nourishes the greatest number of noble and happy human beings, and that man is the richest who, having perfected the functions of his own life, has also the widest healthful influence over the lives of others'; and

With Tennyson, who 'doubts not through the ages one increasing purpose runs, and the thoughts of men are widened with the process of the suns'; and that 'the face of death is turned towards the sun of Life.'

# Appendix two
# Opening Dates of Buildings, with Architects and Condition in 2010

1890, Blackwater Institute, Cornwall, J Symons & Son. Under restoration as village hall.

1892, Perranporth Convalescent Home, Cornwall, J Symons & Son. Converted to apartments.

1892, Whitechapel Free Library & Museum, Potts & Hennings. Incorporated into the adjacent Whitechapel Art Gallery.

1893, Haggerston Library, Kingsland Rd Shoreditch, Maurice Adams. Facade preserved and rebuilt as apartments.

1893, Willesden Cottage Hospital, Newman & Newman. Incorporated into Willesden Community Hospital.

1893, South London Art Gallery, Camberwell, Maurice Adams. Remains open.

1893, St Day Sunday School Room, St Day, Cornwall, J Symons & Son. Used as parish church.

1894, Convalescent Home for Workingmen's Clubs & Institutes Union, Pegwell Bay, Converted back to a hotel, the Pegwell Bay Hotel.

1894, Miners' & Mechanics' Institute, St Agnes, Cornwall, J Symons & Son, Remains open.

1894, Mithian Institute, Cornwall, J Symons & Son. Remains open.

1894, Chacewater Literary Institute, Cornwall, J Symons & Son. Converted to apartments.

1894, Falmouth Cottage Hospital, Cornwall, H C Rogers. Age Concern Day Centre.

1895, Wood Green Cottage Hospital, Chas Bell, Demolished. Sheltered housing built on site.

1895, Hospital wing for West ham Hospital, Lewis Angell. Demolished. Site redeveloped.

1895, Convalescent Home for Caxton Printers Union, Limpsfield, A Saxon Snell. Converted to apartments.

1895, St Bride Printing Library, Fleet Street. Remains open.

1895, Home for Men, Chalfont St Peter, Keith Young. Remains part of Chalfont Centre, NSE.
1895, Newlyn Art Gallery, Cornwall, J Hicks. Remains open.
1895, Camborne Free Library, Cornwall, Silvanus Trevail. Remains open.
1895, Redruth Free Library, Cornwall, J Hicks. Remains open.
1896, Hayle Institute, Cornwall, Silvanus Trevail. Remains open.
1896, Shepherd's Bush Library , Maurice Adams. Closed 2009.
1896, Home for Little Boys, Swanley, H Spalding. Part of the Furness School.
1896, Tilbury Cottage Hospital, Rowland Plumbe. Demolished 1982.
1896, Convalescent Home for Charing Cross Hospital, Limpsfield, J J Thomson. Marie Curie Research Institute until 2009.
1896, Nunhead Free Library, R P Whellock. Remains open.
1896, Liskeard Cottage Hospital, Cornwall, J Hicks. Converted to sheltered housing complex 2009.
1896, Falmouth Free Library, Cornwall, W H Tresidder. Remains open.
1896, Truro Free Library, Cornwall, Silvanus Trevail. Remains open.
1897, Extension to the Haggerston Library, Shoreditch, Maurice Adams. Facade preserved and rebuilt as apartments.
1897, Convalescent Home for Metropolitan Hospital, Staplehurst, Chas Grieve. Converted to residential use.
1897, Dulwich Public Library, C Barry & Sons. Remains open.
1897, Home for Women, Chalfont St Peter, E G Shearman. Remains part of Chalfont Centre, NSE.
1897, Edmonton Free Library, Maurice Adams. Closed. Converted for use as a mosque.
1897, St Ives Free Library, Cornwall, J Symons & Son. Remains open.
1897, Liskeard Free Library, Cornwall, J Symons & Son. Remains open.
1897, Bodmin Free Library & Technical School, Cornwall, Silvanus Trevail. Library remains open.
1898, Pitfield Stree Library, Hoxton, Henry T Hare. Closed. Part used by the Courtyard Theatre, part apartments.
1898, Home for Men, Chalfont St Peter, Maurice Adams. Remains part of Chalfont Centre, NSE.
1898, Passmore Edwards Settlement, Bloomsbury, Smith & Brewer. Private Conference Centre (Mary Ward House).
1898, Acton Cottage Hospital & Nurses Home, Chas Bell. Administration building for Care Home.
1898, Victoria School for Disabled Children, Bournemouth, F Warman. Demolished but school remains on new site.
1898, Technical Institute, Camberwell, Maurice Adams. Remains as part of the University of the Arts, London.
1898, St George in the East Library, Maurice Adams. Destroyed by bombing in WW2.
1898, West Ham Museum, Gibson & Russell. Closed. Converted for use by the University of East London.

1899, Home for Boys, Chalfont St Peter, Maurice Adams. Remains part of Chalfont Centre, NSE.
1899, Home for Girls, Chalfont St Peter, Maurice Adams. Remains part of Chalfont Centre, NSE.
1899, Borough Road Library, Southwark, Phipps & Bloomfield. Closed. Converted for use by the South Bank University.
1899, Convalescent Home for the Friendly Societies Herne Bay, A Saxon Snell. Demolished and rebuilt on same site.
1899, Holiday Home for Children, Clacton on Sea, Chas Bell. Demolished.
1899, Plashet Library, East Ham, Silvanus Trevail. Closed. Used as Registry Office.
1899, Orphanage for National Union of Teachers, Sydenham, Demolished. Site used for residential estate.
1899, East Ham Hospital, Silvanus Trevail. Remains part of enlarged hospital.
1899, Children's Hospital Ward, Redruth, Cornwall, Sampson Hill. Closed. Converted for use as residential.
1899, Helston Science and Art Schools, Cornwall, J Hicks. Closed. Used as community centre.
1899, County Central Technical Schools, Truro, Cornwall, Silvanus Trevail, Closed. Amalgamated into adjacent library.
1900, Acton Free Library, Maurice Adams. Remains open.
1900, Convalescent Home for Railwayworkers, Herne Bay, A Saxon Snell. Closed. Converted for use as residential home.
1900, Whitechapel Art Gallery, Harrison Townsend. Restored and reopened.
1900, Canning Town Boys Club (Settlement), H C Lander. Closed. Converted for social housing.
1900, Launceston Library & Science & Art Schools, Cornwall, Silvanus Trevail. Closed. Converted for use as apartments.
1901, Administrative Centre, Chalfont St Peter, Chas Grieve. Remains part of Chalfont Centre, NSE.
1901, Passmore Edwards House, Clare Market (LSE), Maurice Adams. Incorporated into extended university buildings.
1901, Limehouse Free Library, Sabey & Son. Closed. Not in use 2010.
1901, Bow Library, Roman Road, Bow, S B Russell. Closed. Converted to public hall, Vernon Hall.
1902, Sutton Cottage Hospital, Surrey, Cecil Sharp. Demolished. Site now used for public house.
1902, North Camberwell Library, Maurice Adams. Closed. Various uses.
1903, Plaistow Free Library, S B Russell. Remains open.
1903, Sailors' Palace, Limehouse, Niven & Wigglesworth. Closed. Converted for social housing.
1904, Newton Abbot Library, Devon, Silvanus Trevail. Remains open.

# Appendix three
# Known Gifts of Books

In addition to the gifts of 500 to 1,000 books that accompanied each building he funded there were many other gifts to libraries, hospitals, convalescent homes, workingmen's clubs, institutes and reading rooms in Cornwall, London and in other parts of the country.

| | |
|---|---|
| School Children of Salisbury | 2,600 |
| Bickford Smith Institute, Porthleven | 100 |
| Bethnel Green Free Library | 1,000 |
| Barking Public Library | 1,000 |
| Battersea Polytechnic | 2,000 |
| Borough Road Polytechnic | 1,000 |
| Cobden Club & Institute | 1,000 |
| Chelsea Polytechnic | 1,000 |
| Chiswick Library & Mission Hall | 500 |
| Crays Library, Essex | 500 |
| Lissom Grove Library | 500 |
| Mortimer Street Library, | 500 |
| Marylebone Library | 500 |
| Nicholas Cole Abbey Club | 500 |
| Paddington Library | 500 |
| People's Palace | 1,000 |
| Poplar Public Library | 1,000 |
| Penzance Free Library | 1,000 |
| Romford Rd Library, West Ham | 1,000 |
| Stoke Newington Public Library | 1,000 |
| Southampton Public Library | 1,000 |
| Salisbury Workingmen's Club | 1,000 |
| St Day Free Library & Institute | 400 |
| Tottenham Public Library | 1,000 |
| Morley Memorial Hall, | 1,000 |
| West Ham Public Library, Canning Town | 1,000 |
| Working Lads Club, Whitechapel | 500 |

| | |
|---|---|
| Yorkshire Assoc of Institutes, Leeds | 1,000 |
| Ramsgate Free Library | 1,000 |
| Camborne Institute, Cornwall | 500 |
| Tuckingmill Institute, Cornwall | 100 |
| Redruth Institute, Cornwall | 250 |
| Mount Hawke Institute, Cornwall | 150 |
| Marazion Institute | 200 |

# Index